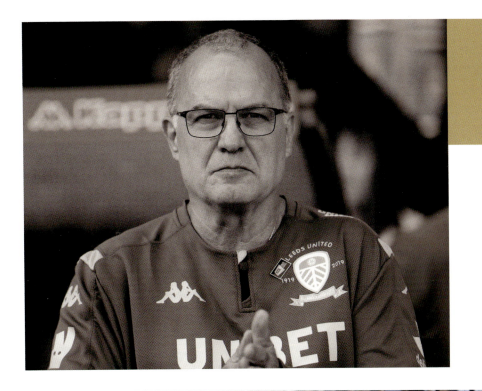

Welcome to Leeds United centenary season.

This is a pictorial record of their fight to escape the backwater of the Championship and return to their rightful place in the Premier League, the best league in the world.

After the heartbreak of last season, when everything seemed in place, teams were flattened, records were broken, lungs and legs exhausted, only to fall short at the last hurdle, there was only one question Leeds United had to answer.

Could they do it all again?

Did the players have the physical and mental strength to again take them through another gruelling season to reach the summit of promotion? Did they have the desire, the ambition and the *cojones* to keep pressing, keep passing and keep winning, to return to the Promised Land?

The rumours were that failure would lead to a break-up on an unbearable scale. Our leader, guru and general Marcelo Bielsa would leave. Our best players would be cherry-picked by richer rivals.

Another slide into the purgatory of the last 16 years seemed possible. It was unthinkable.

It was now or never.

JULY

TRAINING

The hard yards start here. A typical Bielsa training session is punishing and long. They are often two sessions a day and players are allowed a nap or siesta. They often need it; the legendary 'Murderball' sessions are held weekly. It starts with the squad split into two teams. With staff at the side to return the ball the instant it goes out of play and another is thrown in, so this is non-stop football, no fouls, no free kicks. Players are expected to run to a standstill over the sessions. Patrick Bamford said it was '10 times harder than a real game'. Previous teams would fuel up with rice the night before, because the session drained their energy. Even Kalvin Phillips viewed the sessions through his fingers.

PRE-SEASON

VS YORK CITY

Five goals made this a great start to pre-season, with two from Jack Harrison and a rare goal for Adam Forshaw. First of the season for Pablo Hernandez and what turned out to be a farewell goal from Kemar Roofe, thanks for the memories, Kemar.

PRE-SEASON

VS GUISELEY

Goals from our new boys Helder Costa and Mateusz Bogusz won this tight game, which saw a debut for Ben White, who looked great and reserve keeper Kamil Miazek, who took over from Bailey Peacock-Farrell, soon to be on his way to Burnley.

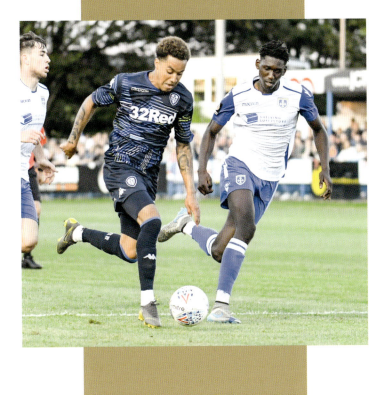

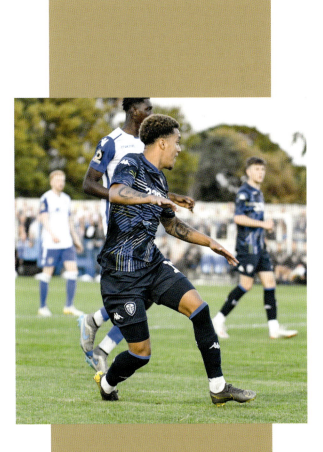

PRE-SEASON

VS TADCASTER ALBION

A great hat-trick from Ryan Edmondson in this 5-1 win included one each from Jack Clarke and super sub Robbie Gotts.

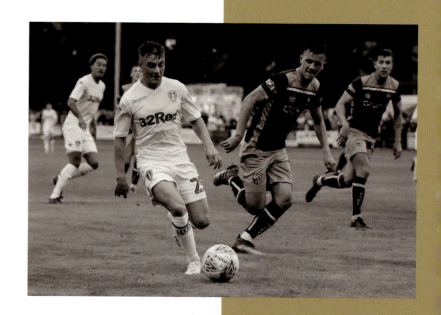

NEW KIT LAUNCH

Leeds United's new home kit was launched at a special event to commemorate the club's 100th anniversary. The new kit was modelled by skipper Liam Cooper, featuring an updated badge, trim and sponsor logos in platinum.

The new shirt proved hugely popular with fans and the club shop was packed. Supporters were thrilled to bits and lost no time in making a purchase for the new season. MOT!

TRANSFER WINDOW

A new season and an exciting new start as, in the words of the team, 'we go again'. Changes were happening already with Pontus Jansson, Kemar Roofe and Bailey Peacock-Farrell leaving the club to join Brentford, Anderlecht and Burnley, respectively. Replacing them were Ben White, a 21 year-old centre half from Brighton, Helder Costa from Wolves' successful promotion team and Illan Meslier, a young France U20 international goalkeeper from Lorient in France.

Last through the door was Eddie Nketiah, seen as one of England's brightest striking prospects, on a six month loan from Arsenal.

The team was ready for a defining season…

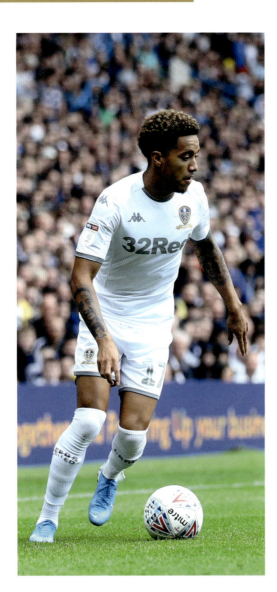

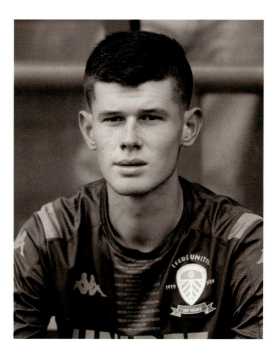

01 ILLAN MESLIER

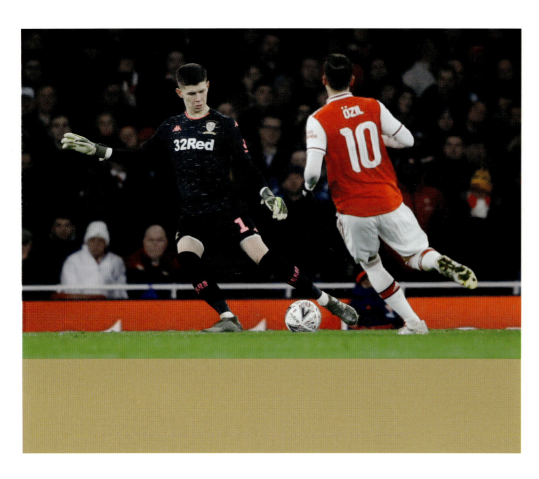

13 KIKO CASILLA

AUGUST

VS BRISTOL CITY
The season kicked off at Bristol City, still fancied but still some way to go. However, they were blown away by Pablo's opening rocket and in the second half, his set-up for Patrick Bamford's sweet header. Jack Harrison finished them off. It was just the start we wanted.

Bristol City 1-3 Leeds United
Sky Bet Championship
Sunday 4th August 2019

Leeds United 1-1 Nottingham Forest
Sky Bet Championship
Saturday 10th August 2019

Salford City 0-3 Leeds United
Carabao Cup First Round
Tuesday 13th August 2019

Wigan Athletic 0-2 Leeds United
Sky Bet Championship
Saturday 17th August 2019

Leeds United 1-0 Brentford
Sky Bet Championship
Wednesday 21st August 2019

Stoke City 0-3 Leeds United
Sky Bet Championship
Saturday 24th August 2019

Leeds United 2-2 Stoke City
Carabao Cup Second Round
Tuesday 27th August 2019

Leeds United 0-1 Swansea City
Sky Bet Championship
Saturday 31st August 2019

VS NOTTINGHAM FOREST

The first home game of the season and we started well... Bamford hit the bar, narrowly missed another and, on another day, could have had a hat-trick. Then Pablo got his second of the season and it looked like we were rolling. But several missed chances later and a pinball goal gave them a point.

VS SALFORD CITY

Our first cup tie away to the Class of 92's Salford City saw the new boy Eddie Nketiah make his debut and open his scoring account in a comfortable 3-0 win. A rare Gaetano Berardi goal (from a corner!) and storming run and shot from Mateusz Klich rounded the night off.

"The performance of the team is increasing day by day and game by game"

MARCELO BIELSA

VS WIGAN ATHLETIC

Revenge for last season's defeat was sweet. Wigan took the lead then had a man sent off. A tidy Pat Bamford brace saw off Wigan for a nice 2-1 win. Marcelo Bielsa said, "The performance of the team is increasing day by day and game by game. It was a fair result, we could have scored more goals."

VS BRENTFORD

A tough game, a meet up with the returning Pontus Jansson. This was decided by our Arsenal loanee Eddie Nketiah coming on as super-sub to break the deadlock, with a smart tap in. Relief all round. Welcome to Elland Road, Eddie, you're settling in nicely!

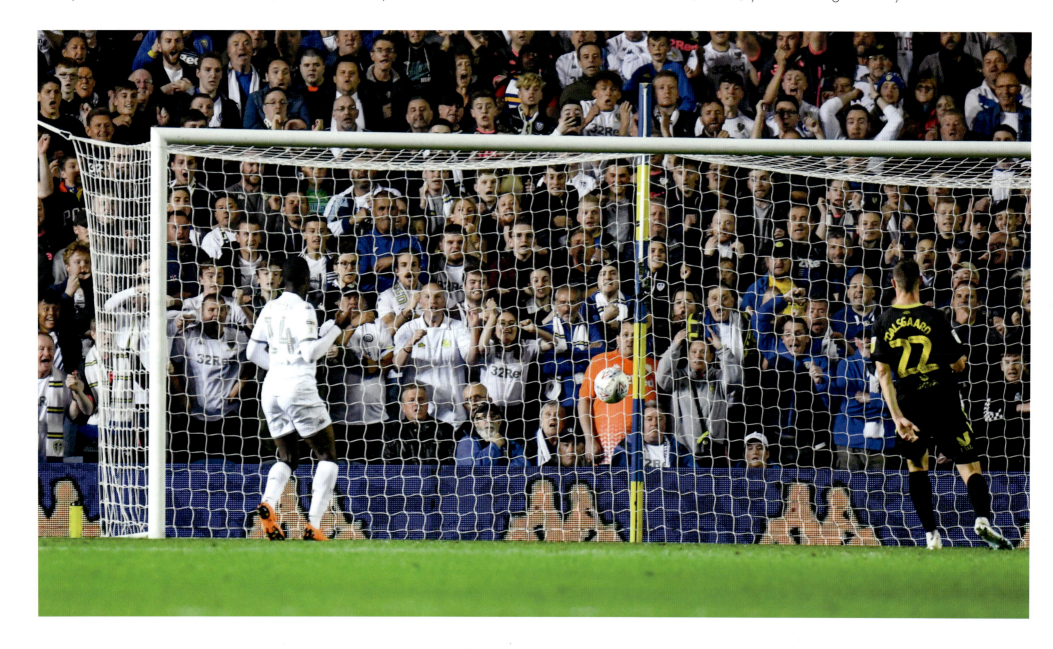

VS STOKE CITY

Is it too early for a goal of the season? We returned to Stoke and Stuart Dallas finished off a perfect example of *Bielsa Ball* for the first of three, with Gjanni Alioski and Bamford rounding off a great win.

In the Carabao Cup three days later, Helder Costa's first of the season and another Nketiah goal led to pens, a Harrison miss and a Stoke win. But let's be honest, we're not that bothered about the Carabao Cup, are we?

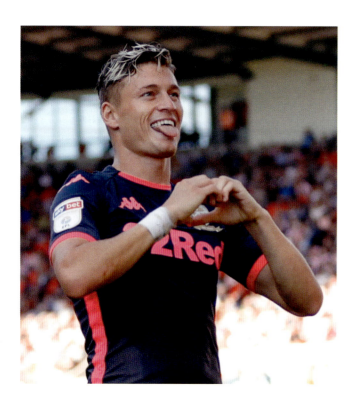

VS SWANSEA CITY
The last game of the month against Swansea saw a frustrating day for the Whites, who had 62% possession and a whacking 21 shots, but switched off in the 90th minute when Wayne Routledge nicked one. Maybe we could find a way to avenge that later on in the season?

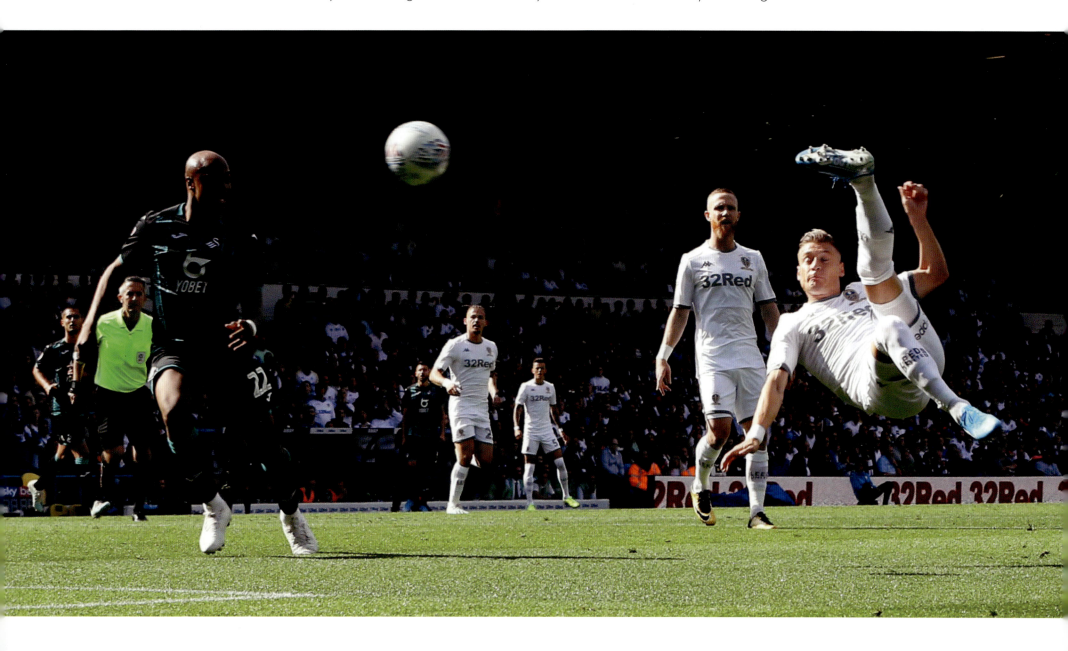

02 LUKE AYLING

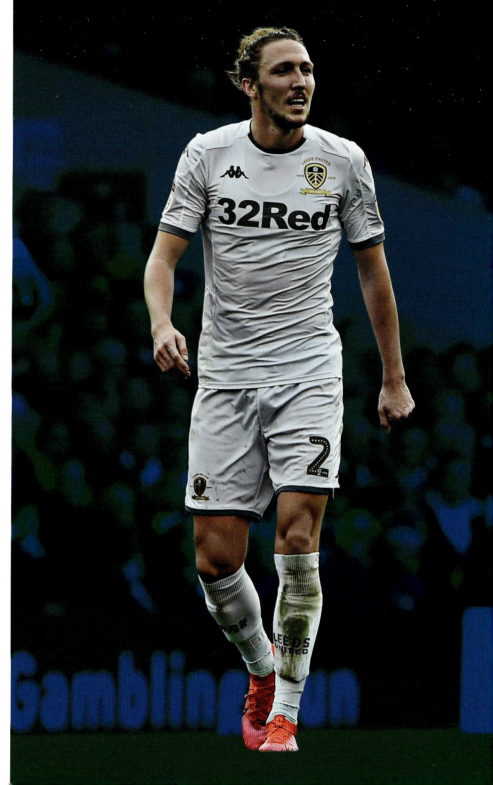

06 LIAM COOPER

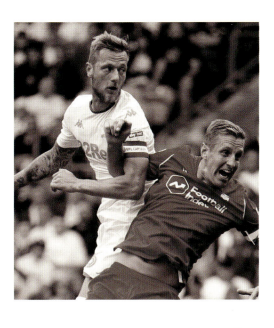

1977-1982	A. GRAHAM
1989-1993	G. STRACHAN
1990-1997	G. McALLISTER
1997-2000	D. HOPKIN
2000-2005	D. MATTEO
2011-2014	R. McCORMACK
2011-2012	R. SNODGRASS
2019-	L. COOPER

MATCHDAY

Even though the game is the most important thing on a matchday, there's plenty of things going on you might not see...

SEPTEMBER

VS BARNSLEY

Our first Yorkshire derby was a gritty affair, Ezgjan Alioski and Bamford tried to wind up Aapo Halme (and anyone else in range). But Eddie Nketiah's second of the season and a Klich penalty settled the nerves. 2-0.

Barnsley 0-2 Leeds United
Sky Bet Championship
Sunday 15th September 2019

Leeds United 1-1 Derby County
Sky Bet Championship
Saturday 21st September 2019

Charlton Athletic 1-0 Leeds United
Sky Bet Championship
Saturday 28th September 2019

VS DERBY COUNTY

It's Phillip Cocu's Derby. Naturally there was an edge to this match after the drama of the play-offs the previous season, but we outclassed a Rams side missing all the loanees that almost took them up, but only led by a Dallas-forced O.G. Then Klich missed a pen and, of course, in the 91st minute they equalised against the run of play, for a draw. It felt like a defeat.

VS CHARLTON ATHLETIC

Lee Bowyer pulled Charlton up into the Championship and proved sticky opponents. Leeds had 72% of possession, but even with Helder Costa making his league debut, we couldn't get a goal. A bizarre winner for Charlton off a Casilla punch out only made it more frustrating. We don't like London, do we?

03 BARRY DOUGLAS

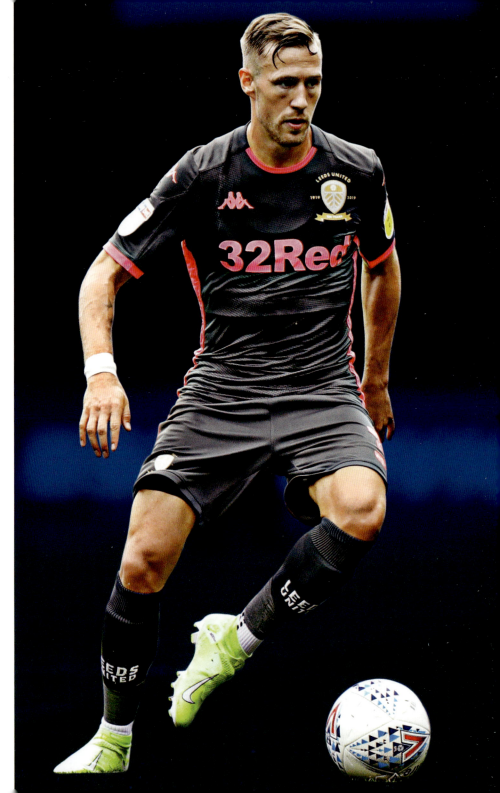

28 GAETANO BERARDI

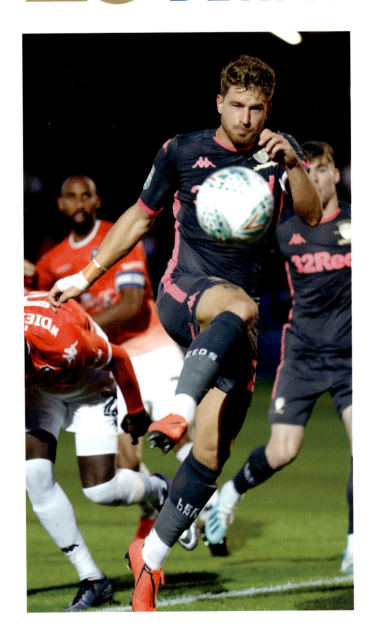

THE FANS

"The most significant thing in football is the love the fans have. When we have something that gathers and unites people, it's a privilege to be part of."

MARCELO BIELSA

OCTOBER

VS WEST BROMWICH ALBION
Our rivals returned and it was a tough game, no four-goal demolition this time, just a few chances and a lot of hard tackles. We took injuries to Cooper and Shackleton, but Gjanni was the difference with a deflected cross. A hard, grinding win, but it put us on top of the division.

Leeds United 1-0 West Bromwich Albion
Sky Bet Championship
Tuesday 1st October 2019

Millwall 2-1 Leeds United
Sky Bet Championship
Saturday 5th October 2019

Leeds United 1-0 Birmingham City
Sky Bet Championship
Saturday 19th October 2019

Preston North End 1-1 Leeds United
Sky Bet Championship
Tuesday 22nd October 2019

Sheffield Wednesday 0-0 Leeds United
Sky Bet Championship
Saturday 26th October 2019

VS MILLWALL

A chain of events: a penalty that shouldn't have been, a sending off that wasn't (and got rescinded), not much went right. Gjanni got an equaliser straight from the kick-off, but it wasn't enough... 2-1. It's that London again.

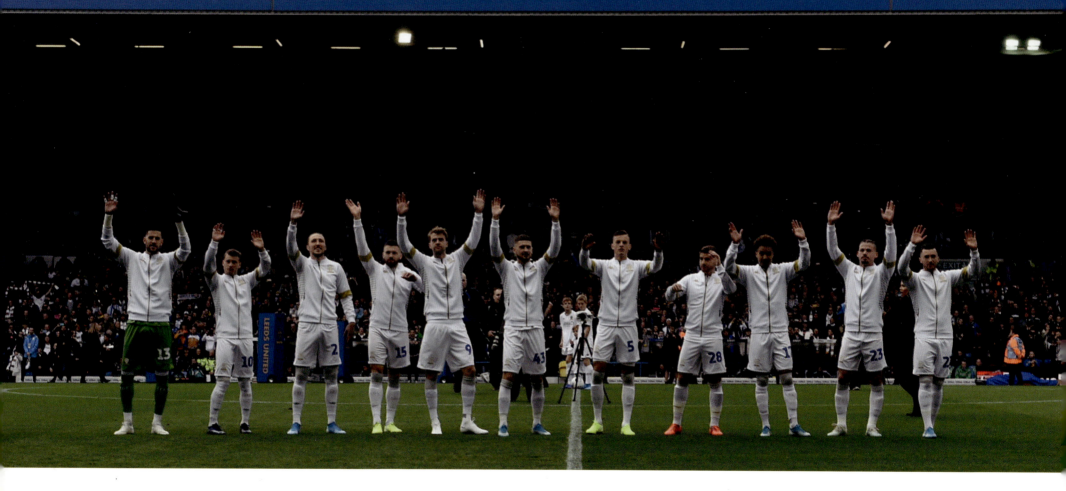

VS BIRMINGHAM CITY
Our 100-year anniversary and Kalvin Phillips stepped up. For Leeds' centenary we had a Leeds lad scoring the winner. It was written by the gods. 1919-2019 MoT.

CENTENARY CELEBRATIONS

The Official Centenary Gala Dinner: A Night of Legends featured 50 Leeds United greats starting from the early 60s Revie days through the Wilko era, David O'Leary's Champions League battlers to the present day. Gary Kelly, Vinnie Jones, Brian Deane, Tony Yeboah and Gordon Strachan were there... but see who you can spot... clue: those 'young kids' are actually the present day squad!

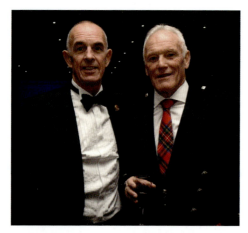

CENTENARY CELEBRATIONS

LEEDS CIVIC RECEPTION

This formal civic reception allowed the city of Leeds to express its thanks for the club and its players. Legends Trevor Cherry, Terry Cooper, Gordon McQueen, Eddie Gray and Joe Jordan were there from the club's golden era. Eddie Gray accepted the Freedom of the City of Leeds for all members of Revie's 1967-74 team. Current Chairman Andrea Radrizzani spoke about the heritage of the club and its important relationship with the city.

SALEM CHURCH BIRTHPLACE OF LEEDS UNITED

A blue plaque was unveiled at Salem Chapel in Leeds to celebrate the club's 100th anniversary at the chapel which is the club's birthplace. Leeds United chairman and owner Andrea Radrizzani was joined by club legend Norman Hunter and captain Liam Cooper to answer questions from the audience, who were made up of fans sharing the same birthday as the club - 17 October.

CENTENARY CELEBRATIONS

CENTENARY GALA
In Conversation with Leeds United Icons
The final celebration of our Centenary birthday was a more informal affair as LUFC greats Lucas Radebe, Tony Dorigo, Luciano Becchio, Jermaine Beckford and Tony Yeboah discussed their life and times at Leeds and what the team and the city meant to them.

VS PRESTON NORTH END

This was a tale of our usual dominance with plenty of chances, then we conceded a late goal. But Eddie got the equaliser with a looping header. Phew. Back up to second, two points behind West Brom.

VS SHEFFIELD WEDNESDAY

A typical Yorkshire derby: rubbish weather, not many chances. As the boss said, "It was a match you could either win or lose." We drew 0-0.

NOVEMBER

VS QUEENS PARK RANGERS
Loads of chances, a disallowed goal and their keeper had a blinder. However, a first start for Tyler Roberts brought a sharply-taken goal and Jack Harrison got a sneaky second.

Leeds United 2-0 Queens Park Rangers
Sky Bet Championship
Saturday 2nd November 2019

Leeds United 2-1 Blackburn Rovers
Sky Bet Championship
Saturday 9th November 2019

Luton Town 1-2 Leeds United
Sky Bet Championship
Saturday 23rd November 2019

Reading 0-1 Leeds United
Sky Bet Championship
Tuesday 26th November 2019

Leeds United 4-0 Middlesbrough
Sky Bet Championship
Saturday 30th November 2019

VS BLACKBURN ROVERS

On a day Elland Road honoured the armed forces, Leeds were locked and loaded: Patrick Bamford broke his duck with a cool penalty and then set up Jack Harrison for a sweet finish for 2-1.

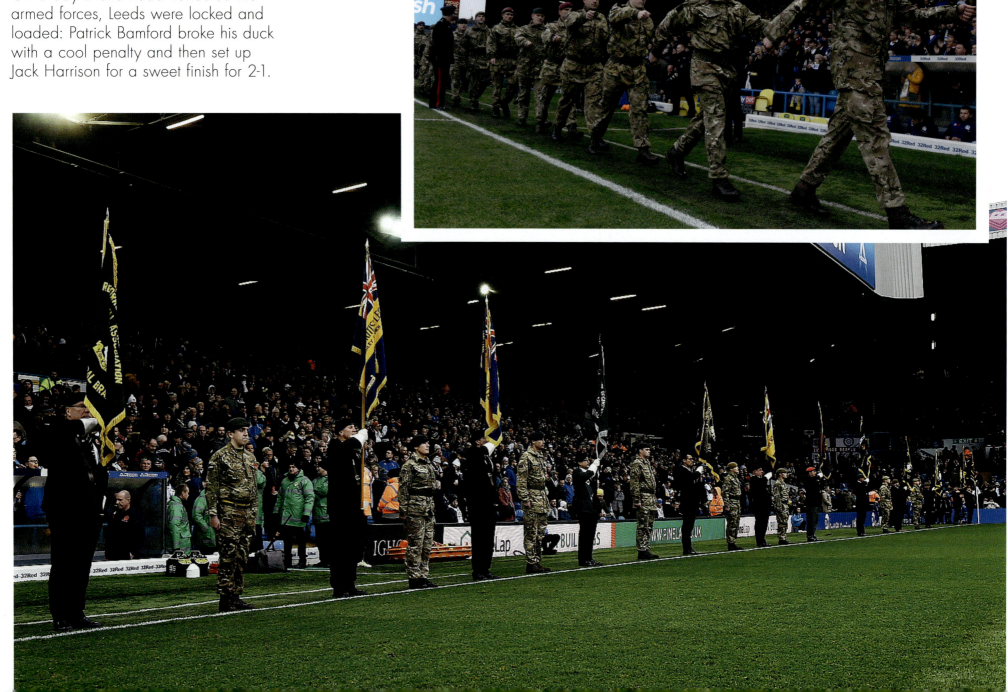

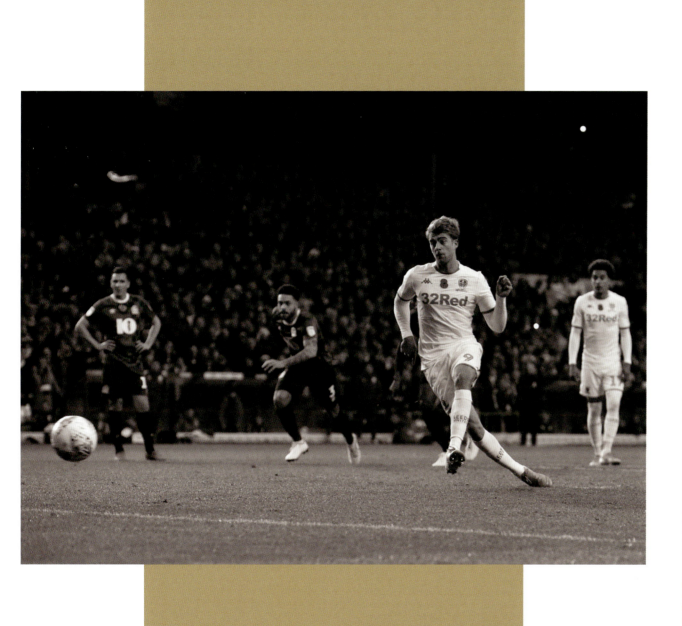

VS LUTON TOWN

Overall, we ran the game with Bamford finishing off a sweeping box to box move by White to score. He also pressured the Luton defender to score an own goal in the 90th minute. The crowd loved him and, of course, he loved them back.

VS READING
Tight, not many chances, but kept going, kept going, going and going, right up to the 87th minute. That was when Jack Harrison got on the end of a great cross from Costa and sealed the three points.

VS MIDDLESBROUGH

Boom, 4-0! From minute three we were at them and Bamford's diving header set it off. Klich's deflected shot, then Costa's persistence and, finally... a goal from a corner. An arcing top-corner job courtesy of Klich. Honestly, it could have been seven.

15 STUART DALLAS

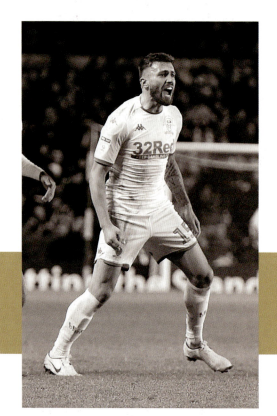
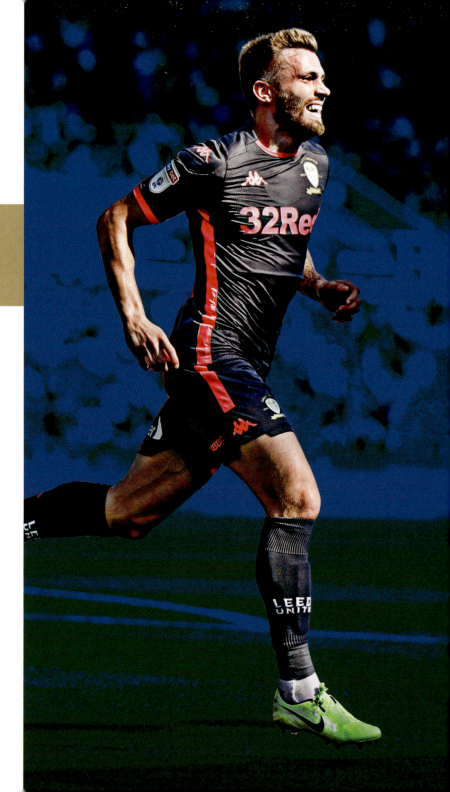

05 BEN WHITE

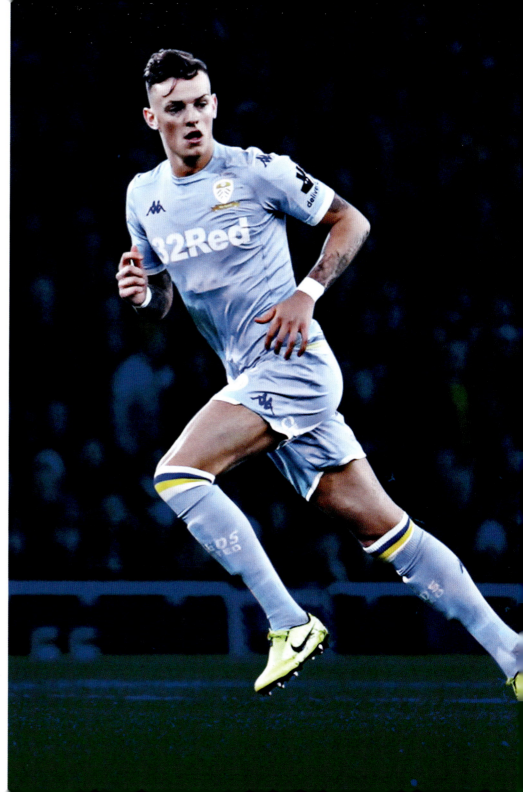

THE NEXT GENERATION

The Leeds under 23s have been a powerhouse for the club, regularly feeding the first team and historically producing great players at the highest level, such as James Milner, Fabian Delph, Lewis Cook, Danny Rose and Aaron Lennon. The current crop are already establishing themselves in the first team squad, with Ryan Edmondson, Jamie Shackleton, Pascal Struijk and Leif Davis getting debuts and match minutes. Robbie Gotts, Mateusz Bogusz, Oliver Casey, Alfie McAlmont and Jordan Stevens are also appearing regularly on Marcelo Bielsa's bench and playing a part in the future of the team.

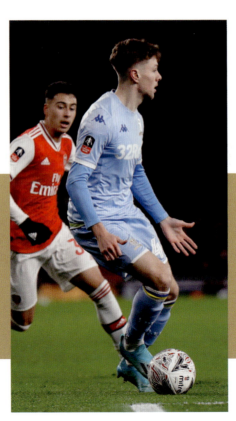

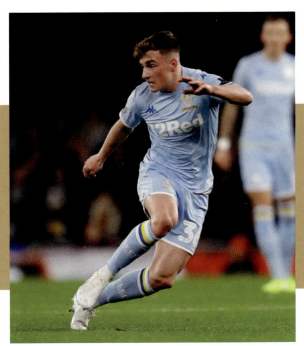

DECEMBER

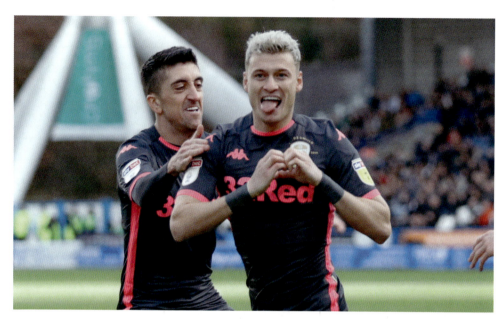

VS HUDDERSFIELD TOWN
A great derby and plenty of chances were flying in at both ends. At the start of the second half, Alioski scored a peach of a volley (from a corner!) and then Pablo with an untypical header in. Add in two great saves from Casilla and it's our sixth win in a row. And we go top.

Huddersfield Town 0-2 Leeds United
Sky Bet Championship
Saturday 7th December 2019

Leeds United 2-0 Hull City
Sky Bet Championship
Tuesday 10th December 2019

Leeds United 3-3 Cardiff City
Sky Bet Championship
Saturday 14th December 2019

Fulham 2-1 Leeds United
Sky Bet Championship
Saturday 21st December 2019

Leeds United 1-1 Preston North End
Sky Bet Championship
Thursday 26th December 2019

Birmingham City 4-5 Leeds United
Sky Bet Championship
Sunday 29th December 2019

VS HULL CITY

Another 'derby' and we rode our luck, with Casilla making excellent saves and near misses from Bamford, Hernandez, Harrison and then an own goal forced from Costa. Then from a Hull shot cleared off the line, we broke away and Alioski bagged the second. Smash and grab.

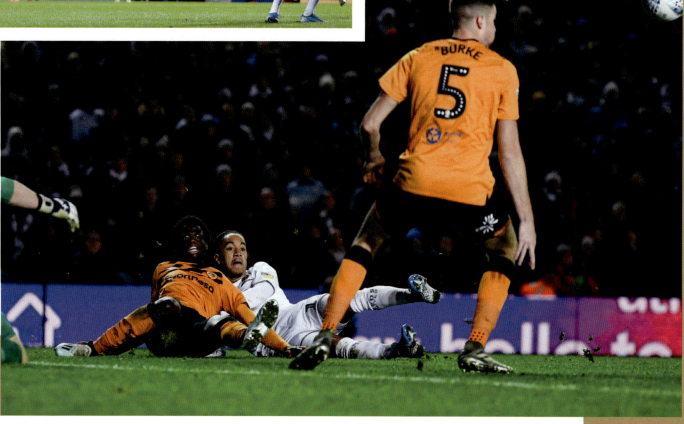

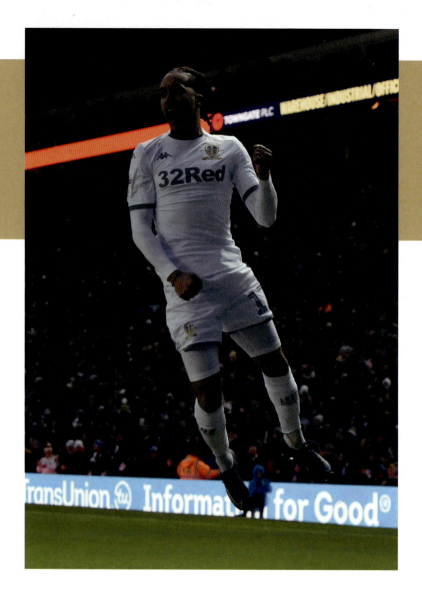

"I knew about Cardiff City's strengths and we didn't resolve it. There is no way we should have drawn that game"

MARCELO BIELSA

VS CARDIFF CITY

How did we go from the best football we'd played in the first half and leading 3-0, to a bizarre collapse at 3-3? Excellent goals from Costa and Bamford wiped out by lack of concentration. It would be the start of a bad run after seven wins on the bounce. The boss took the blame: "I did not get the preparation right because I knew about Cardiff City's strengths and we didn't resolve it. There is no way we should have drawn that game."

VS FULHAM

In a game where we had the most possession and shots but couldn't convert, we lost Pablo after six minutes and they got a soft penalty. Kiko saved two certain goals and Bamford got an equaliser, but to no avail. 2-1. London... again.

VS PRESTON NORTH END
A Christmas hangover and a dropped point after they hit us on the break. Incessant pressure led to a last minute Dallas equaliser. We never give up.

VS BIRMINGHAM CITY

No, you read the score correctly, 5-4 Leeds. We've had crazy games under Bielsa but this takes the biscuit and the whole bakery. 2-0 up with crackers from Costa and Ayling, it was: pulled one back, equaliser, took the lead, equaliser, took the lead, then equaliser (91), winner (95). Stuart Dallas spoke for many when he said, 'I'm just glad I was playing in it rather than watching it.'

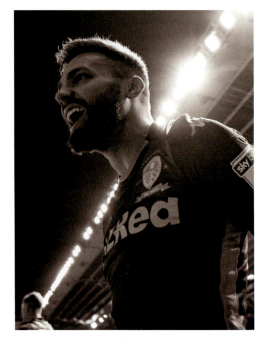

23 KALVIN PHILLIPS

04 ADAM FORSHAW

FREEDOM OF THE CITY

The Leeds 'Golden Era' team received the city's highest honour at a special ceremony held at Leeds Civic Hall, which saw players and representatives from the famous Leeds United team of 1967-1974 receive the prestigious Freedom of the City Award from the Lord Mayor of Leeds, Councillor Eileen Taylor.

Former players in attendance included; Norman Hunter, Johnny Giles, Allan Clarke, Mick Jones, Paul Reaney, Frank Gray, Terry Cooper, Peter Lorimer, Gordon McQueen, Mick Bates, Eddie Gray, David Harvey, Chris Galvin, Trevor Cherry and Sean (Jimmy) O'Neill.

Speaking about the honour, Eddie Gray said, "If Don were here today, he'd say, 'United we were, united we still are and but for a few aches and pains, we'll keep on Marching on Together.'"

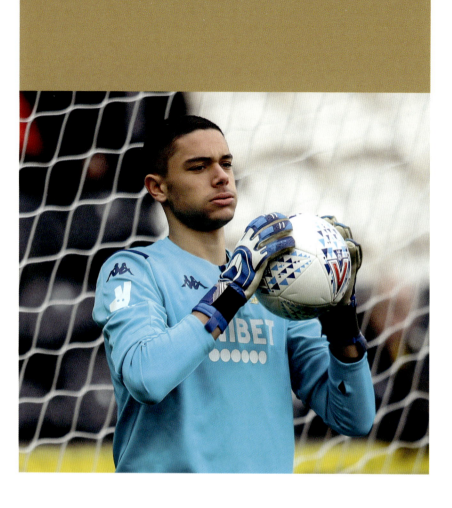

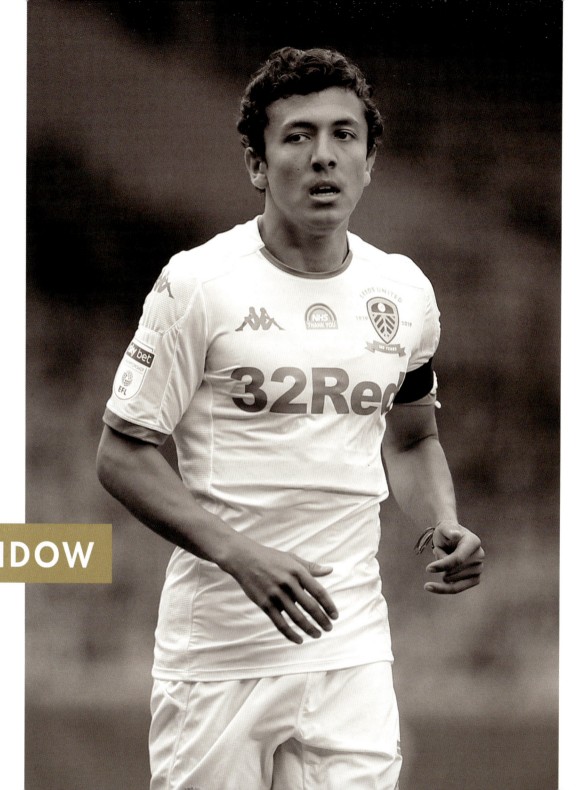

JANUARY TRANSFER WINDOW

The January transfer window brought in three new players to help push the team forward for promotion. We welcomed a goalkeeper, Elia Caprile, 18, from Italy's Serie B side Chievo Verona, and Ian Poveda, 19, a highly regarded winger from Manchester City's under 23 team. After weeks of negotiations, we also recruited a new striker to replace Eddie Nketiah, Jean-Kevin Augustin, 22, from Red Bull Leipzig.

JANUARY

VS WEST BROMWICH ALBION

From a ridiculous head-tennis WBA goal after two minutes, it was toe-to-toe all the way and, to be honest, Casilla stopped three goals and kept us in it. This was Nketiah's last game of the loan but he couldn't make an impression. Bamford came on as a sub and scored with his first header, ironically off Semi Ajayi, who ended up scoring at both ends. Joint top at the start of 2020.

West Bromwich Albion 1-1 Leeds United
Sky Bet Championship
Wednesday 1st January 2020

Arsenal 1-0 Leeds United
Emirates FA Cup Third Round
Monday 6th January 2020

Leeds United 0-2 Sheffield Wednesday
Sky Bet Championship
Saturday 11th January 2020

Queens Park Rangers 1-0 Leeds United
Sky Bet Championship
Saturday 18th January 2020

Leeds United 3-2 Millwall
Sky Bet Championship
Tuesday 28th January 2020

VS ARSENAL

This was the game where we could measure our progress against a great Premier League footballing side. Were we only good against Championship sides? No way. Meslier in goal and Robbie Gotts debut, this was a young side who played without fear and with verve, skill and intent. 58,000 (and a large TV audience) saw us take the game to Arsenal. Leeds had 15 shots in the first half, more than the Gunners had ever faced in one half of football. It was only after half-time they began to play and won with a scrappy goal from Nelson.

Arsenal boss Mikel Arteta said of his team: 'Sometimes they have to experience themselves how tough and how hard it is going to be. I watched a lot of Leeds games and they battered every team, every three days. It was good for my players to learn and to suffer on the pitch. It was like going to the Dentist.'

"I watched a lot of Leeds games and they battered every team, every three days"

MIKEL ARTETA

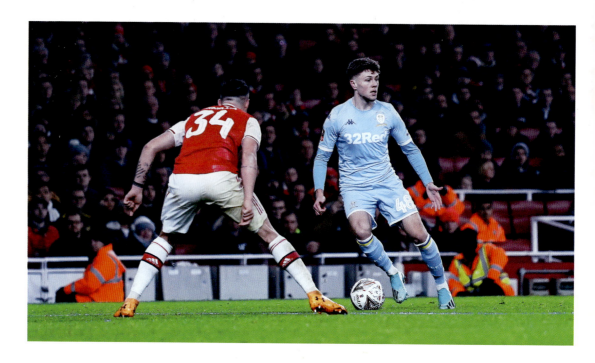

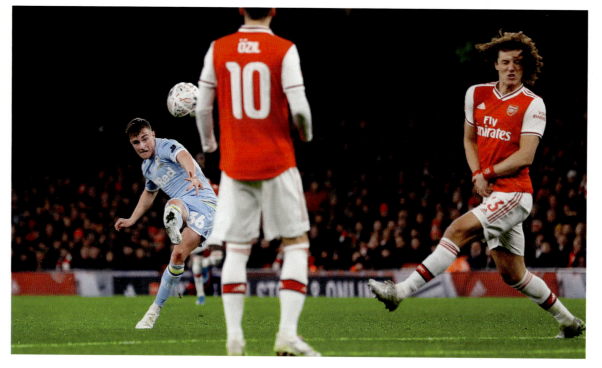

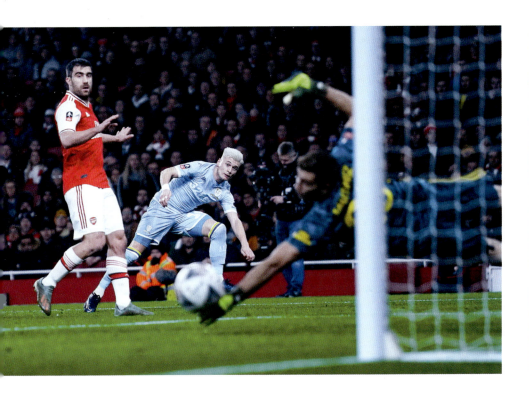
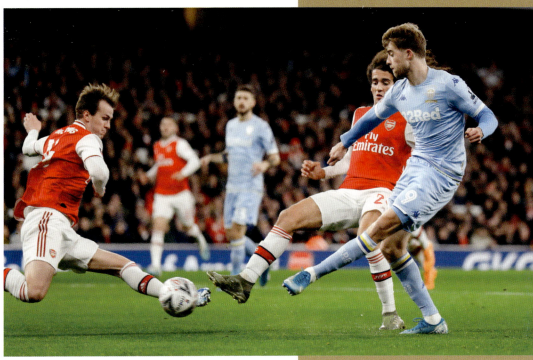

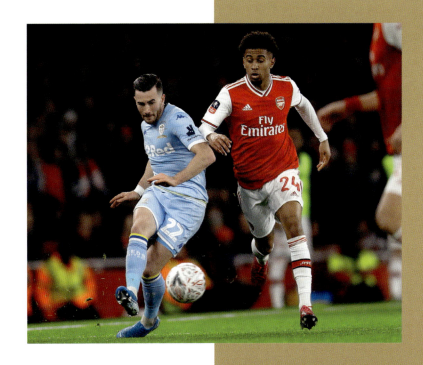

VS SHEFFIELD WEDNESDAY

We gave Garry Monk's Wendies the usual battering but, again, couldn't break through: near misses, half chances, good saves.; Jack Harrison had the best chance but narrowly missed... and then their only two shots on target went in on the 87th and 94th minutes.

VS QUEENS PARK RANGERS
Back to London and this time would be different, wouldn't it? Not really; a fluke/handballed goal, a saved penalty, Pablo hit the post and Kalvin getting sent off in frustration summed it up.

VS MILLWALL

Millwall, and a chance to get things back on track. Except we went a goal down after four minutes then 2-0 down with a needless penalty. How would we respond? Thankfully, we remembered how good we could be and scored three goals within 15 minutes for the win. Bamford with a real poacher's goal, Pablo with the leveller and a brilliant diving header from our number nine. Three points, please. Top of the league.

43 MATEUSZ KLICH

17 HÉLDER COSTA

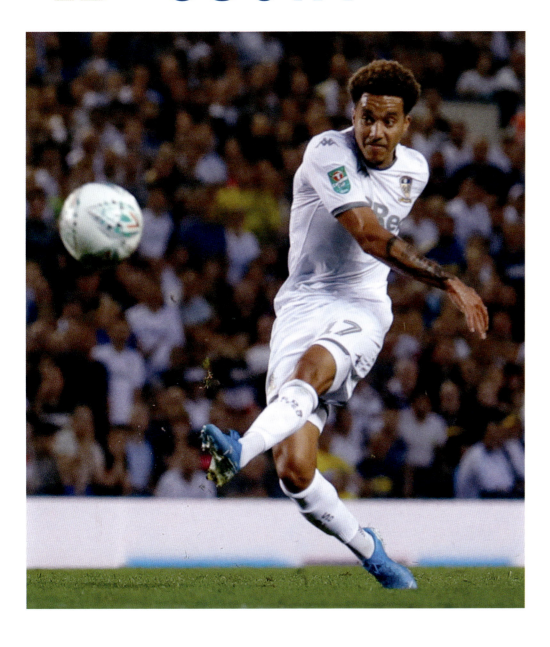

FEBRUARY

VS WIGAN ATHLETIC

Wigan, if you recall, beat us with 10 men last year and derailed our season. This time we had 77% possession. 19 shots, 15 chances; hit the post, three cleared off the line... they beat us 1-0. A Hernandez own goal. From a corner. We dropped to second.

Leeds United 0-1 Wigan Athletic
Sky Bet Championship
Saturday 1st February 2020

Nottingham Forest 2-0 Leeds United
Sky Bet Championship
Saturday 8th February 2020

Brentford 1-1 Leeds United
Sky Bet Championship
Tuesday 11th February 2020

Leeds United 1-0 Bristol City
Sky Bet Championship
Saturday 15th February 2020

Leeds United 1-0 Reading
Sky Bet Championship
Saturday 22nd February 2020

Middlesbrough 0-1 Leeds United
Sky Bet Championship
Wednesday 26th February 2020

Hull City 0-4 Leeds United
Sky Bet Championship
Saturday 29th February 2020

VS NOTTINGHAM FOREST

The poor run continued and at Forest nothing went right. A soft goal before half-time, we ran the game but a last minute breakaway meant 2-0. Even Jean-Kevin Augustin couldn't make a difference on his debut.

As Luke Ayling pointed out after the match, "We play nice football up to a certain point but after that, we don't make any clear-cut chances." He was right, our 11-point lead over third place at Christmas had evaporated. Something needed to change.

VS BRENTFORD

This was a big one. We hadn't won in 10 weeks and the team had called a meeting after the Forest game where Bielsa stood up and spoke passionately to the players. He let them know how far they had come and how good they have been and could be. He received a standing ovation. We came out blasting and created chance after chance. But, out of nowhere, Casilla let a simple pass-back slip under his foot and we were a goal down. This was it: lose and we could drop to fourth. We kept attacking and from a corner, their keeper fumbled a cross and skipper Liam Cooper made sure. A draw, yes, but the belief was back.

VS BRISTOL CITY

Like a hurricane, back came the intensity, the drive and a win. Cooper, Costa and Dallas all came close. Then after a spell with about ten shots on goal, Luke 'Bill' Ayling slotted it in against his old team. And it didn't end there; Bamford had one ruled out for offside, home debutant Jean-Kevin Augustin almost got a second and, finally, Pablo Hernandez hit the post. A one-nil hammering.

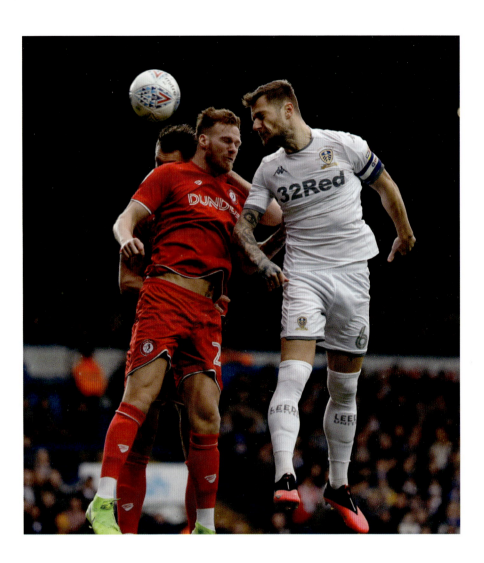

VS READING

More attacking, more chances with Costa, Alioski and Klich going close. Kiko was tested but we upped the revs. And who was there to drive us to a win? Pablo, jinking, turning and twisting, scored through a sea of defenders.

Reading Head Coach, Mark Bowen, said: "They are a well-oiled machine and I am sure they will stay in the top two."

"What I like about Leeds is when we are winning, we attack. And when we are losing, we attack."

PABLO HERNANDEZ

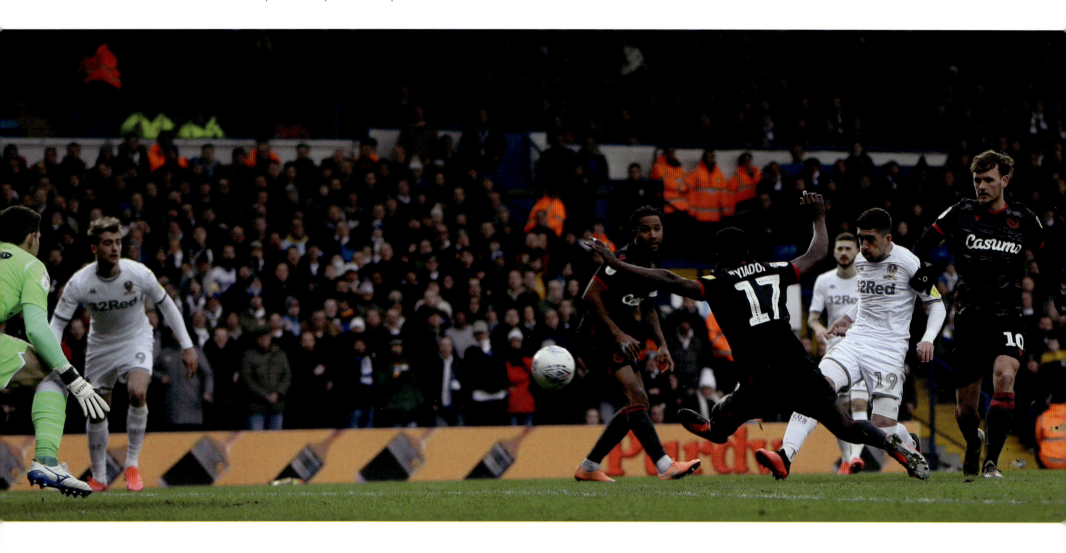

VS MIDDLESBROUGH

The well-oiled machine rolled into the Riverside and up against Jonathan Woodgate's Middlesbrough. This wasn't the 4-0 pasting of November, but Bamford should/could've had a hat-trick, corners were launched endlessly and the Boro' keeper played out of his skin... but not enough to keep out Mateusz Klich, back in the goals again. And very pleased to be.

VS HULL CITY

Leeds torpedoed Hull with a four-goal victory. First, a deflected fluke from Luke after five minutes set the tone and Hernandez then got a sweet second. Harrison hit the post and when Roberts replaced Bamford, he finished off a flowing six-pass move, with a cracking shot, set up by Klich. Three minutes later, Klich floated a great ball for Tyler, leaping like a salmon to bag his second. Illan Meslier made a quiet debut and was virtually unemployed. A great game.

19 PABLO HERNANDEZ

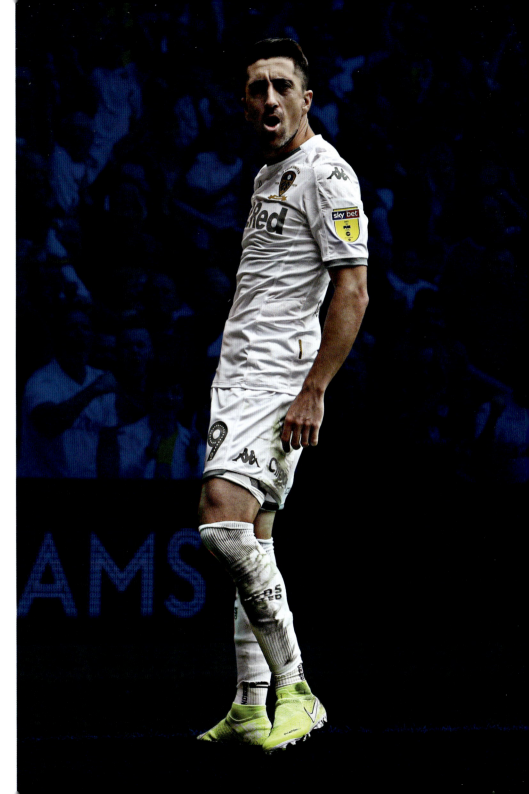

MARCH

VS HUDDERSFIELD TOWN
After two minutes, Luke Ayling leapt high in the air to blast Leeds ahead with a mid-air volley that nearly broke the net. If you were there you will never forget it. Parents will tell their children about this, kids will practice it in the garden. Even the celebration was special – Bill going full guitar hero – hair unleashed, sliding on his knees like Jimi Hendrix. Bamford got a poacher's second, but Ayling was the rock god of the afternoon. Come on, feel the noise!

Leeds United 2-0 Huddersfield Town
Sky Bet Championship
Saturday 7th March 2020

11 TYLER ROBERTS

LEGENDS WE LOST

Covid-19 affected millions across the world and changed our lives. The Leeds United family also suffered with three of our most treasured legends claimed by the pandemic. Between them Norman Hunter, Trevor Cherry and Jack Charlton were the defensive backbone of Leeds from the 60s to the 80s. We will never see their like again. Rest in peace lads.

NORMAN HUNTER

Norman Hunter was more than a legend, he was an icon, someone who people outside of football could recognise, for his relentless tackling and innate skills as a player. But aside from the 'Bite yer legs' legend, who terrorised strikers in the UK and across the world when playing for England, there was another side to Norman Hunter - shown here at the LUFC Panto at the City varieties in 1975.

TREVOR CHERRY

Trevor Cherry moved from Huddersfield to be a great defensive stalwart and ultimately, captain of Leeds United and England. One of his most famous goals was at Wembley in 1974 Charity shield against Liverpool.

JACK CHARLTON

Jack Charlton was known around the world, as an international manager, pundit and coach. At Leeds, he was first a teammate of Don Revie, who then became his finest defender and longest serving player with 773 appearances. He was the core of the great Leeds team with Norman Hunter and Billy Bremner, his room-mate on away days.

JUNE

VS CARDIFF CITY

After the break and all the anticipation, this was spoilt by two unforced errors which gave Cardiff the win, their only shots of the game. We had plenty of attempts but no goals. Bamford blocked a Roberts goal-bound effort and Alex Smithies had the game of his life.

Marcelo Bielsa said, "We could have won, we should have won. We created enough chances to score the necessary goals. Now we have eight matches left and we cannot think everything is set."

Cardiff City 2-0 Leeds United
Sky Bet Championship
Sunday 21st June 2020

Leeds United 3-0 Fulham
Sky Bet Championship
Sunday 27th June 2020

Leeds United 1-1 Luton Town
Sky Bet Championship
Tuesday 30th June 2020

VS FULHAM

Ok, the big battle. A six-pointer with third-placed Fulham and the chance to put space between us and a challenger. After a dirty elbow by Mitrovic on Ben White's jaw, Pat Bamford hit an early goal - an absolute peach - after a superb breakout, hit first-time off a Costa cross - a signature Bielsa move. Bamford turned defender and then cleared a dangerous Fulham attack. We put the hammer down in the second half with Alioski finishing off a Klich-Harrison counter-attack. The final gem was Harrison running onto a slide-rule Pablo pass to beat the keeper. Mitrovic? He was as quiet as mouse and Fulham were done.

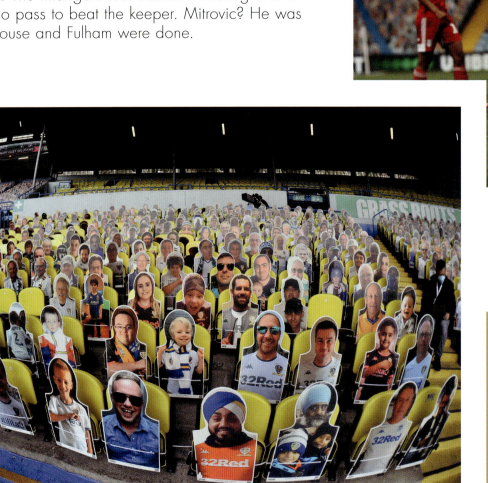

VS LUTON TOWN

Bottom of the table Luton drove the bus onto the Elland Road pitch, parked up and waited for the onslaught. It came with bells on. But... a quick break and they score. After endlessly battering their goal, Dallas found space and stroked in the equaliser. Bamford and Costa so nearly got a winner, but it was a point. Four more than West Brom.

14 EDDIE NKETIAH

09 PATRICK BAMFORD

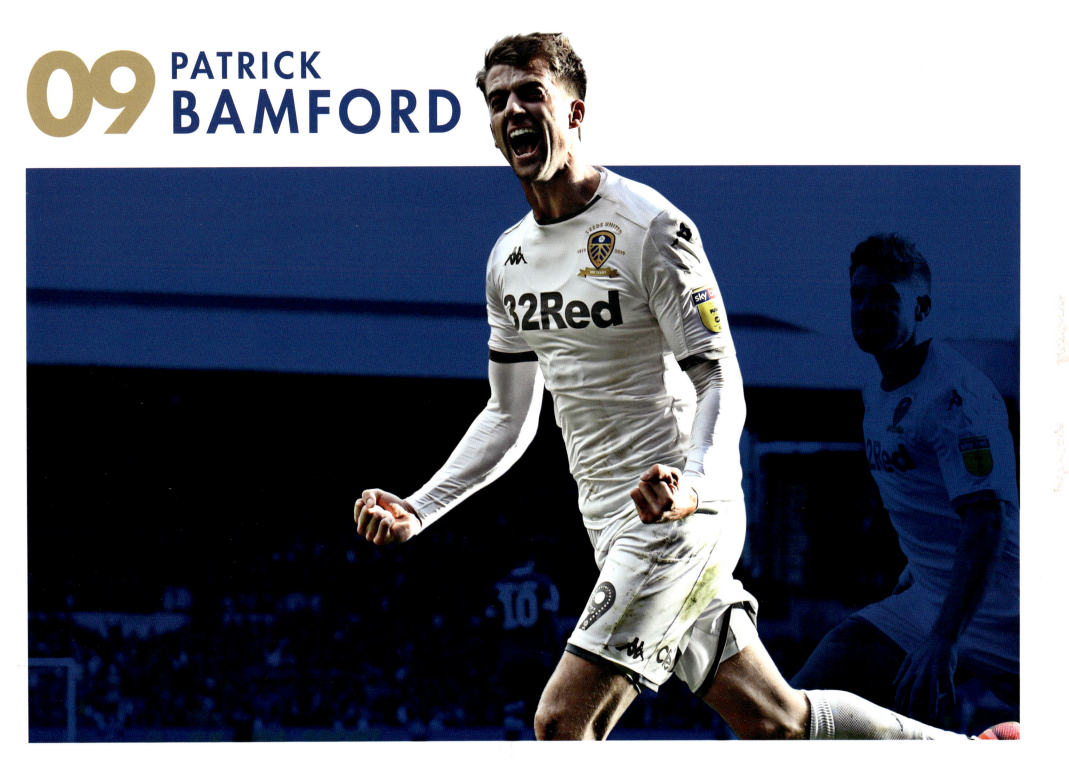

JULY

VS BLACKBURN ROVERS
Getting nervous? Not Patrick Bamford, who slotted in a fifth-minute opener after Klich robbed their centre-half. Blackburn hit the post and wasted their own chances, until Kalvin Phillips hit a perfect free-kick for 2-0. Blackburn pulled a goal back and Klich sealed the win with a dipping shot under the keeper. 3-1. Still top. It's getting close now!

Blackburn Rovers 1-3 Leeds United
Sky Bet Championship
Saturday 4th July 2020

Leeds United 5-0 Stoke City
Sky Bet Championship
Thursday 9th July 2020

Swansea City 0-1 Leeds United
Sky Bet Championship
Sunday 12th July 2020

Leeds United 1-0 Barnsley
Sky Bet Championship
Thursday 16th July 2020

Derby County 1-3 Leeds United
Sky Bet Championship
Sunday 19th July 2020

Leeds United 4-0 Charlton Athletic
Sky Bet Championship
Wednesday 22nd July 2020

VS STOKE CITY

Momentum is building and this was our biggest win of the season. The surprise? It could've been much, much more than 5-0. Stoke worked from the Luton playbook, defending like tigers: men behind the ball, kicking off the line twice. They lasted 44 minutes when Costa was hacked down in the area. Klich made the penalty look easy. Scrap the Stoke team talk. Two minutes after half-time, Costa celebrated his permanent deal by running onto the smoothest Dallas pass for 2-0. Next up, Liam Cooper hitting a first-time shot off a Pablo cutback. Then a superb breakaway, Ayling's perfect pass, a Costa cross, Bamford dummies for Pablo to hit a curving first-time shot into the net: El Mago! The perfect day was finally crowned by a perfect last-minute half-volley from Bamford. Wham, Bam thank you ma'am!

VS SWANSEA CITY

Swansea play a similar style to us and have always proved tough to break down. This game was no different. Chances came and were missed: Dallas, Harrison and Bamford's diving header too close to the keeper. Nothing was happening for us. Into the 89th minute, when most teams would settle for the draw, who are you gonna call? Hernandez. He looked for the ball, saw a sliver of space in the bottom corner, waited and struck. 1-0. Top of the league. Three to go. It feels different to last year.

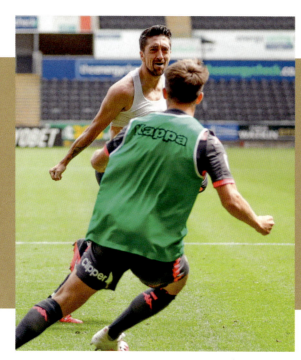

VS BARNSLEY

Barnsley were fighting for their lives, took the game to us and were unlucky not to steal the points. They pressed, pushed and attacked.

Bielsa and the coaches were raging on the touchline and changed our system three times to try match the Tykes, but still they came at us.

Until, we had a breakthrough attack, when Dallas fed Pat Bamford, who pulled it back for Tyler Roberts… but Barnsley defender Sollbauer intercepted and put it in his own net. 1-0, against the run of play.

It was a fraught, untidy game and by the end, players, manager and fans were exhausted and relieved. It was like the old days.

Except we were almost promoted!

VS DERBY COUNTY

Thanks to West Brom losing to the Terriers and Brentford being beaten by Stoke, we were promoted and crowned champions before a ball was even kicked at Pride Park. This was the start of the party season with seven changes, probably due to the celebrations of the previous two nights, featuring Struijk, Poveda and Shackleton. Roberts came close and Poveda had a goal disallowed, then Derby had the temerity to score first, so we retaliated a minute later with Captain Hernandez placing it past the keeper. Jamie Shackleton rammed home from a Roberts through ball and Derby then gave us an own goal for good measure. Salute the Champions!

VS CHARLTON ATHLETIC

Old boy Lee Bowyer needed a win to stay up, but Leeds weren't in the mood for favours. Before the game Bielsa had asked them to play like champions and respect the honour. They did and Ben White scored his only goal of the season - a gorgeous volley from the edge of the area. Dallas finished off a lovely give and go for the second. Unbelievably, we scored direct from a corner with Roberts heading in a Pablo corner, and then Struijk, majestic in the Kalvin role, stroked a weighted ball to Poveda who laid it on for Jamie Shackleton to get his second in two games. Perfecto. We won the cup, we're going up as Champions!

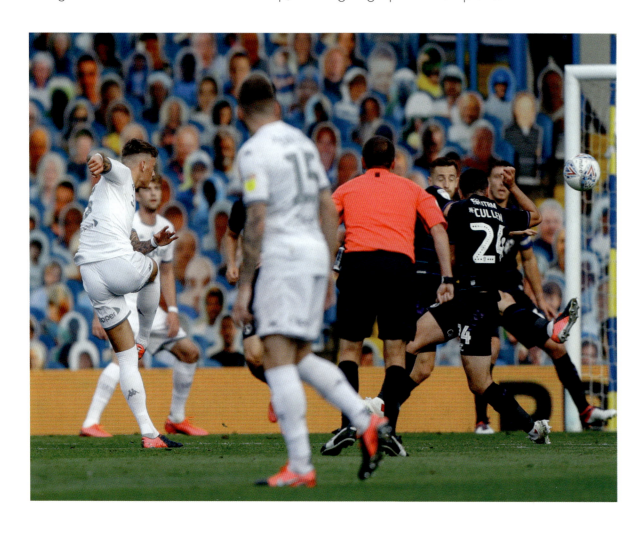

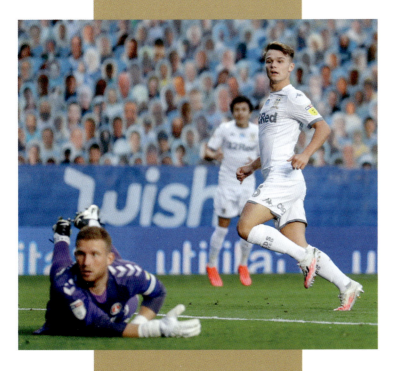

Grazie, Mr Radrizzani, this is the moment we've waited 16 years for...

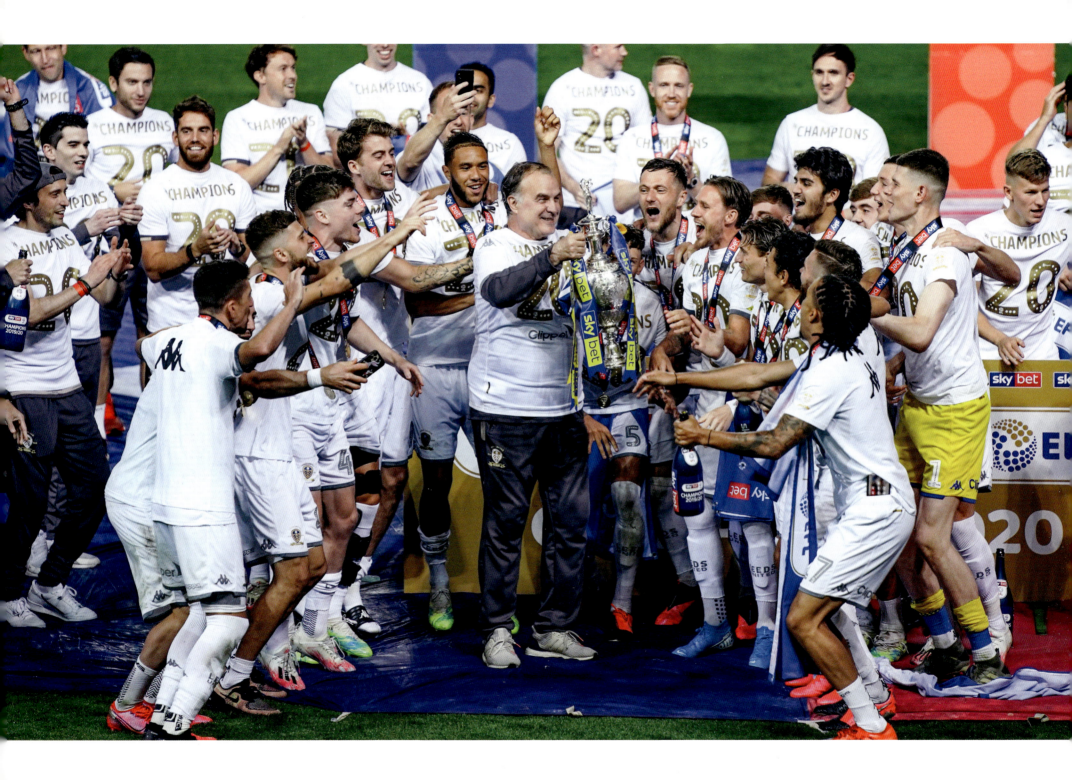

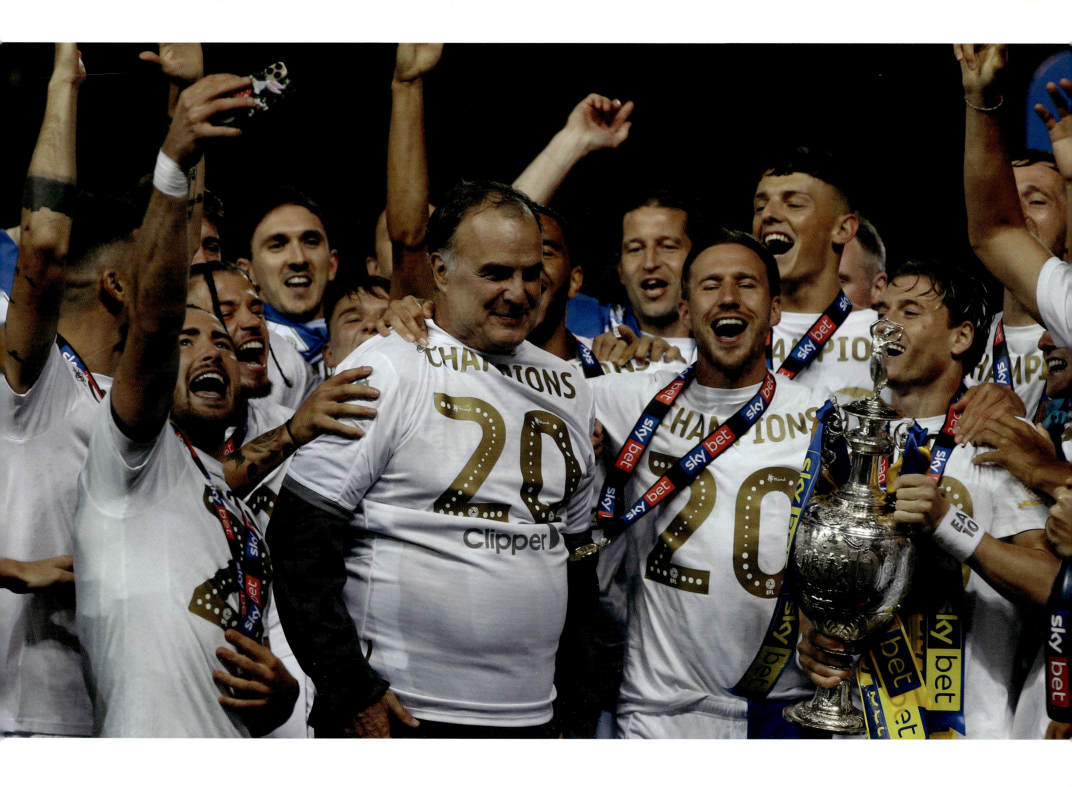

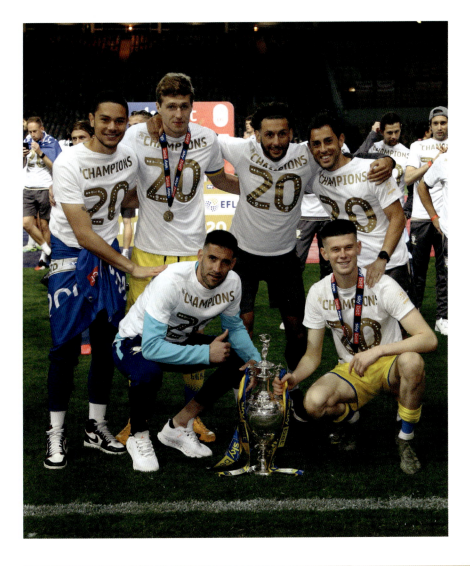

Pain temporary, glory eternal. MOT.

Winter Papers

Edited by KEVIN BARRY and OLIVIA SMITH

CURLEW
EDITIONS

Published in 2018 by

Curlew Editions Ltd
The Barracks
Ballinafad
Co Sligo
Ireland

Editors: Kevin Barry and Olivia Smith

Editorial Advisory Panel: Jen Coppinger, Shane Curtin, Michele Horrigan, Hugh O'Conor.

Designed by John Foley at Bite! Associates, Cork.
Printed by Waterman Printers Ltd, Cork.

Printed on 120gsm Munken Pure by Arctic Paper.
The text of this book was set in Calluna and the folios were set in Geotica, both typefaces designed by Jos Buivenga, exljbris Font Foundry.

© copyright remains with authors and contributors 2018.
All rights reserved.

No part of this work may be reproduced or utilised in any form or by any means, electronic or mechanical, including photocopying, recording or by any information storage and retrieval system without prior permission of the publisher and authors.

ISBN: 978-0-9933029-3-0

www.winterpapers.com

Acknowledgements: Joan Barry, John Foley, Cormac Kinsella, Lisa Sheridan.

Curlew Editions gratefully acknowledges the financial support of
The Arts Council/An Chomhairle Ealaíon.

What turn out to be the most important creative decisions in an artist's life can often, at first glance, seem not to be connected with the artistic practice at all. Central among these decisions is the matter of location. Where the artist or the writer or the musician decides to live is going to seep into and influence the work in defining ways. An artist feeds on the very air around herself, and taps on the ground until it is open to a kind of dreaming, and slowly but certainly, over time, the place will lend its taints to the art; the work will change in response to the location.

For reasons all too frequently essayed, the matter of where to live has become a difficult one for Irish creatives. The city, as a living, pulsing entity, can be the enlivening force for so much artistic work, but when the market makes the city an obstacle to pursuing the art life, the effect is a deadening of the creative spirit. In the annual Fossett's Circus of this book's perambulations around the country for promotional purposes, we have unsurprisingly found that the Irish cities with the lower rents, like Limerick and Belfast, tend at the moment to be the most artistically vibrant.

The good news is that for a small country we've got a whole lot of space. Every hidden corner and overlooked county of this dark, wet, haunted and very beautiful island can provide sustenance and fuel for the artist – the sources are out there, in many unexpected places, and the work that will result will be something to behold.

CONTENTS

CONTRIBUTORS 6

INHERITANCE Elske Rahill 9

AN INTERVIEW WITH MYNAMEISJOHN by Peter Murphy 19

HORSES Eoin McNamee 29

'IS IT STILL THE SAME?' – FICTIONS OF HOME Selina Guinness 34

A POLAROID DIARY Oonagh Kearney 41

I, THE FLOCK Mike McCormack 51

LEONTIA FLYNN AND DOIREANN NÍ GHRÍOFA in conversation 56

TAKING LIBERTIES Leontia Flynn 67

MAUDE, ENTHRALLED Doireann Ní Ghríofa 68

NO DANCING Jan Carson 70

BRYGHT GEHENNA Wendy Erskine 76

THE CHILD OF PRAGUE IN THE PHONE BOX Anna Leask 85

THE TURN Aiden O'Reilly 89

A CONVERSATION WITH BEN KIDD AND BUSH MOUKARZEL
by Mark O'Connell 95

EIGHT NON-SEQUITURS Stephen Brandes 103

THREE SPINS, A WEDNESDAY Danny Denton 111

THE GERMAN PRINCESS John Gallagher 117

AN INTERVIEW WITH MARIA NILSSON WALLER by Róise Goan .. 123

THE ATTENTION OF OTHERS Jill Crawford 129

OCTOPOLIS Yvette Monahan and Rosie O'Reilly 135

AN INTERVIEW WITH DÓNAL LUNNY by Siobhán Kane 146

STARVING Lisa Harding 154

TARAHUMARA Dylan Brennan and Liliana P. Brennan 160

ORANGES Cathy Sweeney 169

A FAREWELL TO MEATSPACE Ian Maleney 173

CONTRIBUTORS

STEPHEN BRANDES lives in Co. Cork. In 2005 he co-represented Ireland at the Venice Biennale and has continued to exhibit nationally and internationally. Recent solo exhibitions include: Parc du Souvenir, Talbot Rice Gallery, University of Edinburgh, 2016; The Last Travelogue of A. Sitzfleisch, Norfolk & Norwich Festival, 2014; April 22nd – from the Last Travelogue of A. Sitzfleisch, RHA Gallery, Dublin, 2013.

DYLAN BRENNAN is the author of Blood Oranges (The Dreadful Press), Guadalupe & other hallucinations (The Dreadful Press), Atoll (Smithereens Press) and co-editor of Rethinking Juan Rulfo's Creative World: Prose, Photography, Film (Legenda/Routledge). He lives in Mexico City.

LILIANA P. BRENNAN is a photographer, printmaker and furniture designer based in Mexico City. Her photography has appeared in The Ofi Press and Abridged.

JAN CARSON is based in East Belfast. She has published a novel, Malcolm Orange Disappears, a short story collection, Children's Children, and a micro-fiction collection, Postcard Stories. Her novel The Fire Starters is forthcoming from Doubleday in early 2019.

JILL CRAWFORD is Northern Irish. Until recently, she was an actress. Her fiction has appeared in The Stinging Fly and n+1. A story is forthcoming in Faber's anthology of New Irish Short Stories. She received the 2017–18 John Boyne scholarship at UEA. She is writing a novel.

DANNY DENTON is a writer from Cork. His first novel, The Earlie King & The Kid In Yellow, was published by Granta Books in February 2018. He is writer-in-residence for Cork County Libraries.

WENDY ERSKINE lives in Belfast. Her debut short story collection, Sweet Home, is published by The Stinging Fly Press.

LEONTIA FLYNN has published four collections of poetry with Jonathan Cape. Her most recent, The Radio (2017), was shortlisted for the T. S. Eliot Prize and won the Irish Times Poetry Prize. She won an AWB Vincent Literary Award in 2015.

JOHN GALLAGHER is a lecturer in early modern history at the University of Leeds. His first book, Learning Languages in Early Modern England, will be published by Oxford University Press in 2019.

RÓISE GOAN is the Artistic Director of The Local Group, a new company making performance projects in off-the-grid locations with communities of place and interest. She also works as an arts programmer and as the Guest Dramaturg at Vooruit in Belgium.

SELINA GUINNESS is the author of The Crocodile by the Door (Penguin 2012). She was The Arts Council Irish Writer Fellow 2018 at the Oscar Wilde Centre, TCD and is writing a novel set in contemporary Budapest.

LISA HARDING is an actress, playwright and writer. Her debut novel, Harvesting, won the Kate O'Brien Award and was shortlisted for the Kerry Group and Irish Book Awards. It has been optioned for the screen. Her next novel is called Overspill.

SIOBHÁN KANE is an academic and arts journalist. She has run the collective Young Hearts Run Free since 2008, putting on arts events in unusual spaces, raising money for the Simon Community.

OONAGH KEARNEY is an award-winning film-maker based in Cork. She is currently finishing her Arts Council film Five Letters To The Stranger Who Will Dissect My Brain and writing her first feature film with the support of Screen Ireland.

ANNA LEASK, a Shetland native, currently lives and works as a photographer in the the north west of Ireland.

IAN MALENEY is a writer from Offaly, living in Dublin. A collection of essays, Minor Monuments, will be published by Tramp Press in 2019.

MIKE MCCORMACK is the author of two collections of short stories, Getting it in the Head and Forensic Songs. His latest novel, Solar Bones, was published in 2016 and was awarded the Goldsmiths Prize and the International Dublin Literary Award.

EOIN MCNAMEE's latest novel is The Vogue.

YVETTE MONAHAN is a Sligo born, Dublin based, photographer. She creates visual narratives, which reveal stories hidden deep in living places. Her book, The time of dreaming the world awake, was published in 2014.

PETER MURPHY is a writer, spoken word performer and occasionally an actor. He has published two novels, John the Revelator and Shall We Gather at the River (Faber), and released two albums with the Revelator Orchestra. He performs under the named Cursed Murphy. His first single is Foxhole Prayer. He is at work on his third book.

DOIREANN NÍ GHRÍOFA writes both prose and poetry, in both Irish and English. Her most recent book is Lies.

MARK O'CONNELL is a writer who lives in Dublin. His book To Be a Machine was published by Granta Books in 2017, and was awarded the Wellcome Book Prize in 2018.

AIDEN O'REILLY's debut short story collection Greetings Hero was published in 2014. He studied mathematics, and has worked as a translator, a building-site worker, a mathematics lecturer and a property magazine editor.

ROSIE O'REILLY is an artist and maker. Her work is informed by her studies in the philosophy of consciousness and sociology and her work in human and environmental rights.

ELSKE RAHILL grew up in Dublin and lives in Burgundy, France, with her partner and four children. Her work includes the novel, Between Dog and Wolf, and the short story collection, In White Ink.

CATHY SWEENEY's short fiction has appeared in The Stinging Fly, The Dublin Review, Meridian, Banshee, Egress, The Tangerine, and elsewhere.

INHERITANCE

Elske Rahill

1. One Body

> 'Woman/mother is monstrous by excess; she transcends established norms and transgresses boundaries. She is monstrous by lack: woman/mother does not possess the substantive unity of the masculine subject ... She is morphologically dubious.'
> Rosi Braidotti, Mothers, Monsters and Machines

You will be my first and only daughter but for now you are the wrench of morning sickness, a thickening waist, pelvis ripening to a cradle of hiccups.

I cannot read; can't work. I wake into exhaustion and vomit off the side of the bed. Slanted on pillows, I turn stray words like little grains; snag-threads of things I have read, things I might write.

I have downloaded a Notepad app, but the effort of reaching for the phone sets a fresh ripple of nausea going. Neon-yellow heaves up from my gallbladder, blossoms garishly on the duck-egg pillowcase, fills a crack between the floorboards. I use a towel from the laundry basket to swab at the bile, strip the soiled bed. Too queasy now to seek out clean sheets, I lie very still beneath the softly naked duvet, holding the phone close above my face. I have forgotten the phrase I thought worth noting.

My last entry, despatch, from a sleepless night, reads:

Q – What is woman and why do we fear her (hate her)?

A – All men (and women!!!) come from woman > woman means mother (psychically) > maternal body exposes the impossibility of pure individuation/subjecthood. A threat to notion of SELF

SO woman = mother = terror/abjection/liquid pre-language

[just for men (i.e. Oedipus/Orestes)? or for women too??? What about daughters???? WHO IS THE DAUGHTER? Electra? Iphigenia? Athena? And who the Mother??? Clytemnestra? Jocasta? Demeter???]

The shape of the letters is ugly and hysterical; a kind of violence in all that punctuation and, in the grandiosity of those mythic names, a suggestion of madness. I delete the note slowly; a twinge of hurt as the arrow blinks back each character, like scrubbing out evidence of some beloved crime.

I have no stretch marks, but shadow-grey veins ink up under my skin with the conviction of an ancient map. A fine trail cleaves my belly from navel to pubic mound. On inspection I see that the line is made of downy fur. My vulva fattens, doubles in length, and is pelted, suddenly, with unruly frizz. I use the mirror to take a selfie of my naked body and WhatsApp it to my sisters with the caption 'I am turning into a wildebeest'.

They send back emoticons: a yellow face with a smile and tears of laughter; a yellow face with an O mouth and shock-round dots for eyes; three tilted yellow faces, four tears this time, framing the faces like falling petals, and a laughing mouth and the words, 'Eek; you are morphing!' Then, a minute later, 'Did this happen on the boys?'

'No.' I write, 'must be a girl thing. Will it go back to normal?'

Two sisters have lost interest now. The third – she has a baby girl, she should know the answer – sends a yellow face with no mouth, only two bewildered eyes: 'Dunno.'

One afternoon, the house to myself, I rear up, lurch from bed and move mutely through the rooms, emptying drawers, cleaning behind cupboards. I fill eight bin bags with clutter and leave them by the door with A4 sheets sellotaped to their sides, DUMP and CLOTHES BANK written in orange highlighter pen. Then I rearrange the furniture and hoover and mop all the floors and hang up some baby clothes and vomit for a long time, kneeling over the toilet, and retreat to bed where I frantically knit you a pink-and-blue striped sweater from four-ply merino wool. I run out of pink before the second arm is finished, drop the nest of needles into my lap, and weep.

It will be soon, I think. Soon we will come apart: a mother and a daughter.

*

2. LITTLE OEDIPUS

'With a few additions and subtractions, our imaginary still works according to the schema set in place by Greek mythology and tragedy.'
Luce Irigaray, Body Against Body in Relation to the Mother

'I have whored you!' shouts your five-year-old brother, dropping his Lego project into a clatter of bricks. 'No kissing!'

We hear him stomping up the stairs – 'Stop that WRITE NOW!' – and your father laughs and rubs the belly-swell of you, making loud kissing noises for your brother to hear, watching the landing while I wrangle back into the straps of my top.

'We need to get a bedroom wall,' I say.

The children's bedrooms are downstairs, but the attic floor serves as the master bedroom and as an office and a laundry room, separated only by spindly clothes horses and carved wooden screens. The attic steps lead straight down to the always-open living room door – a room with a stove and cracked floor tiles, three armchairs, a perilous sea of Lego, overfull bookshelves, and an Xbox. From there, every attic sound can be heard. This is how we are caught watching Netflix late at night. This is how we are caught kissing on a Sunday morning. We need bedroom walls but first we need to put in more air-vents and knock a second skylight into the 100-year-old roof. That part, I am told, is 'complicated'.

'... or a door at the top of the stairs, at least ...'

'Oh Mammy!' cries your father, throwing his voice campy over my shoulder. 'So nice to have kisses with you!'

'Let's just price a skylight, let's just see ...'

Your brother arrives at the top of the stairs, eyebrows low and a totemic grimace teetering between mock rage and sincere danger.

'No kissing!' he says. 'Don't kiss him, Mammy! Promise!'

'I can't promise that, baby. It's okay for Mammy and Daddy to kiss ...'

He turns to your father – 'Mammy loves me, not you!'

He bows his head and grits his teeth and charges, one fist drawn back for a punch, the other clutching the slack waist of his pyjama bottoms, wire-hinged elbow wagging behind him. The bones of his arms are fine, butter-muscled as frog's legs, so frail it makes a tearing pain in my mouth. He leaps onto the bed and pushes your father in the chest with both hands, forgetting his pyjamas which immediately drop to his ankles. Your father pretends to fall onto his back.

'Ahhh!' he cries. 'Help, Mammy!'

'*My* Mammy!' shouts your brother, his voice breaking into giggles, struggling against your father who is clutching a tiny wrist in each hand, head tilted back to avoid a headbutt – 'He's got me!'

'I'm going to punch your willy off!'

'Careful!' I shout, just cross enough to shock him into silence, 'Careful of my tummy.'

Red washes up from his neck and for a moment his lip folds towards tears, but then he turns and rubs my belly in circles with his palm, 'Sorry Mammy. Sorry little baby. It's Daddy's fault.' He pats my belly, kisses it – you, kisses you – and hitches the waist of his pyjamas up to his ribs.

'I need to put an elastic in those pyjama bottoms.'

'Is the baby going to drink your boobies?'

'Yes.'

'I wish I could do that. Can I drink your boobies?'

'Not any more. You're a big boy now.'

'Don't worry little baby,' he says, pulling up my top and whispering in at you through the blood and muscle and waters, his fingertips tapping gently on my skin.

'I will mind you my little baby. I will be your Daddy.'

'Hey,' says your father, who has zoned back from reading a long review under a picture of Sigmund Freud in a garden, 'I'm the Daddy.'

'No, I'm the Daddy,' says your brother, 'And I am married with Mammy. It's my baby!'

'It's all of our baby,' I say, unfolding the journal from where your father tossed it, and trying to find where I left off last night. I read a bit of it in the bath, but the nausea was too bad and I had to stop. Anna Freud doctored her father's findings, hiding letters, skewing results – that's as far as I got.

'I want a baby in my tummy,' your brother says.

'Boys don't have a room for growing babies. Only women can grow babies.'

'NO!' he shouts, standing upright on the bed, fists tense by his side. 'Why tan't boys have babies in the tummy? I want to born a baby!'

*

3. Polis

> 'Aeschylus presents to us a picture of human development from its roots to its most advanced levels. One of the ways in which his understanding of the depths of human nature are expressed are the various symbolic rôles which in particular the gods come to play. The variety corresponds to the diverse, often conflicting impulses and phantasies which exist in the unconscious and which ultimately derive from the polarity of the life and death instincts in their changing states of fusion.'
>
> Melanie Klein, Some Reflections on The Oresteia

You are, in the words of the online pregnancy forums, a 'Rainbow Baby'. All this pretty term means is that you were preceded by a miscarriage. It was my first planned pregnancy. We 'tried'. I had even consulted the web on how to conceive a girl through carefully timed abstinence. When, at the twelve-week scan, the sonographer showed us an embryo with no heartbeat, it felt like a kind of hubris. Who did we think we were?

It was a 'missed miscarriage' which means that the embryo stops but the womb doesn't get the memo – it stays pregnant, plugging away at its task, tenderising breasts and gums, swelling proudly. They said this could go on for months before my body caught on that there was nothing there but a dissolving clump of cells. To make it stop, the embryo had to be surgically removed.

I had never had an epidural before; I'd never had any birth interventions except, once, a dizzying lungful of gas and air. The surgeon stood by the door in vast white scrubs plucking at her gloves, while the anaesthetist slid a needle between the discs of my spine. The numbness billowed down through my bum and thighs, swelling into my toes, puffing my nerves into little popcorn clouds. Lying on the operating table I could still move my legs, but they felt faraway and very large and stuffed with something vaguely dangerous, like fibreglass. Images came in on me like memories of a vivid dream – the squeaky legs of a blow-up doll and the red-ringed well of her mouth, the waterlogged feet of Ophelia left to bloat in the lake beneath all those sodden muslin skirts. As the lower half of me deadened, my breath began to trip on itself. The nurse sedated me and as I began to lose time I could feel my body stiffen into cold, cold marble, very white, and it must be that I've seen it somewhere, because I knew every curve of it – a statue of the goddess Athena, veiled like the Virgin Mary, the folds of her gown covering her from chin to toe tips, and empty beneath, no body to her at all, the veneer of peace in her downturned eyes, and a secret sneer on her closed lips.

We read The Oresteia trilogy in classics at school. We did Oedipus Rex, too, and the boys got a rise out of it – 'He fucked his mother,' they liked to say, 'He fucked his mother, eurgh nightmare!' – but our teacher preferred Aeschylus to Sophocles, so most of the term was spent reading The Oresteia over and over.

It begins after Agamemnon has sacrificed his daughter, Iphigeneia, for the sake of his men. In the first part, he arrives home only to be murdered by his wife, Clytemnestra, who has learned of the rape and slaughter of her child. In the next bit, her son, Orestes avenges his father's murder by killing his mother. He is consequently haunted by 'creatures of the night', scantily clad, smelly, spirit women born from blood – the Furies, who embody the ancient laws. In the last part, The Eumenides, Orestes calls on the civilised world to free him from them.

'So I don't know if we have any feminists amongst us,' said our teacher, a short man with a round face and rust-brown cork-screw hair, 'but the girls in the class should be glad to know that it's a girl – the goddess, Athena, who is the voice of justice and civilisation. It is *wise* Athena who brings about the solution and establishes the ...'

And we said 'polis' and he wrote it on the board – *POLIS*.

The play, he said, is about the establishment of the civilised western world – it is the foundation of western culture, democracy, decency. We had to learn lines from it. Athena says, 'I am for the man in all things' and 'Let all your wars be fought abroad.'

Athena's solution is to disprove Clytemnestra's mother-right. 'The real parent,' she says, 'is the man,' and Athena herself, a motherless daughter sprung from the head of Zeus, is living proof of this. Defeated by Athena's reasoning, the Furies have no choice but to retreat to caves, where token libations are made to keep them at bay.

I liked the play and I liked its resolution. I sympathised with Orestes. His pardon felt like victory. If I could have denied my own mother-ties, I would have.

But the Athena I felt that time, with the sedation working in waves and the surgeon scraping out my pregnancy, was a cold, cruel man's woman, disgusted with my blood, my sex and with all the heat of my body.

After an epidural the feeling starts to come back like ants walking down the veins, but the flesh feels foreign. It was like inhabiting a great plastic doll. I remember the supervised piss I had to take afterwards, before they would let me go home, trying to figure out the right impulses to release it and unsure of my success, then wiping the dead place; the clumsy, muffled scrunch and clunk. 'Yes,' said the nurse, 'you had a pee pee. I heard it.' It made me think of Barbie dolls, the horror beneath their tiny clothes. The hollow tap of my touch on myself, like sound turned inside out.

It was a relief when the operation was over and after a few weeks I began to wonder if I was a little bit glad of the miscarriage, if perhaps it was for the best. How foolish of me, how risky, to try to make a daughter – what could that mean for me?

I have no schema for us; I don't know our story.

*

4. Navel Place

'If there's one thing that's been repressed here's just the place to find it: in the taboo of the pregnant woman.'
Hélène Cixous, The Laugh of Medusa

Printed on the floor is a jolly silhouette of a very pregnant woman with a high ponytail. The motif is repeated every few steps, leading to huge thick metal doors like the doors of a giant elevator. To the right of it is an intercom with a bell and, painted on the wall, the words 'Urgence' and 'Maternité'.

I squat by the doors, rocking on my heels, drifts of sweet-orange soap rising from the warm spread of my thighs. Under the hospital lights I can see how grubby these trainers are, and how poor my attempt to shave my knees, but my body is clean, at least. I had a bath before leaving the house, which eased the pain but sped up the contractions, and it was clever of me to wear a shortish dress, which can be hitched up easily in 'urgence'. I exhale slowly.

'Okay?' says your father, 'will I rub your back?'

I shake my head.

'I find,' he says, raising a finger in mock-expertise, a smile jerking the edges of his lips 'breathing to be a great help.'

'Thanks for that. Thanks for your help,' my breath breaks, jagged with laughter. 'Don't make me laugh.'

'Remember to breathe,' he says, eyebrows raised and a flinching gaze, and I realise he is half in earnest, at a loss for any better advice.

'Shush,' I flap my hand at him, sinking to a crouch, swaying down into this task, bouncing and arching to make way while with a great quake something shifts and parts for you – 'Just shush.'

The metal doors shut slowly behind us. Beyond this point there is a sinister, cool stillness and everything glows aggressively pale – pale beige, pale green. It doesn't smell like birth, but like disinfectant, covering something darker. Below the silence, the hum of an air conditioner or hospital machinery; the yip of a faraway monitor.

In the pre-labour room your father is dressed in a blue gauze cap and apron. The young midwife sticks a bulky cannula into a vein on my wrist, and says she'll be back in a minute to take a blood sample. They keep blood at the ready, just in case, she says, and she waits for your father to translate because somehow my French is failing me now. Her lips touch very lightly as she watches him translate, her eyes stretch round. She has freckles over her nose and cheeks and when she speaks she sounds like a child reciting information recently learned by heart. I ask if I can take off the monitor now and her face tightens in quiet anxiety, but she nods. She is still nodding reassuringly to herself as she closes the door.

This might be her first day on the job – we both suspect it, but won't say so until afterwards.

Instead I say, 'We have reached an age when doctors look twelve.'

'Speak for yourself,' he says, and then, 'She's fine. She's nice. It's fine.'

There is a streak of dried blood on one leg of the bed, an auspicious shape to it – a tadpole tail and then a great blob at the end, as though it has been flung there in a moment of high drama.

'What do you think happened?' I say, thinking of forceps and that huge, slant-bladed scissors a midwife almost got me with once.

He rubs at it with a ball of toilet paper and disinfecting handwash. 'Urgence,' he says.

Squatting in the en-suite now, your father stooping to shower my back, the cannula makes an itchy, wrong sort of pain and I can see it moving in my vein, pressing up under my skin while I lean on my hands. When this is over, I think, there will be a bruise.

The midwife asks if I am having a contraction and your father nods, 'Oui. Oui oui ...' Face filling with bravery, she kneels, arms outstretched, but she doesn't touch me. 'Souffles,' she says, and as he translates 'breathe,' I catch your father's eye, the twitch at the edge of his mouth, then the confusion on the midwife's face when we both laugh.

With yogi grace, she sits on the birthing ball and rocks back and forth to show me how to use it, asks again if I'm sure I don't want gas or an epidural. I can tell she is being careful to be respectful, not to force anything, and I am grateful for that, but – is it my foreignness, or the fact that I keep flipping onto all fours? – while your father translates she eyes me sideways, nervously, like a kindly child with a wild animal in need of help.

I lean forward on the ball and a loud, long roar comes opening from the place you are, and it feels like breathing and release, like making space inside space, but I can see the midwife jump and even your father stands back a little, his eyes bright, but I can't stop my cry.

'Shhh,' says the midwife, approaching me carefully, palms up as though to remove a weapon; 'Souffles, shhhh,' but the cry is part of the opening, like the groan of a great entrance stone rolling back. She calls for someone else – an older, stringy-necked woman who stands at a distance, muttering instructions.

I roar longer and louder and I keep roaring because I like it, it feels good, it feels like a heralding. The older midwife tells me to stop and she looks not only angry but disgusted and I can feel what a horror I am to her; I can see snarls of naked women in dark, dank caves, dribbling and spewing and bleeding, shrieking raucously, haunting matricidal boys as they move away into the world, howling against daughters sacrificed for winds and wars. It feels good to make noise like this, noise that stretches up out of the room but because of their faces I try to read the sounds I am making and I can hear rage in my voice, though I don't feel angry, and the high, long vowels of protest, which is not at all what I mean, but there is glorious defiance in opening my mouth and letting them ring out and I can't stop.

In the calm between contractions I can feel my veins vibrate with life – mine and yours, and it is so tranquil that I try again to apologise for all the silly fuss. The sweeter midwife asks me to get up on the bed so she can measure me. She says I'm five centimetres and I smile an imbecilic smile, full of physical pride, while the other midwife shakes her head and explains that she shouldn't have brought me in here yet –

I am telling your father not to mind her, that you're coming soon, when the next contraction gallops in on a shriek and I won't say sorry this time because fuck them you will be my first and only daughter and I'll bring you in the way that works and I let everything open and I turn on all fours and howl with what is not pain, but the pure force of your life coming through and it feels like a kind of summoning, like all those dark and bloody rights growing bright and joyous and dancing, dancing you into life.

My waters pop and spill and there are bright jellyfish of blood in them and I see concern crease your father's face because there wasn't blood with the others and the young midwife asks politely if I can lie on my back so she can measure, but I say no, I have to do it this way, head on the paper-dressed bed and back stretched taut – you seem to push your own way out, bending my muscles to your needs and I can feel your head unfold as it leaves me and I roar with the strength of you while the stringy midwife scolds me and your father translates, 'Now is not the time for shouting. Now is the time for pushing,' but you shoulder your way out now, and we have you.

The moment before your first cry is a chink in the fabric of this world;

outside death, the cusp of life. I will remember it as a long and silent second, but perhaps there is sound, and perhaps it is quick. You are cauled like a hag as they lift you up. You raise your head just a little, purse your mouth, a granite-grey fist slowly uncurling, and one navy eye slivers open. You seem to me magnificently large and growing, filling the space you have entered like a great profanity of earth and rock and grass and blood, like some ancient goddess pulled from the bottom of a buried sea.

*

5. Memory Map

> '(Culture) denotes an historically transmitted pattern of meanings embodied in symbols, a system of inherited conceptions expressed in symbolic forms by means of which men communicate, perpetuate, and develop their knowledge about and attitudes towards life.'
> Clifford Geertz, The Interpretation of Cultures

At sudden sounds your arms spring up and your hands splay and curve and your mouth – your tiny, milk-scented, peaked and blistered and fleshy lips – make a delicate little O. This is called the 'startle reflex', from when you were a falling baby chimp, reaching to cling to your mother's coat or the branches of a tree, to save yourself from landing on the forest floor. I lift you to my chest and 'Oh,' I say, 'oh oh oh' because of your smell, your little turkey sounds, your toe tips like a string of berries in my palm, and you sleep then, clinging for safety to your chimp mother.

What other history is in you?

Your vulva is a mighty swell like a great red plum and white syrup flows from the opening; so much of it, and I cannot explain why this makes me so chuffed.

I show one of the nurses.

She tells me it is normal, and not to be surprised if there is blood too. Sometimes newborn girls menstruate, she says; a dress rehearsal.

On your wrist, a tiny pink bracelet says your father's name. Every time I see it I think of a phrase, 'The matrix of his language', and I have been in such a different place that I don't know what that means. Then I realise I haven't been saying words to you, but only making sounds, and not even human sounds but the sounds made by whales and cows and wood pigeons. So, I try out words on you: 'Baby girl,' I say, and 'My daughter,' and then, again, just 'oh.'

At first your father cries whenever he holds you; a proper red-eared, lip-trembling cry: 'Oh,' he says. 'What will we do? What can we do? She's too lovely. We love her. Oh, we love her so much.'

Your three brothers come to see you.

The middle one holds back, as though afraid his very presence is too boisterous, too uncouth, as though he has just entered a church wearing the wrong shirt. The eldest just looks at you and smiles and smiles and when he tries to speak, tears blink onto his lashes.

Your youngest brother is spilling with giggles, stamping his feet – 'She is here,' he says. 'She is here, she is here can I hold her can I kiss her?' But then when I change your nappy he recoils at the little pegged omphalos: the bloody, putty twist where we were joined. 'I don't want to see that!' he says. 'I hate that.

Please cover it Mammy I don't want to look at it!'

The Notepad App won't work, so at night I use a biro to make notes at the back of a book your father brought me:

Separation through parthogenetic phantasy, i.e. sprung from the head of Zeus/rib of Adam etc? – misogyny. i.e. Athena pardons matricide, suppresses furies; splits and denies the mother. Boy cannot mourn or repair a hidden wound.

Later in the night, while you feed, I open the same page and write
Daughter
And then
What is our past? Our schema? What kind of stories can we make?
And the next morning
Persephone???

One thing I learned, years after school, when I had already become a mother of boys, was that the real matricide in The Oresteia is not the murder of Clytemnestra, but of Athena's mother, Metis, raped by Zeus and then eaten up, her maternity appropriated. Athena has been duped – she is no brain-child born of man, but the child of a wronged and denied mother. In his play – the play that we learned in school, the play that is the foundation of our decency, our culture, Aeschylus has occluded Metis, robbing Athena of her motherline, cutting her off from her sex. The very foundation of the polis is built on a lie – the splitting of women into Athena and the Furies. Perhaps we can claw our way back through that story? Perhaps if we uncover the lie, we reconcile them.

Visitors come and they pass you around and tell me you are pretty and who you resemble. I look at you from across the room and there you are – you look like you, just like you. I am suddenly impolite, spilling milk through my nightdress, stretching my hands out for you, a cry clamouring in my throat.

'My baby,' I say, 'give her back.'

They have brought you clothing – white and many shades of pink and printed with small pictures of things that threaten the naked, mottled beauty of you: a birdcage motif; a little house; glittering stars.

The first time I shower I do it very quickly; so quickly that I don't rinse my hair properly and have to do it again. I come out of the bathroom in my towel and you are screaming with your whole body; your mouth wide, the square tip of your tongue cupped in your gums, trembling, and your chin – oh no, the perfect heart-point of your chin pulled up like a button, quivering. You cry the way all newborns cry but under it I think I can hear your voice. And I am not even sitting down before you wriggle to the breast, feeding frantically. There is so much you already know.

New mothers can be a bit unstable – is that why the windows don't open? They ask about baby blues and I tell the nurse my mind is fine.

But then when I stand with you, I have an image of dropping you on the lino floor. I see it and hear it – your head cracking and your stillness then. When you flail and bob at my breast I can see how easy it would be, if a moment – and that's all it would take, a moment – of madness hooked me, and in a twist I could break you, the delicate neck that took so many months to grow to perfection; each tiny vertebra and the fatty, furred rolls of your skin. Is that what you see, too, in your moments of terror? Are they your fears given to me or mine projected on you?

I used to know about this stuff, but I can't remember what psychic phase you should be in now – whether you want to consume me or destroy or repair me, or even if I can believe any of that anymore. I think my mind is just fine but this must be a sort of madness, an oblivion to taboo because now, with you here, I believe we can unsplit ourselves.

Today you are two days old and at visiting time they come again – your father, his lip folding again at the sight of you – and your brothers. You are feeding when they arrive, and they all lean to look at you. 'Hello,' they say, 'hello. You're here. You're here. Hello.'

I am still tender-bellied, careful with myself when I lift up out of bed. From months of habit, my five-year-old pats my deflated tummy, kisses it through the polka-dotted nightdress. 'Mammy,' he says. 'There you are.'

IT CAN'T, IT WON'T, AND IT DON'T STOP

An interview with MYNAMEISJOHN
By Peter Murphy

For starters, we're situated in the middle of the largest and oldest standing stone circle in western Europe, about fifteen minutes' drive outside of Limerick city, baking in the freakish sun. Our spirit guides for the day are one John Lillis, aka mynameisjOhn – producer, DJ, and, along with God Knows and MuRli, a member of Limerick's foremost hip-hop exponents, the Choice Prize-winning Rusangano Family – and a 22-year-old MC named Aaron Hayes (aka Hazey Haze), who performs with young contenders Same D4ence.

'If you brought, like, twelve MCs and a camera out here,' Lillis remarks, casting his eye around the Bronze Age monuments, 'this'd be a great place to do something.'

As if to test that notion, he asks Hazey to deliver an ad-hoc rap so your reporter can get a flavour of what's happening at grass roots level in Limerick. Hazey obliges, squatting like some sort of shaman's apprentice, before issuing a guttural Shannonside rasp:

'Some fear the violence
But for who's reared inside it
I declare we're writin'...'

As he scatterguns the words it occurs that the art of MC freestyling, once perceived as year-zero modernist in the days of Public Enemy and NWA, far predates rock 'n' roll and recorded music itself. The combination of raw vocal tone, sprung rhythm and implicit call-and-response is as ancient as any bardic rite. Today, in the savage mid-summer heat, it all makes sense.

Hazey is from the Island Field region of Limerick city, which John Lillis reckons might well have served as template for our co-editor's novel City of Bohane. And while at first glance the Island might not exactly look like a 21st century Celtic Trenchtown, take a drive around the enclave and you'll spot the characters, like the lopsided-walkin' dude we see with a giant marijuana leaf tattooed on his bare chest, bound for the river.

Asked to summarise Limerick's hip-hop scene, Hazey, who once told his mother that his ambition is to have a statue of himself replace the icon of the Virgin Mary in the centre of the Island Field, describes it as 'like a hot jar that won't close' and Lillis laughs in response.

'There's something about the group Aaron is in,' he says, 'that you can get the Bohane thing coming off it. Even when he's talking about the castle over-looking the river. *(To Hazey)* I don't think you've read it, but ye're like fuckin' characters out of this book. It's a book this dude Kevin Barry wrote, half based between Limerick and Cork, but you don't know if it's set in the future or the past.'

Hazey: 'Sounds sick.'
Lillis: 'Do you watch Peaky Blinders?'
Hazey: 'I do.'
Lillis: 'It's like Peaky Blinders on acid.'

*

John had met us off the train a couple of hours earlier. An autodidact and a polymath, he knows his countercultural song-lines: within minutes of our meeting, he's referenced freak philosopher and novelist Robert Anton Wilson's 1980s collaboration with Dublin psych-punk legends The Golden Horde.

'I read Prometheus Rising at 28,' he'd said, 'and that was probably the most important book I had read at that point. There's a chapter in it called The Thinker and the Prover, and the second EP I made was off the back of that. The first EP was off the back of Adam Curtis – there was a line in that documentary (The Century of the Self) that said, "There is a policeman inside all of our heads, he must be destroyed."'

'So I thought, "What those guys are doing through writing or documentary making, I'm going to try and get at through sampling. That's gonna be my thing. I'm going to find the books, I'm going to find the thinkers, and I'm going take those ideas and try to translate them through music, and if it makes no sense whatsoever to the public, that's completely fine, because this is an individual process." I can't write the way that Robert Anton Wilson wrote, no way, but I can take a couple of lines that he said and chop them up.'

Over lunch, off the record, we'd discussed Freud and yage and shamanic practices and grief therapy. As well as overseeing Rusangano's rise to prominence, Lillis has for years been heavily involved in youth music education programmes. He'd suggested meeting up with Hazey and taking a drive around the city before lighting out for the Neolithic territories.

And here we are, talking about the inherent energy of places, how Limerick city had for decades borne the burden of a ghetto reputation. And while the lads' social circle still includes an outlaw caste who can't venture out to the pub for fear of reprisal attacks, these days the city is more Interzone than no-go zone, all hot colours and Do the Right Thing heat-haze. Maybe it's simple photosynthesis, but there's a feeling of regeneration afoot. When I ask John if he believes a place's energy can be rehabilitated, or if it's an inter-generational curse, he's emphatic in his answer.

'It can be *one hundred per cent* rehabilitated.'

'In the last five years,' Hazey adds, 'I met some genuine people, *real* people, people that give you hope.'

Lillis: 'There's no way that we could have done what we did unless we knew that there was this generation coming behind us. We would have been doing shit for years, but it felt like imitation. *(To Hazey)* And then when we started meeting all of ye, it was like, "Alright, these guys are about to overtake us in a big way, real fast." And that was a kick in the arse for us, even teaching, someone would ask a question and I'd be like, "He knows more than me." I'd have to go home and google that shit. And I don't mean in a competitive way …'

Hazey: 'Just raising your bar higher.'

Lillis: 'You see this 22-year-old kid who's on the path – it took me until I was 32 to get on the path. He's on it ten years before me – brilliant. Limerick definitely has a different energy at the moment, but the one thing to remember about energy is it's always transforming, it's never going to stay in that mode. It's inevitable that in two to three years' time that energy is going to pass to somewhere else. You just can't keep it. You can't hold it.'

Hazey: 'Sometimes when it's gone, you have to just face that.'

But by the same measure, when the wave is there, you have to ride it.

'When we were doing Rusangano stuff, we moved at hyper-speed,' Lillis

recalls. 'The level of gigs that we were doing ... We were doing it all ourselves, there was no management, there was no tour manager. We lived it. We absolutely lived it (*laughs*). I remember me and God Knows going to a small town in west Limerick and playing to four women in their 70s on deckchairs. That was one of the early shows.'

'But one of the best things was that when there were amazing things happening with Rusangano, like supporting Snoop Dogg, I was also a carer to someone who was very ill at the time. So you'd go into this imaginary world of "This is going to happen, this is going to take off," or whatever, but when that gig was over and you took off that African shirt and jumped back in the car, you're like: "Oh yeah, I gotta get back for twelve o'clock to give that medicine." Those are very grounding things. I think it's vital to have that side as well. No matter how successful you are, a point comes in everyone's life where you're sitting on the toilet and you're like, "Fuck, there's no toilet paper!"'

For all his vision, Lillis, as you may have gathered, is a pragmatic operator, and one whose openness to business and municipal opportunities reflects hip-hop's tradition of hard-nosed realpolitik, a self-starting, self-sustaining ethos often spurned by indie kids. Maybe it's a class thing. Either way, it dovetails with local arts departments' and government bodies' awakening to the possibilities of the artist's social role. All three Rusangano members have worked closely with Music Generation in the areas of mentoring and education. This, Lillis, asserts, only validates rather than undermines their counter-cultural credentials.

'People outside your field are like, "Look, even if I don't understand what you do I can see that there's value in it, and if you're willing to structure this in the right kind of way, we're all willing to get behind it and support it." The new mayor of Limerick is a mad hip-hop fan. You can have people in the hierarchy or positions of authority actually recognise you, whereas before the arts were this area where it was like, "Ah, give 'em a bit of money and shut 'em up." Artists don't live the same traditional life as someone with a nine-to-five, but their views and opinions are as vital, and we need to input these into everything, whether it's the architecture of the city, the way the city is socially run, or the programmes that are put out there for young people.'

And what of the old freak flag bearer's refusal to engage with The Man at all costs?

'The hippy ideology doesn't work because you don't contribute, you're opting out. If you want real change, reshape the system. If you want a peaceful society where everyone is equal, get a fuckin' job and pay some taxes. If you had told me that ten years ago, I would have been like, "Fuck that, man." But we pay our taxes. We want to give back to society. We want to make sure that programmes like Music Generation get state funding.'

'I remember I was interviewed for a community music job at one stage and I was asked, "What would you do in Limerick city?" And I said I'd build it around rap music. And someone at the table asked me the question, "Yes, but a lot of parents in the Island Field wouldn't like their fifteen-year-old kid rapping and using explicit lyrics." And I just started laughing at them. I was, like, "A fifteen-year-old in the Island, the chances are his father is only 36 and has every Tupac album. You're totally out of touch." And you could see the person was looking at me going, "Am I?"'

So much of MC culture is about self-identification through place. Even if your home turf is portrayed as a war zone by media channels, there's an element of pride in having come through the rough times.

'That's one of my main things,' Hazey responds. 'It's not Hazey from Limerick, it's Hazey from *the Island,* Limerick. I want to make sure that the Island is recognised, not just everything bad down there, not just, "The Island, *full o' rats!"* We want to be known for music as well.'

With that, at John's urging, he performs a piece called A Beauty Named Shannon, a journey into the dark heart of the region's suicide-cluster legacy that has silenced rooms around the city.

'The Shannon river goes, the Shannon river flows
Just to go and swoop these few bitter souls
Under the bridge like trolls …'

As soon as Hazey has delivered the final line, an American lady who's been prowling around the stones' perimeter shouts her approbation. It transpires that she and her husband are musicians from Chicago. After she says her few words and moves on, Lillis shakes his head.

'It's amazing that you can be sitting in a 5000-year-old stone circle in Ireland …'

HAZEY: 'And a woman from Chicago says, "Nice rap!" This *must* be a place for musicians. Let's do a gig!'

But first we need to get out of the heat. The burn is real.

*

Half an hour later, sitting outside the Commercial Bar in the city centre, we order drinks and get to talking about the Rusangano Family's origins, an alliance made between first generation emigrants from Togo and Zimbabwe, and a hip-hop fan from the west of Ireland. The group's debut album Let the Dead Bury the Dead, released in 2016, was forged from Lillis's sonic, philosophical and political studies (voices sampled include Alan Watts and MC-poet Denise Chaila) and God Knows's and MuRli's explorations of their own national and cultural identities.

'I first heard Public Enemy at ten,' Lillis says when probed about formative listening experiences. 'I used to listen to Apocalypse '91, and be like, "I have no idea how this music is made. I can't get it." At thirteen I got my first James Brown tape and there was some, like, *"Aaaow!"* in it, and I was like, "That's in the Public Enemy tape!" How did they get it off that tape and onto this tape? And the layering was phenomenal. Anyone who's making that argument that sampling is not real music, if you look at it in the Puff Daddy sense, absolutely, I'll agree with you. But if you look at it in the Bomb Squad kinda way, that is collage on a whole other level. Even art-wise, the only art that for a long time resonated with me was collage, because straight away, I was like, "That's hip-hop." I could make that correlation, in that there are certain people who can do that sound collage in the most fucking amazing way. And that's what I felt about Public Enemy.'

'And to link it with Let the Dead Bury the Dead, I made a mistake when I was first getting into sampling, in that I thought you would take a kick from one record, a snare from another, a yelp from this, and they all had to come from different records. And it's only in the last five years that somebody told

me, "You just sample one track and put some drums underneath it." And I was like, "Shit, I've been sampling forty tracks on every song." And they were like, "That's cool, but you can do it in a different way." And I was like, "I *can't!*"'

So how did he meet the other two Rusangano members?

'The very first time I met God Knows was in Limerick city about eight years ago. An American DJ whose origins were Irish, Billy Jam, he was on a radio station called WFMU, an off-kilter freeform radio station in the States. But he decided to do a transatlantic broadcast from Limerick city, as an exposé of rap happening in Ireland. And it's funny when you look back on it now who was in the room when that happened. The Rubberbandits were in the room, I was in the room, Naïve Ted was in the room, God Knows's crew came through on that day as well, and none of these people knew each other. I was DJing for the radio show, and God Knows was being interviewed, and suddenly he stopped the interview and was like, "*Bang* that rhythm!" And I was, like, "Who's this young fella?" He was 16. And the energy off these dudes was insane. He was in a four-piece called True Blood Soldiers, and I'll be honest, I wasn't a massive fan of the music they were making. The lads had quite a strong Christian background, so I saw them perform and I thought, "There's something there, but the Christian thing isn't sitting right with me."'

'And maybe two years later I was working as a youth worker in Clare, I had to put on under-age gigs for kids, and the basis for anything back then was your typical bassist-guitarist-drummer-singer. I was programming youth stuff around Ennis and I just wanted different shit. I knew how I felt when I was growing up, it was like, 'I can't go and see another four-piece do a Wonderwall cover version.' Particularly at that age, 16 to 20 years of age, bands aren't really that good or they haven't found a personality. So I remembered those guys, True Blood Soldiers, I thought they'd be a great act to put on 'cos they were completely different from any other band.'

And what was the response?

'The teenagers of Clare were petrified of it – the Public Enemy thing. They had all these syncopated dances, some of the kids were laughing, 'cos when you're scared of something, you'll laugh at it. And the thing that I was saying to those kids afterwards, "If you watch any of those guys, they know how to *perform*. Whereas you're getting up and you're playing music, but you're not *performing*. This is different."'

'And it's funny, but I would've gotten to know God Knows and MuRli in a whole other light now, I've gone to weddings and I see how they celebrate, there's no alcohol but there's dancing *in* the church, and that dancing continues until five o'clock in the morning, and it's the most phenomenal level of dancing. It's show-offy but in this really fantastic, friendly, competitive kind of way. It's class. You see how ingrained dance is in that culture. I don't think pale, pasty, shy, retiring Irish people will ever get that spirit of dance. I drive around with God Knows all the time and I'm petrified that he's going to crash the car because the music is always turned to 11 and no hands on the wheel. It's all a performance.'

'So anyway, I ended up hanging out with God Knows a couple of times, talking about life. I thought he was a fascinating character, I wanted to understand him as an individual. And the thing I said to him when we had first done stuff was, "No mention of God anymore. No mentions of Jesus or the Christianity thing. If we do a forty-minute EP and it's you going, *'I love Jesus,'* that isn't gonna work, but if we do it in a different context, I think we can make something interesting." I remember writing the very first press release we put out, and it was, "What would happen if a Christian and a pagan came together and decided to make an album?"'

The old Saturday night/Sunday morning blues-versus-gospel dichotomy. So where was MuRli at this point?

'I didn't really know MuRli, he was on the periphery. Our stage show was good, but it needed a little something else, and I remember saying to God Knows, "If we could bring one more person into the fold …" and he was always: "MuRli. MuRli. MuRli." And it wasn't that I didn't see it at first, I thought he was really good, but then I got to know him as a person and I was like, "Oh my god!"'

Why?

'MuRli is hands down the smartest person I've ever met. I think the inner confidence that MuRli has is unshakeable. He's sent from above. I don't know how else to put it. God Knows is on fire at all times, he is burning up, you can't sit him still. But MuRli will sit there, like a buddha, for hours. There comes a point when you're talking to MuRli and the third eye emerges and light just beams out of him, and you're like, "Dude, you're as deep as you can get."'

*

The big turning point in the Rusangano saga was of course the 2017 Choice Prize win. There were many fine albums released around that time, but Let the Dead Bury the Dead was the only true manifesto on the list. Its scope was Irish but also internationalist, spiritual, political, social and artistic. And sound-wise it was richly layered, complex, bristling with invention.

'We had an album title a long time before we had anything else,' Lillis testifies. 'It was just a turn of phrase, we were on the way to Galway, and my dad was very close to dying at that particular time, and whatever God Knows said, he said it as a throwaway comment: "Ah, let the dead bury the dead." I said, "*What* did you just say? Where did you pull that out of?" And he said, "It's a Bible quote." So he told me his context of it. And I was like, "*That's* the album title. That's the direction we're going. Because it means something to you, but it means something else to me." And the whole time we were making it, for all three of us, it was to try and find the truth in that phrase. And as soon as the phrase was there, it was kinda, like, "Oh yeah, all we have to do now is make the album."'

'But the Choice Prize *was* the turning point, and we were definitely delighted to get that level of recognition. But it was also a turning point in that I felt, "You've crossed over …" It stopped being a Limerick and Clare thing and became a national thing. It was, like, "We can't hold this anymore."'

Was that scary?

'One hundred per cent. But that's down to control issues on my side. That's something that I was quite uncomfortable with, where you realise it's got legs. It started as a baby but now it's talking and walking by itself, and you have to let it go and do its own thing.'

Consequently, Lillis has been careful in his curating of the group's public image. They've avoided media saturation and advertisement-soundtrack ubiquity. They never ended up doing children's shows.

'When the email came in and said, "Hello, this is RTÉ, we're just wondering do you do Christmas carols, or cover versions?" that was a particular moment,' he says with a chuckle. 'Up until that point we had responded I think to every single email that came in. And that one just went into the WhatsApp chat straight away! It was like, "I think there're mails we need to just ignore from here on in!"'

Since then, Lillis has been taking his time, reassessing his role not just in the music industry, but the world in general. He's no rap fundamentalist, but rather sees Rusangano as part of a wider movement that might include writers, poets, teachers and filmmakers.

'Sometimes I think we have as much in common with the older tradition of storytelling,' he considers. 'When we were being interviewed early on, people would automatically go, "Oh you're part of this new movement of rappers or people from migrant backgrounds in Ireland," and I was saying, "Actually we've more in common with acts like Lynched." Or even Girl Band to a certain extent. The energy that Girl Band put off on stage, that's what we were going for. And the way that Lynched would tell old stories in a contemporary way in their songs.'

'And Blindboy isn't necessarily part of the rap scene in Limerick, but he's certainly like the godfather. To give him a bit of context, when I first started doing music, I was part of an early school of rappers in Ireland, and I remember hearing the Rubberbandits for the first time, and for me, in a really good sense, that was the nail in the coffin. I got the irony of what they were doing in their early rap tracks, taking the piss out of the shit that we were doing, which was kind of like, "Yeah, we're Irish and we smoke hash and we make rap songs." And then they just took it and flipped it on its head and said, "This is how ridiculous you sound. And we're going to do it in a comical kind of way." And as soon as that mirror was held up and you saw the shadow side of yourself, it was like, "I've gotta do something different."'

And so it proved. Lillis conjures me a closing statement before the three of us drain our beers and head our separate ways.

'I don't want to look on music as the thing that pays my bills,' he concludes. 'I do different jobs on different days. Music is my wife, but I don't want to spend all my time doing it because that's going to take from it in some way. For a large portion of my life, all I could ever think about was being on a stage, performing, that was the goal, and I couldn't look at anything beyond it until that happened. And that was one thing the Choice Prize did. It was, like, "That's it. You know now that you've done it. You know that those things you imagined in your head when you were 14, when you used to dance in front of the mirror, holding a fake microphone, they've actually come to realisation."'

'Now I want to explore all the things that go with it.'

HORSES

Eoin McNamee

They came in from the island at mid-morning on a broken down punt. The island lay half a mile offshore. It was uninhabited with a bird sanctuary at one end and the Haulbowline lighthouse at the northern tip. There were four men and three women. The men wore black suits and looked like street figures from long ago. Lost citizens photographed on the avenues of forgotten cities. The women wore long skirts with embroidery in the hem and tied their hair back from their faces. On the way in from the island the skirts fluttered like tattered ball gowns.

The Lights had been built for the men servicing the Haulbowline lighthouse. Helen had leased it for a season. The doors were wooden, heavy-bolted, the planking studded. In the winter, shingle from the beach was thrown against the seaward wall. The Haulbowline horn sounded when there was fog. There were parts of the winter when whole weeks were given over to mournful sounds.

The house was rented from Patterson. The Lights had been his family home and he had let it to holidaymakers for years. He skippered the pilot boat in the channel between the shore and the island. He said he'd worked the oil industry in the Shetland Islands for ten years to earn money for the boat. He'd called it the Voe after the oil terminal at Sullom Voe. He said that in the summer there was no nightfall. She wondered what a Voe was. She thought of it as a dominion of light.

He said the foreign workers spent a day and night at a time out on the island, gathering whelks and razor fish. They wore torches on bands around their heads and followed the tide out at night to gather the shellfish. When they were finished they waited for dawn in a derelict birdwatchers hut. The shellfish were packed in hessian sacks and were put in the back of a van when they came ashore. Every night Helen could see the lamps moving in the dark.

Patterson came to the Lights every week to collect the rent. He was a lay preacher and spoke in the square in the town on Saturday evenings and he came after preaching. He looked out of the window at the torchbeams moving down the island beach. The night seeded with their light.

'They'd want to be careful out on that island. The beach slopes then it drops off into the deepwater channel. Put a foot wrong, you're in the race. All sort of sunk boats down there you could get snagged in. You don't want to see a body's been in the water for a week or so.'

'I saw a few. I nursed in the Royal.'

'Come to one of the missions,' he said. 'There's all sorts of people there. There's a social side to it.'

'Maybe.'

'If you want to go out to the island I could take you out in the Voe. This time of year you drag your hand in the water and it lights up with plankton.'

'I have MS,' she said. She was trying to think of herself as crippled. There would be palsies. She saw herself following people down the street, wheedling.

'You never said you were ill.'

'They say I'll experience fatigue, sudden losses of function.'

'If you fell in the house, who would know?'
'Nobody.'

She had a scan in the Royal. The nurses were all new, Phillipinos and Polish. She didn't know any of them. She was told to remain absolutely still in the machine. When she was small she'd been good at hiding games. She knew that you didn't go far, that the best way was staying right under their noses not breathing, not moving. She didn't know that these withholdings had stayed with her through the years of work. The stillnesses of airing cupboards, of shrubberies after rain. Places you could go when the machine rotated, when it made the otherworldly sounds, the bone-noises.

The scan came on a gelatined plate like a negative from early photography. If you looked closely there would be men and women in old-fashioned costumes, sombre with the burdens of forgotten worlds.

There was a storage room under the stairs in the Lights with a shelf of board games and puzzles, Monopoly and draughts, the boxes frayed and repaired with yellowed sellotape. There would be missing pieces, half a deck of cards. There were sun-faded towels hanging from brass hooks. A feel of long-gone summers to the room, sand carried into the house beneath your feet. The smell of sun cream. She opened a shoebox of photographs and newspaper cuttings.

lady captains day at Sand Park golf club

the bride wore a dress in silk taffeta with diamente inset

She knew she was intruding on someone else's history but she didn't care. She was tired of her own. She imagined a family coming in off the beach, a summer storm darkening the windows. They would play board games in front of a driftwood fire. There would be laughter, dry lightning in the sky out beyond the lighthouse. She would be wearing a summer dress. She found an embroidery of wild mustangs. They galloped across a yellow stitched background. She brought it out and put it on the wall beside the kitchen.

In early February she went for a walk on the beach. On her way back she sank to her knees in the sand. The tide started to come in around her. The beam from the lighthouse passed her at timed intervals. She smoothed her skirt around her knees. Everything around her was in motion. There were hailstones in the air. Wind swaying the marram grass. Clouds blew across the moon. The night was a dance and she was going to sit it out.

The foreign workers were launching the punt from the jetty. A young woman walked through the surf to Helen. She tried to help Helen to her feet, then she put her arms under her and carried her to the Lights. She could feel the girl's hands under her thighs. She knew there was muscle wastage. She would feel birdlike, the bones like something from early flight, delicate struts and flexors. The girl had black hair and a blue gaol tattoo below her right eye.

The girl was wet through. None of Helen's clothes would fit her. Helen pointed to the room under the stairs. The girl went into the room and came out with a faded red and black dress. She took off her top and skirt as though she had been given an order to strip in a room with a single bulb and a metal locker. Helen saw how young she was and thought there would be a vulnerable beauty, an orphan pallor, but there was scarring on the girl's groin and collapsed veins on her legs. Helen saw the needle tracks when she lifted her arms to pull the dress over her head. The girl went over to the mustang embroidery and stood in front of it for a moment. The wild horses were in full gallop. They tossed their manes. Dust rose from the ground under their hooves.

In May, Patterson set up a tent mission in the field beside the beach. Men and women gathered around a harmonium and sang hymns across the empty beach. Helen didn't go but one night she walked across the beach to the big tent when all the cars were gone, parting the flap to enter. There was a smell of grass and wooden benches stacked in the middle. Patterson was there on his own. He looked tired.

She asked were there horses on the island?

'No,' he said. 'It's what the gangmasters call the workers. Horses. They need somebody for a job they take a minibus across on the ferry and head east on the autobahn. A few days and they come back with as many as they need.'

Patterson told her about the cities where the gangmasters found their work crews. Edge-of-the-world-places, abandoned industries and run-down suburbs. Minibuses waiting outside bars and cafes near mental hospitals and drying-out facilities, snow whirling in the squares, their pale clientele shuffling on frozen pavements.

There were missions in the tent all summer. The voices of the preachers carried to the Lights. She had never been to one of these meetings but she knew that people came to the Lord during them, that they were washed in the blood of the lamb.

Patterson said that the Horses lived in the net store behind the jetty. She washed and dried the young woman's clothes and brought them to the store. The jumper and skirt belonged to some era of threadbare fashions. The cloth was worn, the stitching was poor, darns under the arms.

The net store had a behind-the-lines feel to it. There were broken pallets on the ground. It smelled of spilled marine diesel. They all looked furtive. She looked around for the young girl but she couldn't see her so she gave the clothes to one of the older women. One of the men had a cut on his arm and had taped a child's nappy to it with insulating tape. They were their own crime and their own forensics.

The missions ended but the empty tent stayed up. At night she heard its white canvas crack in the wind.

In June the young woman went missing from the island and Patterson found her body at the lighthouse. He said she'd gone out too far the night before, that she had stepped out into the deep channel.

She was lying on the deck of the pilot boat. Her eyes were open. Helen wondered what she had seen. It would be a kind of universe down there in the black tidal race, plankton going past like pulsar streams. The Horses stood on the jetty looking down on her. There was nothing to be done. There was no loyalty and no betrayal. One calamity was very like another.

Helen wondered if there had ever been a girl walking home from school. A city on the edge of wheatfields. A block of apartments on the outskirts, just beyond the last metro stop.

When they lifted her onto the jetty one of the men took off his heavy glasses and leaned over her, his lips moving slowly as though he was not speaking but letting each word fall from his mouth onto her waterlogged face. No one tried to stop him. There might be ancient words of pleading in their language. There might be expressions of calling back.

A week later she met Patterson at the pier. He was washing the boat's decks. She asked him what had happened to the girl's body.

'Congregation paid for a cremation,' he said. 'Plenty more where she came from.' A Voe she thought was a vast unearthly space. It left no room in the heart for anything else.

She stayed in the house. She was too tired to walk on the beach. The man with the heavy glasses came to the door in the evening. He had a parcel wrapped in brown paper. He was wearing a frayed overcoat and looked like an envoy from a distant country. He looked past her as he handed her the parcel.

He stood for a moment as though there were some message that she might send back but there was nothing. She watched him walk to the end of the path and walk out the road past the mission tent where he was lost in the mist rising off the shoreline fields as if he came from a city that was dreamed of but never built.

She opened the package on the kitchen table. It was the red and black dress the girl had taken from the storage room. She ran her fingers along the hem and felt detailing she had not known was there, thread in faded gold. She went into the room under the stairs and brought out the box of photographs and clippings. Family groups on sun-dazzled beaches. Damp stains on the emulsions, the paper spotted and foxed. Helen thought of the settings without them. The unpeopled beachfronts scoured by the wind, the overgrown beauty spots. Where had they gone, the mothers in angular sunglasses and arcane swimming costumes, the children with concave chests?

She found the cutting she had been looking for. It was dated thirty years earlier.

> *The honeymoon was spent at the Lights, and for going away the bride wore a loose-fitting coat over a cherry and black dress trimmed with gold lurex thread, and black accessories.*

Where was the bride who left her cherry and black going away dress in the Lights, the gold thread tarnished with the years? She wondered if the newly married couple had played Ludo or whist while the darkness gathered, stormlight to the north. She wondered if they laid bets, gamed with each other, what the forfeits were?

She saw the Horses working at a car wash which had been set up in an abandoned garage in the town. They shuffled around the cars in coats and broken shoes, down at heel vaudevillians with buckets and sponges. None of them looked up when she said hello. They could only be sad and remote. They could be rescued from others but they could never be rescued from themselves.

The hospital took more photographs of her brain and sent her cross sections. There were unmapped worlds.

Patterson had said there were no horses on the island but she didn't believe him. When they were alone on the island the horses would come down to the tideline at dusk. They would scrape at the frozen ground with forehooves. They would flare their nostrils and their breath would smoke in the cold air.

The tent stood in the field like a tabernacle into the first months of winter. She went as far as the end of the garden using crutches so she could see the beach and the island. The tide going out, the black water flow just offshore. She remembered what Patterson had said about boats sunk in the channel and wondered if there was still passage seaward, if there was someone she could ask to take her to the island. It had appeared close to the shore when she had first come but now it was further away. Late in the winter she started to see lights on the island shore again. The air was clear and she could see faces under the torches, bent downwards as though they prayed at the edge of the sea, as though they knelt to the evensong of themselves.

'IS IT STILL THE SAME?' – FICTIONS OF HOME

Selina Guinness

Our home, Tibradden, is often used as a film location. We seem to specialise in low-budget, or no-budget, productions that require someplace close to Dublin on the fraying hem of grandeur.

I. 'I THOUGHT IT WAS GOING TO BE A FAIR FIGHT, MICHAEL?'
   King of The Travellers, writer/director Mark O'Connor.

There are three Travellers on coloured ponies riding round the Nineteen Acres. The shotguns, slung crossways on their backs, jog up and down as they trot bareback up the hill. They've been out hunting. The one that shot a pigeon wears a pork pie hat. Over their shoulders, the Poolbeg chimneys approach more closely through the haze than I've ever seen them before.

They moved the vehicles in over a week ago. It hasn't stopped raining since. They'll be here another fortnight. The site is pure muck; the drive beneath the cedars has been tracked and churned by the wheels of heavy motorhomes and caravans. Kids, authentically wet, peer at me through the smoke. I've no business being here, but I'm curious. I've my youngest on my hip. He has an appetite for fire and he struggles to get down.

A plaster Virgin Mary stands behind the site. She's slung with plastic flowers and rosaries, her gaze delicately averted from the puddle at her feet. A smiling villain is due to drown in it this afternoon. The nephew, bulling to avenge his da, drags his uncle across the site, and pushes his head down, and down again, until the holy water fills the porches of his ears. A few wives shout for help but no one intervenes.

Out in the sheep shed, Padraig is making glycine glass to shatter when the hatted man is thrown through the window of a pool hall. He plays taverners' cricket with my husband on the Theatrical Cavaliers. He reaches up to the shelf behind, and carefully lifts a clay plaque down to show my elder son. 'We'll set that in the tree tomorrow so as not to damage the bark.'

'I want to show you something,' the nephew tells his sweetheart. They name the Spanish chestnut that stands out front an oak. Each spring, its hollow trunk is home to a great spotted woodpecker that stays for a month or two before heading on to Wicklow. By now, it's long gone. The nephew bends to point out the initials they carved there together as kids –

JPM ♡ WP
Friends Forever

And you can hear the birds singing as the coloured ponies pick their way through the forest towards the rival camp where WP lives. It is Halloween. The riders are tripping out on mushrooms. Their golden masks glint beneath the trees. A bonfire party burns the other side of the stream. And you know this will not end well when the ghost of the old King appears to his son, JPM.

A maroon jeep jerks to a halt at our front steps and the flat-capped land-owner leaps out, already shouldering his rifle. This house is his, and the land, though the title isn't quite legit. We see the nephew canter across the field out front. A crack, and he crumples, slumps and slides off the horse cityside, away from us.

My youngest son, perched on his daddy's shoulders, slaps his face with glee. We have stood out here this past half hour and seen them lift the sods and lay a mattress in their stead. They have covered it with grass. This is how you get away with murder, over and over again. The settled people don't understand that the Traveller on the coloured pony doesn't mean them any harm. He only wants to meet his girl who is running to him from the trees. They want them gone, and as the daylight goes, pity for it, so do we.

It is November 5th and my children are agitating to be fed. This same night, a match is thrown and a caravan burns. By the time, the helicopter lifts off for the final shot, we understand how purposes mistook have led to deaths put on by cunning and forced cause. Go, bid the soldiers shoot.

II. 'They've gone and now I'm the lord and master.'
   Clean Break, directors Gillies MacKinnon, Damien O'Donnell; writer, Billy Roche.

The blonde daughter, pale beneath her freckles before this ever began, is hustled out of my sons' bedroom by a balaclavaed man. The daylight on the landing confuses me. It is dawn in Wexford, but this family are sleeping through the flat grey light of an October afternoon. Then I remember. The gang were not admitted until my own children were safely out to school. So dawn was ever in doubt. There is one among the gang who already regrets his involvement in this sorry plot. He sits, conscience-stricken, behind the wheel of the white van, glancing anxiously towards our house.

The kidnapper steps courteously aside on the stairs and raises his hood as I pass. The house has character, he says. He has just carried the bank manager's wife out of our bedroom, his hand clapped over her mouth to stifle her panicked cries. 'Sshh, sshh,' he insists, as he presses her against our front door to manacle her fluttering arms. She is wearing silk pyjamas a pretty shade of red and the skin around her eyes is luminously taut. The paint on our front door is black with grime around the lock.

Her husband is marched into the drawing room and ordered to sit down. He selects the armchair where my mild-mannered Uncle Charles used to sit and do the crossword. The green velvet tablecloth my grandmother used for bridge has been draped over the back of it to hide an ugly stain. The walls are hung with brown paintings from country auctions. Some unlikely Chinese prints add colour to the shot. The stylish wife who walks her saluki by the disused docks would not stomach that lamp so prominently positioned beside our couch. The kidnapper takes out a pack of smokes and lights one. The banker is unperturbed; it's almost as if he knows the man. Out in the hall, his daughter is forced to kneel on the Persian carpet while her mother weeps bitter tears, her gag slipping.

And if this is not how it was nearly forty years ago, it yet comes close to how I imagined it, lying awake at a similar age in that girl's bedroom, listening out for the covert tread of balaclavaed men approaching up the stairs. For an armed gang did come to raid this house in the days when the Provos did such things. They took Joe Kirwan from the gate lodge and made him plead at the kitchen door for Muriel to admit him. His son had taken ill, he said, he needed

to call an ambulance. And once inside, they took Kitty, Muriel, Kathleen, Joe, Susie and Joseph to the coal cellar and locked them all in, saving Charles, whom they pistol-whipped through every corner of his house. Then one of them, a conscience-stricken patriot, asked my grandmother whether there was not perhaps one item she would like to keep? And to her great surprise, he returned to the cellar where they'd tumbled in quilts and eiderdowns, for it was late December and they feared her dying with the cold, bearing her silver christening bowl and made a show of balancing a little silver spoon in it. As if, she said, this one gesture were enough to redeem him as a gentleman. For all their violence, they were not discourteous.

The last day of the shoot falls on Halloween. In the downstairs bathroom, I paint Kim's face a persuasive shade of zombie green; his brother's bone-white as a skeleton. They have promised, I remind the men upstairs, to be gone by witching hour when the trick or treating must begin. Soon, I say to them, that doorbell will ring and I must admit these masked and painted children, and reward them for their terror. They'd better hurry up now and remove the hostages from the scene.

III. 'KENSINGTON 3487?'

Foyle's War; season 7, episode 2, 'The Cage'; writer Anthony Horowitz, director Stuart Orme.

The most soignée in a long series of wives to inhabit our hall raises the receiver of the Bakelite telephone. 'Kensington 3487?' she enquires. Her hair is coiffed in an elegant chignon. 'Yes,' she says. No more is necessary for her to ascend the staircase and fetch the small valise she has kept packed and ready for this moment when, like all good spies, she is recalled to East Berlin.

Her husband sits on the couch in our drawing room, bent on solving the crossword in the London Times. He is mildly perplexed by the telephone call, the sound of her footsteps making for the front door, her failure to answer him when he hails her, 'Darling?' When the inspector calls, he turns to show him the honeymoon photograph displayed beside the artless head of a crocodile. 'We were about to have dinner,' he explains. 'Everything seemed normal.'

This must be how wives disappeared in the good old days, when any unexplained step beyond the natural range of ten yards from the kitchen or flower room would be greeted as a vanishing act by their stupified men. Still holding the silver frame, he confides to Foyle in hushed tones, 'I can assure you my wife *loathed* communism.'

This husband, as it happens, also plays on my husband's team. On sunny days, I post myself on the boundary, and graze surreptitiously on the cricketers' lavishly-catered teas.

IV. 'Let's throw a lifeline to the wilderness!'
   Dare to be Wild, writer/director Vivienne de Courcy.

The crew arrive in late autumn requesting mayflowers. I have learned the only seasons film-makers will observe are those of the financial year. Everything else can be arranged. And so holm oaks supply leafy summers in November, and a hot water bottle revives a child who must step barefoot into the December stream again and again and again. I despatch them to the Ladies Meadows where the gnarled hawthorns mark lost hedgerows, and the rushes grow more thickly than the Department of Agriculture deems feasible to graze.

A stony-broke, idealistic, young landscape gardener, a boho version of the real, has a sketchbook full of grand designs she wishes to enter for the Chelsea Flower Show. She loves the wildflowers first identified in the thickets and pastures of her native Cork, though few of them are named: the pimpernel, stitchworts, vetch and lady's bedstraw that here escape from gorse fires to bloom in these fields. On screen, the hawthorn punctually effloresces a lavish shade of cream. The arch-druid, Prince Charles, strays into her circle of granite standing stones and admires it as his own. And I am not the least surprised when the spy's former husband, now captain of the Theatrical Cavaliers, shows up to chair the judging panel and awards this Celtic garden gold.

V. 'I was lonely for a context. You think these are your surroundings but you know in your heart, they're not.' Eavan Boland.
   Is it Still the Same?, directors Charlie McCarthy and Declan Recks.

The reins hang slackly from the bridle. The forelock sweeps over an eye. This coloured pony arrived by crate and sea from Yorkshire. It belongs to Mel, my step-daughter, a present from her grandfather, sent over by her mother as a gift-horse for my son. But what is this pony doing here? It is not huge or threatening, but a dappled steed fit only for a damsel in the best of coupon dresses, rocking between nations, upstairs in the playroom of the Irish ambassador's London residence.

Winter Papers

VOLUME 4

IRELAND'S ANNUAL ARTS ANTHOLOGY

Edited by KEVIN BARRY and OLIVIA SMITH

· VISUAL ART · PHOTOGRAPHY · MUSIC ·
· DANCE · THEATRE · FILM · FICTION ·
· ESSAYS · POETRY ·

An annual anthology for the arts in Ireland and beyond – stories, interviews, essays, reportage, photographs, more.

Featuring

Stephen Brandes	Selina Guinness	Bush Moukarzel
Dylan Brennan	Lisa Harding	Peter Murphy
Liliana P. Brennan	Siobhán Kane	mynameisjOhn
Jan Carson	Oonagh Kearney	Doireann Ní Ghríofa
Jill Crawford	Ben Kidd	Mark O'Connell
Danny Denton	Anna Leask	Aiden O'Reilly
Wendy Erskine	Dónal Lunny	Rosie O'Reilly
Leontia Flynn	Ian Maleney	Elske Rahill
John Gallagher	Mike McCormack	Cathy Sweeney
Róise Goan	Eoin McNamee	Maria Nilsson Waller
	Yvette Monahan	

RRP €40

WINTERPAPERS.COM

CURLEW EDITIONS

ISBN 978-0-9933029-3-0

'We turned the armchairs on their side there, day after day, and called them horses, and rode them away from this strange house with the fog outside the window and a fiction of home in the carpets on the floor,' wrote Eavan Boland in Object Lessons.

The silver doorknob turns and the door swings open to reveal a blur of heavy curtains downstairs in the dining room. The lens pans round at a child's eye level taking in forbidden things: the polished expanse of mahogany, the stiff-backed chairs. It pauses, and then tracks back to the ornately-framed portrait that dominates the room. The camera lingers longingly on the dragoon's red uniform, the gold frogging, the regimental badge of the 9th Queen's Lancers, a true cavalier. And I wonder how Samuel White, M.P. for County Leitrim, an Orangeman who voted in favour of Jewish and Catholic emancipation, would regard his reincarnation in the dining room of Frederick Boland, De Valera's private secretary, a signatory of the Treaty, ambassador of the Republic to the Court of St. James? The poet's voice explains that her father came from a 'recognisable Ireland, an Ireland that marched towards independence.' And it is hard not to think that, in these circumstances, her parents would have evicted this military ancestor, for all that he considered himself an Irishman, from their new residence: the first occupants of the brand new embassy at 17, Grosvenor Place, a building gifted only two years previously to the Irish state by the Hon. Arthur Ernest Guinness.

And what of the women in this patrilineal changing of the guard? Strangely enough, in my own mother's house, a painting by the poet's mother, Frances Kelly, hangs above her bed. The model relaxes in an armchair, an ochre cushion behind her head, a green cloth draped over her left forearm. The gesture of comfort is as certain as a piece of furniture. You sense the artist and her model are composed in each other's presence. Her lack of clothes is incidental. A swirl of paint confidently suggests the weight of her right breast. A book lies open in her lap, the cup and saucer held lightly upon it. Her head is turned towards the window where a fuller-figured vase stands empty on the sill. It is a noise outside perhaps, that has drawn her thoughts away.

VI. 'It is love / both granite and meadow.'
'Tending', Vahni Capildeo, from Venus as a Bear, Carcanet.

The Trinidadian poet Vahni Capildeo, has stayed at Tibradden, and lists the house as a location for five poems in her collection Venus as a Bear.

The bottom sash is raised high to let the summer evening pour in. The Killers are on stage tonight *and anything goes in a place like this* distorts the chorus of this Dublin pastoral I'm trying hard to write. The traffic on the M50 thrums like a cricket beyond the thistles, already going to seed in the drought. The two rams have moved across from the Ladies Meadows for there is still water in the drinkers this side of the lane. The ewes are bellowing for their attention, echoing the lambs we should be weaning now.

Vahni, you have set our house singing in Venus as a Bear, and tonight indeed, this figure at her desk sings inside the body of your stringed

instrument. Am I not your guest? *Il n'ya pas de* house *hors-texte*. We have dined on puffball and exchanged crocodiles and wolf dogs between our paper zoos. Out in the walled garden, you miss a falcon among the witch hazels, but this lack, this flash of fire in the abyss, sings the joy of freedom in this the place I host, for now.

And to which shepherd ultimately do all these lambs belong? The one who gets them standing on her opening page, or the one who'll feed them, dose them, weigh them, and with any luck, dispatch them heavily to slaughter before the season's out?

And if this essay is a cavalier performance among the theatrical props of other texts, a disavowal of property in other people's words, then let it also be a prayer of sorts that this house remains a welcome, a playhouse where those distinctions between *host*, *hospes*, *hostis*, come not to matter much. For is this not how home is always best defined? Not as a place of identity but a mode of self-effacement; not a return to origin, but a masquerade of hinterlands, where today a woman writes, anxious to leave this house in the able care of others. Her valise is packed. She is waiting only for the call.

A POLAROID DIARY

Oonagh Kearney

A beautiful invitation:

A camera & eight Polaroids

'Off you go.'

I hold the camera up and point it in the direction of several palm trees yawning below the window of a small flat on the outskirts of Cannes. I am here for ten days for the film festival.

Yesterday, before I leave Cork, I am struck by two ironies.

1. A 'working/holiday' booked before the announcement of the 8th Amendment referendum date. I had thought, it will be June. I consider not going. I want to be home canvassing. I buy a copy of Kathy D'Arcy's Autonomy, a load of 'Yes' badges and stickers in my local Together4Yes HQ and 'off I go.'

2. I will be taking my Polaroids while attending a festival known for its glamour and sunshine, as much as for its film culture. This breeds low level anxiety that the Polaroids will be entirely out of whack with the daily life of a film-maker. I look at the positive: 'at least the light will be good.'

*

I like this camera: plastic, bulky, resilient. When I take it out, I notice there are two remaining Polaroids (still to be shot) inside. Immediately, this makes me happy: two spares, two extras, two additional chances to 'mess around', shoot a bogey without consequence, miss a beat without having pressed record. Practice Polaroids if you will. Leftovers from the last pair of hands to hold this plastic wizardry of promise.

I point – assess – redirect – decide – press! Wait – nothing – press again! – swish – light flash – movement – machinations – but nothing emerges.

It would seem my Polaroid camera (I call it mine, though it is not, how quickly I form attachment) is simply going through the motions. A Polaroid that can't polaroid. An 'Instamax' that can't instantize the instant.

Several spontaneous moments are lost before I realise that irony will be, quite literally, my constant and defining companion on this journey.

*

Should I squander these two spares (by removing them and in doing so, exposing them) and load in the fresh, unzipped foil of eight? Days pass, with new distractions, before I take action. By now, I am feeling less confident. To press the red button, no longer engenders a new world. I load up. Point towards the trees – press – and – slither! A thin black cover sheet emerges. But I am not expecting this. I am thrown. I press again. And this time – a Polaroid does emerge.

But no trees just cloud.

One down, seven to go.

Polaroid 1

'Palm Trees'

'Maybe this is what happens when I am too high?'

Polaroid 2

'Cannes' (Assurances)

For fear I might leave it somewhere, I haven't brought the camera out (it's back to 'the camera' again, not mine, for obvious reasons). On the way home from a screening I see the words 'C-A-N-N-E-S' lit up on the hillside. Jazz music plays. It is raining. Shiny tarmac reflects neon. I point and click: 'a little glitz in the group will do no harm.'

The moment charms. And I forget the rain. But jostling home in my bag in the dark, the rain finds my Polaroid ...

Polaroid 3

'Mandy'

I am sitting a the back of the Arcade cinema for a late night screening of Mandy directed by Panos Cosmatos and starring my friend Olwen Fouéré. Weirdly, the screenplay is co-written by Aaron Stewart-Ahn, who I briefly met at University College Cork twenty years ago when he was a visiting Asian-American student. I responded to his ad to be part of a film. The script required me to take off most of my clothes for a sex scene. Desperate as my eighteen year old self was to be part of theatre and film, I decided it wasn't for me. About a year ago, when I joined Twitter, I reconnected with Aaron. He's a decent guy: funny, warm, aware and all these years later, still working in film. This is the Directors' Fortnight. Fair play to him.

The opening credits come up in neon pink: Nicolas Cage, Andrea Roseborough, Ned Dennehy, Olwen Fouéré. I don't know Ned, except through his many roles in Irish film and theatre. In a year when there has been no Irish production at Cannes, I feel immensely proud of these two fine actors, Ned and Olwen, flying the Irish flag.

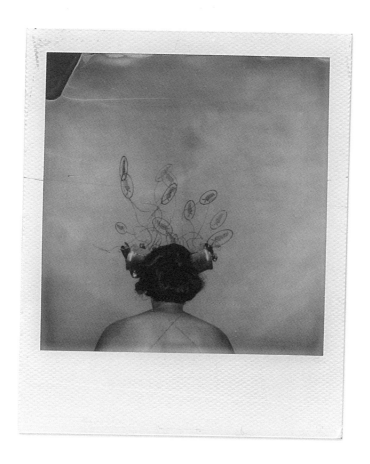

Polaroid 4

'Palm d'Or'

After hours of careful preparation this is her moment to walk the red carpet, decked out in a golden dress and head piece. Who is she?

She is one of the many who come to the Palais daily all dressed up and looking for tickets to a gala premiere that evening. The dress code for men is strictly black tie. For women, anything glamorous goes.

Polaroid 5, 6, 7

'Meditation'

We've always meditated together since we first met.

But until I took this Polaroid, neither of us knew that he always with his hands down, and me with my hands up.

The weather is so fine, we take our practice to the beach where others sit in quiet contemplation.

I stare at the horizon.

I think about the future.

And the past ...

I try to be in the present.

POLAROID 8, 9, 10, 11

'Yes'

8. Back in Cork, canvassing.

One week to go. Hope and fear, the stuff of screenwriting. Every vote counts. I am surrounded by heroes.

9. This is a portrait of the surface of the moon. Or at least this is what I see in the Polaroid taken while driving to Offaly, further and further away from the people I love and want to be with as perhaps, together, we turn the tide of history.

I feel a presence while driving. I look out to my right and see the moon: round, white, almost bobbing. For a moment, I really feel its taut roundness; defined and curved within space, like the earth. A buoyant moon, a confident moon, a moon that is with me, with us.

Two hours later, I pull into the B&B car park and the radio announces the exit polls. Wait a second – this can't be? I sit in the car, glued to Twitter. I pick up my room key, walk to the nearest hotel, order prosecco and find some fellow yes voters with whom to celebrate. Jesusmotherfuckingchrist we did it.

10. Driving home the following evening I listen to so much bad music on the radio, waiting for the official announcement. After what seems like an eternity, and plenty of analysis, the final result comes through: 1,429,981 of us voted yes. I wanted to mark the moment and here it is. The road ahead. Taken just inside the Cork County Boundary.

OONAGH KEARNEY

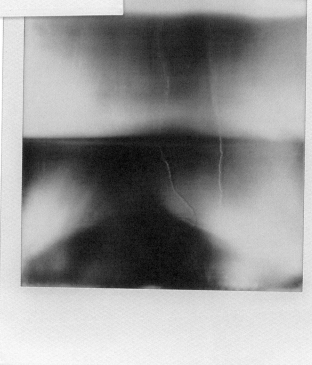

OONAGH KEARNEY

Polaroid 12

'Back to Life, Back to Reality'

The dream is here: clear, open, expansive.

But my desk is still busy, over-crowded, cluttered.

Getting back to work is never as straightforward or as simple as I'd like.

I, THE FLOCK

Mike McCormack

We got word today. Our son Mark has died for the eighth and last time. All his iterates and avatars now finally laid to rest, flesh and bone followed to oblivion. His digital ghosts evaporated.

'Thank god,' Martha breathed, 'over at last.'
'Yes, our prayers have been answered.'
'The longest two years of my life,' she continued. 'Where was he found?'
'Don't ask.'
'I have to.'
'You don't want to know.'
'Yes I do, this is my son we're talking about.'
'Sort of.'
'You know what I mean.'
'It's not good.'
'Of course it's not good, tell me where for Christ's sake.'
'In Lubyanka prison, he was interrogated and he never regained consciousness.'

Martha nodded without further expression. Son or no son, the same news eight times in a row has that deadening effect on you. Our only comfort now is that they will finally issue a death certificate and we can sign off on his life. Our son's life bracketed by certificates, our signatures on both.

Our child finally laid to rest.

Mark was killed two years ago, at his own desk in his own bedroom. At the time, in his early twenties, he was working as a contract coder for a climate change organisation and was preparing an important presentation for an upcoming environmental conference. The day he was killed he had spent several hours modelling the rise in sea levels along a fifty mile stretch of Ireland's west coast. But it was not rising sea levels that killed him. Wounds to his chest and abdomen confirm that in his last moment he had time to turn and face his killers.

The mainstream media glossed over his death as yet another casualty in the endless attrition between various terrorist factions. But no one believes that it was anything other than a government-sponsored hit – a dark cameo in this administration's undeclared war on its own citizenry. Mark, you see, was one of those activists who had made himself a thorn in the side of the government. Since his late teens he had turned his coding skills to the ethical hacking of corporate databases and those bank accounts registered to the one per cent. And whatever monies he skimmed from these accounts he channelled to projects which were as virtuous as they were intentionally shaming. Suddenly banks and oligarchs found themselves the unlikely benefactors of various charitable causes in distant lands – breastfeeding clinics in Bangalore, literacy and educational projects in North Korea, desalination plants in West Africa. All this work on the side of the angels, this saintly work which should have ended when he died.

However, shortly after his month's mind mass, seven images of Mark's face were posted to the homepages of government departments and certain banking institutions. No one knew where they originated from but they coincided with a concerted assault on the accounts of some very high net worth individuals. Soon afterwards they found themselves underwriting small banks which specialised in funding flood relief and inoculation projects in Southeast Asia. It would seem that Mark's saintly work would continue after his death.

So, for the past two years Mark's avatars have stayed one step ahead of those digital bounty hunters which have been sent after them by the security forces, ducking and diving and leaving in their wake a pleasing trail of chaos. But in the last couple of months, each of his seven avatars has been run to ground – some cornered and cancelled, some with their code hopelessly scrambled, some finally reaching the limits of their AI and now exhausted from the chase and finally raising their hands above their heads with no expectation of any mercy. One by one they have been brought to heel until this last one, dead in a prison cell in Lubyanka, signalled the last of Mark's ghosts, his flock finally dissolved.

Looking at the whole thing now I find it hard to decide whether it was all political activism or a work of art. Was it social passion or private inspiration? Or both? I am inclined to think it was both because it would be of a piece with Mark himself, a child who was ever in two minds.

Of course Martha lost interest in all this a long time ago. All emotional interest that is. Now she is merely tidying away the facts, keeping abreast of things. She has long since cried her tears somewhere out of sight, some shaded place which lends itself to the shedding of angry tears.

It's hard to say when we stopped loving each other. Hard to say precisely when the distance between us opened to a fatal fissure – both of us stranded on either sides of a crevasse waving forlornly across at each other. The obvious answer is that it occurred with Mark's death, that his passing marked the end of our marriage. The truth is that we were far apart by then, if we cared to admit it. I think Martha tired of me. And that is as simple as it may be – the loss of love may be down to something as banal as people tiring of each other.

And of course she blames me for Mark's death. My crime is to have handed him a cause and a passion which has now gone and got him killed.

She was never so virulent on the topic as the day we heard of his death. In the kitchen she took a moment to set aside her grief and shock to lay into me.

'Politics,' she choked, 'social justice, it's all a fucking virus and now it has gone and got our child killed. I hope you are happy.'

'He was my son,' I protested.

'You never loved him,' she raged, the words coming forth in a spray of spit.

I opened my hands in a kind of martyred pleading.

'No,' she raged, 'never. You might have thought you did, you saw him do certain things and you approved of these things because in reality they were your things but you never loved him. You and your fucking history.'

And then her voice tailed away into that pale silent rage that has always frightened me.

And now our son is finally dead and there is nothing we can do for him. And precisely because he is dead I have all those wishes a father might want for his son. I would like to think that he stood his ground at the end. As a teenager he distinguished himself as not only a skilful sportsman but also as one in whom there was no backward step. I would like to think that when the end came he drew on this stubbornness and that it stood to him. But of course my wishes would be different had he survived. I am fully aware of that.

And I can see him at his desk, his head bent towards the two monitors he always worked from.

That is where he made his stand. I imagine that when his door burst open he rose with his hands above his head, rising slowly from his chair, pushing it away with the backs of his legs. No doubt he would have some quip on his lips – Mark always had a dramatic sense of the moment, he would have prepared himself for it, a range of smart-arsed comments stacked against this moment.

And that is where they shot him, entry and exit wounds, that is where his heart stopped beating and his pulse running. And that was the precise moment when all hell broke loose

And now we have come to get his death certificate, to sign off on his life once and for all.

And this man in front of us does not look like the sort who should be sitting behind a desk. Some kink in his fate has detoured him from the life of manual labour his broad shoulders and heavy forearms suggest and placed him in this cramped room with its poor lighting and stacks of files. Discarded monitors clutter up the space behind Martha and myself. One of them is trailing a black lead and a plug as if it were its own dismal umbilical.

The man has taken the last few minutes to scan through our documents before he pushes them to one side.

'Everything seems to be in order.'

'Good,' I nod.

There then follows a long pause. I can only guess that he is surprised to find himself in this narrow enclosure. A man with those shoulders and arms would have thought he would make his way through life making room for himself.

'So you can issue the death certificate.' Martha does nothing to hide the note of weary impatience in her voice.

'No.'

'No.'

'There have been developments.'

'What sort of developments.' I can feel Martha stiffen beside me. The sudden tension in her shoulders crosses the distance between us and settles across my neck. The man across the desk is not suited to such clipped exchanges, his idiom is surely a more expansive bluster, not this finicky obstructionism.

'We have received intelligence that more of Mark's avatars have come online in the past few days.'

'He has been dead two years, how could there be more.'

My pause is his invitation to explain but it is a moment before he steps into it.

'Bounty hunters have spent the last two years hunting down all your son's iterates. Last month we tracked down the seventh and neutralised him in Lubyanka prison. '

'You mean murdered him,' Martha charges.

'We know all this,' I say in exasperation.

The man forges ahead without acknowledging our interjections. 'We thought that was the last of them, but yesterday we received information that there has been a new outbreak.'

I crane forward. 'How do you mean? Mark has been dead two years, how can you be sure any outbreak has anything to do with him?'

'His fingerprints are all over these avatars. Their governing algorithms share basic coding characteristics which are as individual and as recognisable as fingerprints.'

'How many this time?' Martha asks.

'Eight.'

'Are there any more?'

'We are pretty sure that we have them all.'

A sudden barking laugh erupts from Martha. It startles me to see her exchange a look with this man across the table. Something tells me that I've missed something.

'What?' I say stupidly.

'You tell him,' Martha urges the man. 'My husband is a history teacher so this is a pattern he has not come across before.'

'Your wife has spotted the significance,' the man says, 'one, seven, eight ... that is a very recognisable numeric progression. But in this context it is more than a sequence, it is a message.'

'If it is a message, I cannot read it.'

'The message says that this is likely to go viral. Any attempt to round up these eight avatars will only generate more and next time the number will be even greater.'

'So what are you going to do?'

The man sits back and shakes his head. 'For the moment we cannot do anything, your son is well ahead of us; it is best to leave well enough alone.'

Martha has already risen from her chair, she is all rage and disappointment. Her voice is a low rasp.

'Congratulations, our son is about to go viral.'

Outside the Registry of Births and Deaths a low winter sun shines across the car park. I had not noticed that at the furthest end of the car park an international insurance firm has a large regional office. Something about it makes me stand and stare for a moment. Martha turns to see me gazing at the blue façade.

'That was his first strike,' she says.

'Yes, that's what I am trying to remember.'

At the beginning of his political activism Mark's first successful hack was to infiltrate the files of this very insurance company and to rename and sell on a handful of their policies to a Dutch bank. He then rerouted the funds to a children's hospital in Gaza. By the time the money was traced, several kids had undergone expensive life-saving procedures on the back of his funding. It was months later before I heard about it and was able to piece it all together but even today I still feel something of the excited pride I felt at the time. I admired his courage and his imagination, the broad mindfulness of the whole thing. But even if it was the start of his successful activist's career it raised a flag with his name on it as a talented and passionate hacker; from that day on there was a target painted on him and looking back at what was then a triumph, it is now possible to see it as the beginning of the end.

I am suddenly overcome. So many things run through my mind and it feels as if the sunlight of this day has found a way into my head. A voice is speaking to me on the edge of this car park.

'Tell me my son is not dead,' it says. 'Tell me that there is a door somewhere behind which he is sitting and all I have to do is push it open and he will turn towards me. Tell me that we will recognise each other and that we will take it from there. Tell me that we are not such awkward men that we would not be able to make the most of this moment. Tell me that we would find the words. Tell me that we are that sort of men. Tell me that I would close the door and pull up a chair and the moment would lend us the proper words. Tell me these things. Tell me that we are not so far gone in awkwardness that we would let the moment slip away between us. Tell me that these things happen outside history and tell me that this is not my fault, tell me that I have nothing to do with it.'

I see the startled look on Martha's face and I realise that I have spoken out loud.

'Let's go home,' she says.

And she is walking towards the car and before I start I am already five paces behind her.

FORM, FLOW, FLUX, AND OTHER F-WORDS

In conversation – LEONTIA FLYNN and DOIREANN NÍ GHRÍOFA

The poets Leontia Flynn and Doireann Ní Ghríofa sat down in Belfast and talked about what it is they do, and how they go about doing it.

DOIREANN NÍ GHRÍOFA: So what do we mean when we use the phrase poetic craft? What is that?

LEONTIA FLYNN: I am unable to think in abstract terms. Sometimes, that phrase sounds really daunting like (extreme Darth Vader voice) 'CRAFT' or alternatively, like when you have a project involving Airfix glue and a plane to assemble (*laughs*). What do *you* mean when *you* say craft, how 'bout that?

DNG: Cheers for flipping it back to me! I first came to poetry feeling very much like a dabbler, and I still have that chip on my shoulder, of fretting that I am very amateurish, though I suspect that every writer has a chip of some shape or other on their shoulders …

LF: Oh, huge. Huge chips.

DNG: … and I suppose *one* of my own chips lies in the insecurities of a person who hasn't a clue what they are doing at all, and is outside of a university system in which everyone appears to be capable of articulating their work in sophisticated terms of craft. My own feels more of a shambles, to be honest, more of a mad combination of chance and daydream and messing. Because of that impostor-esque feeling, whenever people speak of things like 'craft' around me, I immediately feel that terrified sense of 'Oh shit, I'm going to be found out now.' So that's my experience of phrases like craft. Horror.

LF: Seamus Heaney's take – this is from one of the essays in Preoccupations – is that craft is the learning, the inherited, the making thing, the tradition, in some ways the *polishing* bit, and then technique is the instinct, the *winging it* bit, and the inspiration.

DNG: And how does that definition actually feel within your daily practice of writing poetry?

LF: As I get older I can see that it's useful to maybe conceptualise it like that, But you don't conceptualise it when you're getting the poem written, do you? So whatever you call it, it's *after* you've done it. I think the way I've written is changing over time, which makes me think that craft *is* what we practise and technique is what we just *have*. I've always had a strong sense of limit. When I started to write the poems for my first book I just made everything ten lines long. And now I might think why? Why ten? But I couldn't predict what fell into that form, and that was the exciting part. You know the sense of just failing and failing and failing, and then saying 'Right, I'm not doing this anymore, this is pointless,' and somehow then finding it coming out in a way

I didn't think of. So I am really interested in the part I never predicted, which was somehow in the dark.

DNG: Absolutely! Yes, I know that sense of surprising myself within the act of trying to build a poem, and the surprise that swerves up when I least expected it. Such a buzz.

LF: I like the part that isn't quite in control of the process. And the fastness of writing poems. Actually, forget that, never mind craft and technique, I think a better distinction is quick poems and slow poems, and the slow poems tend to be more crafted … and you have to live in between. I don't mind the writing, writing's great, it's all the living in between bit that I can't be bothered with (*laughs*). But then when I have a sense of it, I can return to it with the idea of a sort of formal shape that I can work towards. Your poems are often quite long, aren't they?

DNG: Yeah, I've found myself writing longer poems over the past three years or so. I would love to be able to write shorter poems, I'm always hoping, trying, and failing to write shorter poems, but the failures keep leading me towards these wildly lengthy poems. I seem to need a lot of space to sketch the architecture I need within a poem, to evoke the type of vividness that I want to conjure in the reader, but I really hope I will be able to teach myself to write shorter poems. I deeply envy writers who can communicate a poem within a restricted space. I am always striving for that, and I find the practice is really useful, even though more often than not I fail at it. The gesture or the attempt towards brevity still enriches my poems. Any tips for those of us who want shorter poems?

LF: Well I find that this tendency to write short, or to write poems with restrictions, is just how form works for me. Even when I write essays, I am not someone who is ever going to go over a word limit. You know, ever. I don't find any of this easy. Maybe ease is an interesting part of this as well. I find it all really, really hard.

DNG: Yes, absolutely. I struggle so much more with writing as I go on. It's like the more I dedicate my days to trying to write, the harder it gets. That side of craft is counter-intuitive, isn't it? I would have assumed that any skill a person dedicates their days to must be bound to get easier, or at least quicker, the more it's practised. Not this, though, at least not for me. My current level is Code Red: Excruciating. I find it's harder and harder as I go on. Do you?

LF: Yeah. I mean I think it's incredibly difficult to do. It's all so incredibly hard-won. For me, my earlier poems were an attempt to create a sense of immediacy, and that is not the same thing as writing something in an immediate way. So it was all more difficult than it maybe appeared … and that's the chip on my shoulder. Oh, the chip on my shoulder goes down so far it reaches the pain in my heart (*laughs*).

DNG: We could be here all day talking about the various chips on our shoulders! I'm curious to hear more about one thing you mentioned, the distinction between the self-imposed restrictions you chose in form at this point in your development, and how subsequent external restrictions, like lack of time, came to bear on your poems? How was your craft impacted differently by choosing a certain set of restrictions versus having restrictions imposed upon you from outside, and how do you navigate between the two?

LF: Oh very interesting. Choosing a limit is self-imposed, where I'd say, 'I'm going to spend this long and write for this long.' Something works maybe one time out of ten. So in fact the limits don't appear within the poem. Also I never obey my own deadlines. I don't know how anyone does.

DNG: Do you impose deadlines on yourself? How does that work? Do you mean a time limit to complete a poem in? So in addition to the restriction of form you're imposing on yourself, you are also setting yourself a specific deadline in which to have written the poem?

LF: Well I'll say, 'I'll get this one done by such and such,' just to have a sense of it not, you know, dragging on for my whole life. It doesn't work anyway, because stuff in notebooks – ideas, images, whatever – actually all comes back years later. I'm always amazed by that. But the form comes first for me. So if short poems started me off, then I thought 'Oh I'll do these sonnet-y things' – out of boredom really – and then I got bored again and started writing in five-line stanzas. Again, I don't know why, except maybe they just felt like sonnets with an extra line, they even had that wee shift in the middle, and because I did five or six like that, they started to generate their own momentum and I wrote more and more, and stuff I'd stored from years before all started coming into it. So it felt organic. That's the winging it thing, isn't it? When I stopped I thought *Huh? Did I really do that? Did that really happen?*

DNG: Ah, that process sounds like you're touching on that really hip buzzword of 'flow'.

LF: I haven't heard anyone else talk about this. I always talk about this, even in my class yesterday. So 'flow' is a thing now?

DNG: Yeah! The sense of getting really immersed in any kind of artistic practice to a point where it is all coming together so smoothly that it feels like the world falls away, and afterwards you might sort of think, 'Wow, where did that come from?' It's something I've felt, too. I mean, it's the magic, isn't it? It's the magic of subsuming ourselves in the writing. It's the high every writer, artist, composer, whatever, is chasing. And then in the aftermath of that weird sense of flow, it's hard to even recognise the thing as yours … I sometimes feel like a stranger wrote all my poems because I get so lost in that process, I almost disappear into it. And when I perform my poems at readings I sometimes feel like 'Who wrote this stuff, it wasn't me!'

LF: And when you get into that flow, you're changed as a result of it. I was talking about The Figure a Poem Makes yesterday, by Robert Frost. The idea of a poem as a 'piece of ice riding on its own melting' – you know, where it assumes direction with the first line and then takes us somewhere we didn't foresee. It's so much about his own project, like (*fancy old man voice*) 'Yes Robert, tell us all about your poems now, why don't you!' But after a while I began to think that it was the only way I could understand poetry. There's something within us that wants to say things and for them to sound lovely and rhythmically pleasing. Poems are a completely different way of communicating … It's neurological. I did not know flow was trending right now but I am on board with that. If the kids are all about flow, then I am too (*laughs*).

DNG: You're well ahead of the zeitgeist! I'm curious about what you mentioned about that sense of our repeated failures as poets, and how for you that might involve what you describe as abandoning images or ideas in notebooks, only to find that they rear up years later and stride into a new poem. So maybe you almost have a sense of where that poem rose up from, the seeds of it, at least? I'm trying to remember that quote by Michael Longley – 'If I knew where poems came from, I'd just go there.' Where do your poems come from, and do you recognise them from those abandonments as they arrive, or are they mysterious and unrecognisable again as you coax them out into the world?

LF: This used to sound like some crazy Wicker Man bullshit to me, some witchcraft nonsense. *Oh, High Priest of Poetry, let me commune with the greats on Mount Parnassus*, or whatever. But it's true I never sat down with a kind of project, say, 'Now I'm going to write about Inherited Trauma. Or hey, I'm going to write about Women in Families. Or oh, now I'm going to write about Ghosts.' No, it all felt slightly more fortuitous. And I was excited by that.

DNG: I love the sense of being excited at that point in the process of telling yourself the poem. The point at which it feels quite private as an act of communication, when it's a weird sort of story I'm telling myself, and it's always so strange and surprising to me.

LF: Like some sort of circuit, where everything goes in the right direction and it produces something that can't really be engineered.

DNG: Mmm. Controversial question coming up … In light of what you've just said, that the impulse cannot be engineered … Well, can it be taught?

LF: Hah! Well, right then, here's the thing. You cannot teach somebody to be struck by lightning, really. But you can teach them the crafty bit, so there's a preparedness, and a sense of building good habits, so that when the lightning does strike, we hope that it'll meet with receptiveness.

DNG: Nuala Ní Dhomhnaill has written beautifully on this, how she spends time in the folklore archives, reading and reading, and maintaining that daily habit of writing, so that when that lightning of a new poem eventually does hit, she feel ready for it: as far as I remember, she calls it 'sharpening the metaphorical pencils.' It's match-fitness, I suppose, isn't it? There is a sense of mystery too, isn't there?

LF: I don't know about you but I can be hugely contradictory on this. In one way I say it's a sort of affliction. I mean who wants this personality type? (*laughs*).

DNG: Yeah, absolutely. Who would want to be a poet? We're all total nightmares.

LF: To be always hankering after a poem, yearning for it, condemned to only ever be half-paying attention, and to live in a certain amount of chaos (*gestures to the corpse of a plant on her desk*) because we're not paying attention to the world. And on the other hand, I also say, well, it is just simply a thing you do. The writing itself, it's labour. It's hard work, it's a laborious thing. People think that you're sitting under a tree, knitting blankets for fairies (*laughs*) but there's a lot of heavy lifting. So I want both sides of it: the heavy lifting, but also the stuff that puts you at odds. I think that if you're not at odds with the world, well, you should be. Because writing poetry demands time, labour and concentration, in a really un-concentrating world.

DNG: Oh god, yeah. Is it a life sentence, do you think? Are the pair of us stuck this way for life, now?

LF: Er, yeah. I think so. I really do. Do you not?

DNG: No, I think we are. I think we're done for (*laughs*). Someone asked me recently what I will do with myself once I retire?! And I laughed so much, imagining that one day I might just say 'Now. That's enough of that. Where's my hammock?' As if it might be that easy – to just, somehow, decide to give up writing on a whim.

LF: I did consider stopping publishing, but never writing. Writing is the sense of wonder and awe in response to life that is so necessary for me, I couldn't stop that.

DNG: You do sometimes appear from the outside to be a poet who almost rejects the modern public face of poetry …

LF: Huh? Do I?

DNG: Well I mean especially with the internet. You're not into that side of things, are you?

LF: It's partly that I'm really bad at it.

DNG: I deeply empathise with that sense of wariness, because so much about the internet directly opposes what we are attempting to achieve in terms of our craft.

LF: Well, I'll paraphrase a Yeats quote that says writing is the social act by the solitary person. I think the internet is a marvellous thing, or it was, originally, but not the 'social' element of social media. I write poetry, but when I try to say something 'as a poet' I just end up thinking 'I'm so bad at this, and now I am going to leave.' I'm actually just shy or socially awkward, which is an evolutionarily pointless and very pre-internet thing.

DNG: How did that work its way into your last book, The Radio, with its poem-scenes between that 'awesome voice of the internet' and the persona of an exhausted mother?

LF: A good few years ago I felt social media would change everything – our sense of representation and identity and communication.

DNG: And it really has.

LF: I worried it was all going to become a popularity contest. Poetry has always been relatively unpopular, and had a minority following, so I hoped it wouldn't affect it – but actually it sort of *has*, in a way.

DNG: It seems to me to be developing into an equation which always has the same thing at the end: dollar symbols. Publishing is a business. Even poetry publishing, though the numbers are small, is in many ways an exercise in capitalism. And social media is swiftly becoming an element within the digits of that equation, a development which is increasingly evident in the American literary scene, perhaps less so in Ireland, at least so far.

LF: I see it in universities, too. They've become much more vocational and trades-y, like, 'We're going to teach you to write – now! You're a writer!' but within that system, what will happen to the critical voices who might actually address these issues, and the implications of massively reorganising our ways of communication with each other?

DNG: Yes, and our mechanisms of thought. That seems to me an interesting element in how the internet is developing within our private hours, within our days: the way we think, such a fundamental element of our private lives, something which was always so nebulous, and so malleable, appears to me to be changing in response to the internet.

LF: Exactly.

DNG: And you're at the coalface of this because you are working every day with young people who are grappling with their efforts to become writers, but within a world in which the internet marks their every waking hour. Where is the place for poetic craft within a culture in which there is this fragmentation of thought? How does the internet infect or enrich the craft of our human attempts to make poetry?

LF: I love 1960s handbooks to poetry. Look at Ted Hughes's The Making of Poetry, and it's simply about looking at animals. You know the way it once seemed like all poems were just about that – looking at animals? (*Laughs.*) But he has a thing about stilling your mind to focus and maybe allowing the thoughts to arise like fish in a pond, and if you don't then they will remain like 'fish in the pond of a man who does not fish'. So I asked people if their thoughts were like those last fish – and they said yes, basically. I mean their lives are very distracting. The fragmentation puts the inner life – which is where poems come from – under pressure.

(*Deleted: a long and funny tangent about WhatsApp, internet memes, the place of the viewer in absorbing the evolution of a single meme in internet culture and reading Twitter jokes as living fossils of humour in flux.*)

DNG: I'm really interested in how a poet who is internet-literate may begin to allow the sense of an internet audience to influence their craft. Like, I'm very curious about poets who write the type of short verse which is wildly popular on Instagram, in how writing with the aim of creating something which, above all else, is popular will bring the sense of an audience into the writing process itself. Will this be an element of the writing process for more poets as we continue to inhabit the age of the internet? When you and I are old will we be saying 'Ah, I remember how people used to write poems long ago, even before the internet. The good old days …'

LF: But what about how language influences it … writing in Irish. Obviously you're not outside things like the internet – but does it allow you to be more private in a world where there's no privacy?

DNG: It absolutely does – given that the general readership for poetry is small, the readership for Irish-language poetry is smaller still! Our readers are a tiny fraction of a tiny fraction. I cherish the freedom it allows me. For me the writing process can be quite selfish at certain points, where I'm really just writing the poem for the poem's sake, and I'm merrily oblivious to thoughts of audience, or whatever.

LF: Yes, there's no place for that when you're writing a poem. It constructs its own readers, and I don't think there have to be that many of them.

DNG: Writing in Irish, I don't feel any need at any point in the writing of a poem to censor myself, or to tone things down for any imagined reader. So even in my early books, there's a lot of quite explicit writing on the body, and sexuality, and I might be a little warier with English. So that's really liberating.

LF: I find it weird how people talk about Irish-language literature in romanticised terms, because I love things like how Nuala Ní Dhomhnaill might write about myth but then there'll be a modern object in the next line.

DNG: Exactly! It's one of the joys of reading her work. When bean a' leasa, the fairy queen, rocks up holding a Black+Decker! Amazing … I mean modern life is throbbing through all of Irish-language literature. I feel really lucky to be coming of age in this particular generation of Irish poets. I love how in Aifric Mac Aodha's poems, in particular, you have elements like a nightclub DJ, or a fisherman lifting nets to find a sex toy, or the very modern experience of arsing around on boredpanda online. I love it, but it's not what people expect of Irish poetry.

LF: Oh God, what do people expect of Irish poetry? How does the flow work with writing in Irish? Does it flow more in one language or the other?

DNG: Well I can only speak for my own process here but yeah, it is different in the different languages for me. When I first started to write, I was writing only in Irish and I had a very strong sense of flow, I almost couldn't help myself. Then, because I didn't have any external translator, I forced myself to learn how to translate my own poems to English. At first, there was zero sense of flow in that process for me, it was excruciating trying to make myself write in another language, really counter-intuitive. But then I started to feel a little of that exciting sensation of flow, and I started to write some poems in English. But I needed a sense of restriction still so I wrote a lot in form, and I still cringe a bit at how that book (Clasp) feels to me like a chain of writing exercises like, oh, you know, 'Now write a villanelle. Now write a rondelet.' But in order to carry myself into writing in English, to almost trick myself into that flow, I needed the forms to unlock the door. What you mentioned earlier about choosing the restrictions for your work really resonated with me in that sense. As I've gone on now, I do now get the sense of flow when I write in both languages.

LF: The reason I started translating was because I had to write in what would be shorter time slots, and I didn't want to sit down to the panic of a blank page. So as well as starting a long poem which I knew I would work on one stanza at a time, I wanted to translate something which would be full of, you know, sex, and swearing – because I had a baby. I'd done Catullus at school and I remembered he was really short, and that the diction was clear. That pristine clarity, that bluntness was how I'd wanted to sound. I knew I could always go back to him if I got stuck with the struggle of just keeping things going and return to those translations.

DNG: That's fascinating to me, the effort within the craft of translation to carry over to your own poems that are bring written in parallel the sense of clarity from those primary texts.

LF: Yes, and the rhythm of it, too. The flow you can sense without knowing the words. Sometimes I'd abandon the literal sense of his poem, or just get a vague sense of it and do it by the rhythm mostly. I wanted to see if I could rhythmically approximate the original while also communicating sense. It takes ages though, which is why I stopped. I thought: I want to write quick poems again, actually. That's where I'm at now, after finishing those ten-line stanza poems in the last two books.

DNG: One of my worst habits is that I am always tinkering with my poems, even years after they're supposed to be finished. My own published copies of my books are covered in scribbles. I'm really quite brutally abusive to my poems, ungracious and insulting. I probably shouldn't admit this in public but I often hate my own writing. Like deeply, deeply hate it. I would burn all my books if I could. I think it maybe has something to do with feeling the poem as never being a static artefact, but always in flux, and seeing them all printed and neat-looking just seems so loathsome and fake to me. I mean, I would literally burn them (*laughs*).

LF: (*Laughs*) Oh don't, just hide them – hide them away. The first time my book arrived in the post, I hid it behind a sofa. I actually think your attitude is really sane. When women do it, people go 'Oh, modesty!' or whatever. But there's a kind of psychic confusion in seeing what has been in here (*taps head*) out there. Every time, it's hideous. I deface and revise my published poems too.

DNG: To see the poems which in my head always felt fluid and pure presented as something inert and fixed just seems so … wrong. And it's far from feminine modesty for me, it's a very violent and muscular feeling which is in absolute opposition to the supposed feelings of a contemporary writer, which appears to be all about shifting copies in shops, or from Amazon factories or whatever. What I've been finding in the past year or so – and I'm really still only beginning to find my feet in my own craft, I haven't been doing this very long – is that I'm beginning to feel much more at ease with my poems when delivering them aloud. Maybe because they become somehow temporary then, they are nebulous again, they live in the ear of the listener, where they either float or fall, whichever, but in that way of freeing them to an audience, rather than on a page, they are mine still, and I can hold them and change them and say them however I want. And more importantly than anything, they feel alive to me when I say them aloud, in a way that they don't when I see them all neatly typed in a book. That impulse has fed back now, has looped right back into the craft part of the creation of my poems. Whereas before I used to type silently in composing a poem, completely ignoring all that writing advice of reading everything aloud, now there are many points where you could catch me speaking half-lines of new poems when I'm stuck in traffic, or doing the dishes, or whatever. It is changing me. You could say that this shift in craft is making me even more of a weirdo than I was before (*laughs*).

LF: In an ideal world we would just upload a book directly from our heads, and avoid all that back and forward bollocks. I am also opposed to poetry being reduced to 'content' to be delivered at festivals, or whatever, as entertainment. It just depresses me.

DNG: What about when we create a poem on our own in a room, and then we agree to go do a reading somewhere, and there's that moment right before getting on stage, where you're looking at the words you're about to read out, and looking at all these faces ... Do you ever feel like, 'Why the fuck am I doing this to myself?'

LF: Yeah, why? Why!? It's really, really peculiar. I think, like with the publishing side of things, the idea of public readings is quite irrational or arbitrary. And perhaps all these things will be unrecognisable to people in the digital future.

DNG: Every part of a writer's life, when you pause to think about it, is profoundly weird. Why do we do this? What do we get out of it? Instead of spending all these hours at these dark labours, we could just go for a nice walk, or have a cup of tea, you know? It'd probably be a life with at least a little less angst involved but ... Nah.

TAKING LIBERTIES

Leontia Flynn

Now that the verdict's in,
the voices raised, the arguments advanced
and assets tabled
for a split, the city stops

seeming to ask: 'What now?'.
The streets are bare at noon
as though inhaled. A sense of locked rooms
and hasty consultation

and over the vacant lot
beyond my desk, three herring gulls reel up
protesting: high and white
like ticker tape reversed.

Airborne relief. 'What now'
for words – or for the hate boils
and courses through nervous systems?
Look, I'm pushing back my chair and going home,

'that once-bright casket
from which the jewels have been freshly
robbed', by the river-road
which follows the curve of the earth

and where, left since the workers downed their tools,
the trees on either side
crowd in – weighed down
with both neglect and bounty.

MAUDE, ENTHRALLED

Doireann Ní Ghríofa

for Maude Delap,
after 'Medusae' (Dorothy Cross)

(i) Morning

Seventh of ten, little Maude is running
on Valentia strand again. In her braids,
sea wind unspins, until she skids. Sudden
in the sand, a jelly-bell, lump of glue-gunk
spiked with ink, tentacles spilling
from a fleshy pink, and oh!, it stings.

(ii) Afternoon

The ocean alone.	Alone, the ocean.
And Maude, afloat.	Under her boat,
darkness telescopes	a world of hover and float,
of swim and flit	and gilled throats.
Maude peers past	ling and dogfish, past
pollock and conger eel,	until she glimpses
the bell and tentacle	that she seeks.
All swell and release,	these skewed globules,
crimson- and blue-	streaked. Maude considers
how each one	draws up handfuls
of itself, then lets go,	a lone float. Maude
learns this lesson well;	Maude takes notes.

(iii) Evening

Her afternoon is spent dredging, scribbling
experiments, fizzing air into aquaria,
and feeding her jellyfish. Maude's shelves heave
with specimens, an exhibition of spin and dip.
These clotted blooms cannot hurt her as words do;
No daughter of mine will leave
home, except as a married woman.
Maude knows the etymology of *captivate*,
how it holds both charm and a cage.

(iv) Night

After nightfall, the jellyfish gnaw at Maude,
they call and call, until at last, she rises,
rubbing her eyes. In her fist, a candlestick,
its flame sheltered within fingers grown arthritic.

At the lab, her reflection hovers in bell jars. Aged,
changed, Maude is alone, afloat again, afraid.
And are they there, still, her jellyfish? Or have they
perished too, faded into copperplate curlicues?

Only Night tells the truth. Moonlight spells itself
in a floor all evidence: cobwebs, brick, crushed
glass, filth. All the jellyfish, and all the liquid
once held in her vessels, have evaporated to silt.

Maude ghosts the dark, captive, still, lifting
a hand to the imagined glass that always held her
from the dance. See her, awed – Maude,
our Maude – barefoot, enthralled.

NO DANCING

Jan Carson

*My religion makes no sense
and does not help me
therefore I pursue it.*
Anne Carson, from My Religion

A few months ago, I was working with a group of people living with dementia. They were residents in a care home run by the same Protestant denomination my extended family belongs to. It's a conservative outfit with extremely traditional values. I couldn't believe they'd even allowed artists to interact with their residents. We wrote poems together. We sang – mostly hymns and traditional songs – and my colleague led us through some basic choreography, helping the participants move to music played through a tiny speaker. You could've said we were dancing. It looked a lot like we were dancing. But this particular church isn't keen on dancing, so we called it 'structured movement', and hoped that those passing the dayroom would mistake it for armchair aerobics.

On our third week – bored with endless renditions of Molly Malone and He's Got the Whole World in His Hands – we introduced a livelier tune: Singing in the Rain. I often work with people living with dementia, so I'm well-used to the seemingly miraculous things music can do to an addled brain: lost lyrics are recalled, coordination can improve, and non-verbal participants often appear to temporarily regain their speech. But this was different. This was wild and – given our venue – a little bit reckless. The residents began to dance with a kind of unreserved fury. Some stood up for the first time in weeks, using their Zimmer frames for leverage. One lady took a maraca in each hand and shook them madly above her head. In an armchair, by the window, a very dapper gentleman of ninety two swayed along, clapping his hands and beaming. When the track ended, he cleared his throat and announced 'I used to love dancing before I got saved,' then paused, as if considering what he'd just said, before adding, 'I don't know why I ever stopped.'

I cried all the way home in the car. I knew exactly how this elderly man felt and, while I was glad dementia had loosened his inhibitions, liberating the primal urge to dance, I was also jealous. I wanted a little bit of the looseness he'd managed to find. I'm almost forty. It's many years since I stepped away from the religion of my childhood but I still can't bring myself to dance. It's nothing to do with ability; I'm sure even the most awkward mover can learn the basics. It's not fear, or even the sort of self-consciousness which keeps some people hugging the wall 'til the third or fourth pint kicks in. No, it's a peculiar kind of tightness I've inherited from growing up Northern Protestant. No matter what I do, I can't seem to crawl out from under it.

Not everyone who grew up Protestant in 1980s Ulster had the same experience as me. Back then, Protestantism could look very different depending on which particular brand you subscribed to; where you lived, (rural or urban, border town or port); which class you fell into; whether your folks were heavily into their politics or, like mine, largely apolitical; whether they were big churchgoers or just birth, death and baptism types. I've talked to lots of people who were brought up Protestant. Sometimes these conversations make me thankful for things like trousers, Nancy Drew novels and the television set in our front room which remained silent on Sundays but was otherwise fair game. At other times I've met people whose Protestant childhood was so loose and liberated, I've wanted to scratch their eyes out. These people had beer-drinking parents, pierced ears and Catholic friends they weren't trying to convert.

I can't tell their Protestant stories. I can only tell mine. Lately, I've been exploring it in my writing because I can't see my upbringing reflected anywhere else in Northern Irish fiction. When you can't see your story anywhere, it's hard to believe it's of any worth. But I'm not just writing my own story. There are thousands of people who grew up in very similar circumstances, attending churches in little towns and villages all across the North. Their experience was far removed from the well-documented exploits of Belfast-based Protestants. They grew up Baptist and Brethren (both the ordinary and exclusive kind), Methodist, Elim Pentecostal and Anglican – which we considered a little too Papish, a little too fond of candles and saints – Free Presbyterian, Non-Subscribing Presbyterian and regular, bog-standard Presby, like me. They differed on baptism, communion and predestination, but mostly agreed that women shouldn't be let anywhere near a pulpit. Some of my peers left the Protestant church as soon as they could, some stayed, and some are floating half-way in between, not sure what they are anymore.

I can't speak for every Protestant experience but, within our community, art was largely frowned upon. I once sat through a sermon spelling out the dangers of attending the theatre. It was like listening to a Victorian morality paper. Artists were perceived to be secular in the extreme and therefore dangerous. Safe art could be found in the form of Christian music, films and novels which had gospel-focused messages at the core. For those of us who felt compelled to create, there was little inspiration or encouragement to be found. The church I grew up in had an almost Old Testament fear of idolatry. Any 'graven' or created image was in danger of being worshipped at God's expense. By implication, those of us who chose to create anything were setting ourselves up as idolaters. This, I now know, was flawed theology, ignoring the tremendously rich seam of poetry, art and song which runs through the Bible. It can be traced all the way back to the Reformation, when the desire to be different from the statue-and icon-loving Catholic church led to a brutal stripping back of art from many Protestant churches and rituals. You can still see this theology reflected in the austere architecture and plain surroundings many Protestant congregations worship in.

Bearing this in mind, it's hardly surprising that my experience is rarely explored in Northern art. If you've been raised deeply suspicious of creativity, the last thing you'll do is paint, write or sing about your experience. That art which does exist has usually been created by artists who've already distanced themselves from their religious upbringing. It is often questioning, usually angry and largely inaccessible to those still living within the tradition, or on the margins, trying to raise a dissenting voice. I cannot emphasise how heartening it was to stumble across Jeanette Winterson's Oranges Are Not the Only Fruit, or to hear my first David Bazan record, and to realise there were other people like me, questioning the religious tradition they'd found themselves in. Seeing my struggle represented made it seem valid and helped me feel less alone.

I was born in Ballymena in 1980. Ballymena is famous for having seven towers, most of which have fallen down, and for producing Liam Neeson and the Reverend Ian Paisley. During my formative years, I was only familiar with the work of Paisley. He seemed to be everywhere, mostly shouting. When I was around eight a banner appeared in front of the Seven Towers Leisure Centre which read 'Ballymena Still Says No.' I instinctively knew this was the work of Paisley and his associates. It stayed up for most of my childhood and, for most of this time, I assumed my town was adamantly opposed to line dancing. Line dancing was regularly castigated in the local newspaper. Line dancing led to drunkenness and debauchery. (Q. Why don't Ballymena folk have sex standing up? A. In case they accidentally start dancing.) Line dancing was probably a gateway drug to the mad, drug-fuelled raves which took place every weekend up at Kelly's in Portrush.

There was whispered talk in church circles of 'other denominations' offering line dancing classes in their halls, mistakenly assuming this would be a good way to get the unsaved in. (We were always trying to get the unsaved in.) Such behaviour was considered suspect, at best, and at worst a sign of rampant secularisation. Secularisation did not sit well in Ballymena. ELO had just been barred from playing the Showgrounds under suspicion of moral degeneracy and possibly even Satanism. The God-fearing Protestants of Ballymena had a very long list of things they disapproved of. Some activities, such as sex before marriage and smoking, were definitely sinful. Others, including chewing gum, playing cards, going to the pictures and wearing strappy tops, were not out-and-out sinful but they certainly didn't reflect well.

I was not at all rebellious. I never swore. I never lied. I certainly didn't dabble in intoxicating substances or chew gum. I briefly owned a copied tape of Nirvana's Nevermind but after hearing a visiting youth pastor preach on the dangers of listening to Kurt Cobain, I went home and binned it, shoving the unspooled cassette to the bottom of the wheelie bin in case Jesus might come checking. Everyone looks back at their childhood and cringes. I fluctuate between cringing and feeling outright ashamed. I did things I wish I could take back now. I could make a litany of the horrors. The blood-curdling embarrassment of going 'round the housing estates, distributing Gospel tracts, praying I wouldn't encounter anyone from school, then feeling guilty because wasn't this tantamount to denying Christ? Attending a residential course entitled 'How to convert the Catholic Child.' Evangelistic street drama. (Just placing those three words next to each other is enough to make the stomach lurch.)

What was I thinking? I wasn't thinking. I was a child. I attended church five times most Sundays and never missed a service for fourteen years. (If you're wondering what the Presbyterian Church gives you for this stunning achievement, the answer is a Bible, a truly enormous one.) I went to church-based youth groups three nights a week and, in the summer, spent most of my time at Holiday Bible Clubs. I never questioned anything because I rarely met anyone who wasn't like me. Most of my friends in school had similar upbringings, some were even more churchy. I thought we were completely normal.

I don't want to undermine the way I was brought up. My family are good, kind people. They raised me as they'd been raised, with love and duty. My family have been Presbyterians for as long as the line goes back. Part of me is sad that this tradition ends with me, because there are many aspects of my upbringing I'm thankful for. Sunday School outings to Portrush. Socials, the rural, Protestant no dancing/no drinking equivalent of a barn dance. The enormous pile of home-baked buns and cakes which accompanied every Church activity. I've never known belonging like I knew as a child growing up in a country,

Presbyterian church. Good news was always celebrated. Hard times were faced together, and this was no vague or nebulous concept of support. Christian love was always tangible, never tokenistic. Friends called 'round to sympathise, sometimes sitting quietly for hours when there were no words worth saying. Larders and freezers were miraculously filled when someone took ill. Earnest prayer was always available. These prayers mightn't be eloquent, but they'd always be heartfelt. People sung hymns and really meant the words. It was a beautiful thing to raise your voice and take part in the chorus. I would not be a writer if I hadn't grown up with the lyricism of the King James Bible and the fantastical stories of the Old Testament. These were the building blocks when I sat down to fashion my first stories and I'll always be grateful for them.

Naomi Alderman, in her novel Disobedience, opens each chapter with a description of a Hasidic Jewish practice which strikes her as meaningful. This celebration of Jewish tradition is all the more powerful in light of the fact that Alderman's protagonist has abandoned her faith. When it comes to religious tradition she chooses to hold onto the good and let go of everything else. It's a process I'm currently walking through, and it's a very painful process. Sometimes the anger takes over and I feel like there's nothing worth holding on to at all. Many of my friends who grew up Northern Protestant don't believe anything anymore. They're angry and disillusioned. I don't blame them. It's not easy growing up in a hothouse of fundamentalism and legalistic thinking. But for me there's still something there. I'm trying to work out what I believe and why I believe it. I'm holding on to the true and essential as I weed out the ugliness. It's a painfully slow process. I feel like I've been on this journey for longer than I haven't.

I am a dreadful cliché. I was ruined by books. At fifteen I read Wuthering Heights and everything got turned upside down. I didn't lose my faith, though at the time it felt like I had. Discovering literature, music and film was more like a grand awakening. I fell in love with the unknown in art and this helped me to realise that my God wasn't dead after all, though fundamentalism had him by the throat. I slowly started to see that I was drawn to the mystery of God. I craved awe; I craved a God who could never be fully comprehended. It was the rules and legalism which left me cold. I felt like Presbyterian doctrine was constantly trying to reduce the infinite down to three bullet points and a sermon heading.

As I read more widely, furtively checking suspect books out of the library, I began to entertain independent thought. This, in itself, was a monumental achievement for a girl raised sixth-generation Presbyterian. I revisited passages of scripture which had seemed profound and intriguing before some man in a pulpit explained their mystery away. I considered the idea of worshipping the Lord in the beauty of holiness, which David Park seems equally fascinated by in his novel The Light of Amsterdam. I thought of the fantastical Leonora Carrington-esque images in the Book of Revelation. The parables and allegories of the Gospels. The misery of Job. Later, I focused my master's dissertation on Mark 4v. 10–12, where Jesus is asked why he speaks in parables. He answers, somewhat cryptically, 'that they may be ever hearing but never understanding.' I'd never heard any Presbyterian preach on this passage before. The first time I read it, I felt the roof peel off my tight, legalistic religion. Maybe all the mystery, uncertainty and wonder I found in art might actually fit within the scope of my faith. I could be both an artist and a person of faith. There was space for me to be unsure.

The American poet, Christian Wyman, writes that 'the minute you begin to speak with certitude about God, he is gone.' I wholeheartedly agreed. I could see the Bible was full of ambiguity and room for personal response. Yet Northern Presbyterianism, having its roots in strict Calvinism, elevated doctrine and fixed interpretation over the endless, honest questioning which comes from lived religious experience. The Word always held precedent over feelings and emotions. I couldn't separate the two so neatly. There are so many reasons why I didn't stay in the Presbyterian Church. I felt like I couldn't be honest about my doubts and questions. There was no room for uncertainty within such a constricted view of God. I craved more creativity in liturgy and worship. I found myself increasingly uncomfortable with the doctrine: how Presbyterianism viewed women, Catholics, the LGBT community and those people we charmingly called 'the least of these' and went on mission trips to serve or, perhaps more honestly, convert.

Ultimately, it was the Church's unwillingness to change or compromise which made me leave. By the age of sixteen, I knew I was an artist. It took me another few years to admit it but by the time the process was complete I was certain God didn't view artists the same way my church did. It was not just inevitable that I would write. It was absolutely essential to every part of my well-being: physical, emotional and spiritual. It was a calling. Flannery O'Connor has been my constant companion over the last few years. She speaks a lot of hard-learned truth. In Mystery and Manners she writes 'when people have told me that because I am a Catholic, I cannot be an artist, I have had to reply, ruefully, that because I am a Catholic, I cannot afford to be less than an artist.' If I substitute my Protestantism for Flannery's Catholicism I have the most difficult, yet essential truth I've learnt on this journey. I'm not a writer in spite of my faith – I write in, and through, and ultimately, because of it. I couldn't remain in a church which saw the best part of me as broken.

It's almost a decade since I severed ties with the established Protestant Church. It's also a decade since I began writing in earnest. In a sense one religion has trumped the other. Through writing I discovered some of the open-endedness I was searching for in my early church experiences. I've flourished in a world which values questions above prescriptive thinking. I didn't lose my faith. I found a fuller expression of it through the art I get to make and explore. I've learnt how to lose my inhibitions and loosen my constraints through writing. There's hardly anything I wouldn't explore in my work. I wish this freedom extended to the other parts of my life where I continue to feel constrained by my upbringing. There are so many experiences I still have to grow into. I'd like to be dancing before I turn ninety two.

It's not that I think dancing is wrong. I'm long since past judging. I watch other people enjoying themselves and I feel like I'm on the edge of living. 'In the World but not of the World,' as the Bible verse puts it. This is quite an isolated spot to find yourself in. You are caught between two modes of being. I'd love to lose myself and dance without inhibition. I've tried. I can't. Every time I dance I feel constrained. I feel as if every part of me is ludicrous and I need to sit down. I feel as if I'm veering dangerously close to being out of control and I can't cope with this feeling. I was brought up to fear losing control above all other sins. Living with reckless abandon was pretty much the opposite of Presbyterianism. I could list specific vices to be avoided – drink, drugs, dancing, sex, secular music – but it is not the fear of succumbing to a particular temptation which runs through me like a fault line, it's legalism itself. I followed all the rules for so long, even those that made no sense, that I've retained a kind of muscle memory. I can say with certainty that freedom is a very good thing. But can I let myself enjoy it? Rarely. I'm hard-wired to keep safely between the lines.

In The Days of Rain, Rebecca Stott's memoir of growing up exclusive Brethren, she talks about the same phenomenon. After leaving what she calls a religious cult, her father embraced every secular distraction available – music, theatre, gambling, flashy cars – while ten-year-old Rebecca, craving the rules and constraints she'd grown up with, immediately joined an Anglican Sunday School and set about making it more legalistic. I'm not for a moment suggesting I grew up in a cult but there is something about coming into a newly-found sense of freedom which induces anxiety. You crave the familiar safety you've always found in rule-keeping. It is possible to both say, and actually believe, that something is no longer wrong and yet find yourself so programmed to abstain that you simply cannot get your body in gear.

There's much talk of Catholic guilt but this kind of Protestant shame is as powerful and restrictive. It fears change. It is quick to distance itself from anything it's been conditioned to see as sinful. It struggles to act upon its own human impulses. It is painful enough to watch this struggle play out it in the lives of individuals but it's absolutely devastating to witness the impact it's currently having upon Northern Irish politics. Many of the Unionist politicians who have the power to decide our country's future grew up in similar rural, Protestant communities to my own. While I often want to knock their heads together in frustration, I also understand the tremendously strong ties that bind them to the doctrine and theology which has shaped their worldview. It is a massive leap to step away from, or even to challenge, the religion you've been raised in. Even those whose attitudes have changed are undoubtedly still subject to the same constraints and inherited thinking I struggle with daily.

Thankfully, things are slowly changing within the landscape of Northern Protestantism. There's a marked split between the old guard and the more progressive non-denominational churches, which are on the increase. This is perhaps best seen in the response to the Presbyterian Church's recent decision to exclude LGBT couples and their children from partaking in communion – a widespread condemnation has been provoked, both within dissenting Presbyterian congregations and from many other denominations. While much of the established Protestant Church remains stalwartly stuck in a theology which hasn't evolved since the days of Calvin, others are moving forwards at some speed, embracing new outlooks and reinterpreting both the Bible and the outworking of their faith in light of modern life. Change is coming but change always comes with a cost. It's not easy for those moderate Northern Protestants who're trying to live out their faith with open minds and consideration.

It's not meant to be easy. Many of us, myself included, have made mistakes along the road. You don't grow up sixth-generation Northern Protestant and find yourself free of religious baggage or regret. I've entertained thinking that I'm now ashamed of. I've done and said things and treated people in a way I no longer believe to be Christian. I'd like to undo it all but it's part of who I am. I can only make amends and keep trying. I'm not who I was ten years ago. Everyday I'm a little easier in my own faith. Guilt is no longer my primary motivation. I can change my mind and admit I was wrong. The tightness is slowly losing its hold. I can't dance yet, but I'm getting there.

BRYGHT GEHENNA

Wendy Erskine

In the charity shop windows on the road there's an assortment of goods: a child's wetsuit, say, a Belleek vase, a pair of stripper shoes, a fibre optic light. There are two, sometimes three mannequins, always female. Someone who's made a donation might see their own clothes on the model in the window: their jacket certainly, the same little stain on the sleeve, but the arm at an unfamiliarly jaunty angle, the model smiling in a way they might not.

Inside the shops have started colour-coding the clothes, so that the rails run through the shades of the prism. The tangle of necklaces on display might be draped on a plastic hand. Shoes, bought for a wedding or court appearance and discarded afterwards, still look stiff. There will be a cardboard box of CDs, some still bearing the price labels from long defunct record shops. On occasion there will even be LPs. There may well be a treasure to be discovered by a collector but more likely on offer are pop compilations and light classical. There may well be country and western records, American certainly, but also albums featuring artists from Belfast or Armagh or Tyrone. Some of these will fall into the sub-category of country gospel. A person going through a record box in a charity shop might just come across the recordings of The Devine Family.

They might see the album with Pastor Ronnie James Devine, his wife and his son in a fishing boat. The sky looks ominous and the water choppy, but Pastor Devine's expression is stoical, as is his wife Dorcas's. Eleven-year-old Jamie's countenance is more difficult to determine. On the Christmas record, released some eight months later, they are in a room with an unadorned tree and a log fire. Dorcas Devine is at the table and Pastor Devine stands in front of the fire, one hand on the mantelpiece. Jamie Devine is sitting cross-legged on the floor, apparently reading a book. They might find the Praise album which features a highly tinted mountain scene of the type found on holiday postcards.

The records, if they are to be found, are almost forty years old, perhaps scratched, warped. The production sounds thin, the songs dated and rather Old Testament. The undoubted sincerity is perhaps a little embarrassing and the pedal steel, often too loud, is intrusive. The trilling harmonies of Jamie and his mother are shrill.

Ronnie James Devine has a rich baritone voice. During a short-lived religious phase, Ernie McCormack, the boss of a little Belfast record label, found himself in the pastor's church one Thursday night and, although he got little from the sermon, was struck by the power of the singing emanating from the pulpit. Ernie McCormack had a roster of Irish traditional artists, plus a female country and western singer and her band. He saw a certain commercial potential in the dour figure at the front. The pastor wasn't sure whether entering into a venture with this man was in fact God's purpose but he said that after prayer and reflection he came to the conclusion that he could do useful witness through it. The first record of the pastor's rendition of familiar old hymns was well received. It got airplay on the local Sunday night religious programmes and the pastor performed at any churches requesting his presence.

When it came to Ernie McCormack's attention that both Dorcas and Jamie Devine could hold a tune he decided that they should also appear on the records. The Devine Family: a good gimmick. People would like Dorcas, they would take to her. She was pretty in her own way. And all the old people would love the boy.

The Devine Family started to appear on local television. Jamie's hair was always trimmed for this, the newspaper put down on the kitchen floor, and he could see his mother's hand shake as she cut his fringe. The prospect of appearing on television frightened her. There would usually be some kind of rehearsal, even for live shows. When someone yelled 'cut', Dorcas's hand went to her temple. She always thought it was her fault. If Ernie McCormack was around the studio, he would pretend to cuff Jamie on the ear and then he would give him a pound note. Don't be spending it all in the one shop! he said every single time.

They were occasionally asked onto variety shows. Other familiar faces included the accordion band made up of four generations of the same family and twin magicians. The two youngest members of the accordion band were just a little older than Jamie, but had no interest in talking to him. They pointed and whispered to each other: would you look at the goody-goody wee cocksucker!

It was the final few months of primary school when he first started singing on the records. In his small school there was delight that one of their own should be elevated in such a way. He was required to sing in school assemblies and everyone asked him about being on the telly. When Jamie moved to secondary school however, there was a different attitude. On the first day someone in his new class said, here, you're not that wee fruit that does the singing?

That was the beginning. The school day was long. In the corridors between classes Jamie got used to people pushing him and shouting. Give us a song! Oi you, Holy Joe, what's up with you? Some joker started a way of having fun that was promptly taken up by everyone in the school. It was called I Saw Wee Jamie Devine. I Saw Wee Jamie Devine downing ten cans of Kestrel then having a wank in his front garden. Well I Saw Wee Jamie Devine shagging his ma in Gresham Street while he was eating a burger. Well know what, I Saw Wee Jamie Devine sucking Bobby Sands's dick while he was singing Jesus Loves Me. And so on. Before long there was no one in the school who did not know who wee Jamie Devine was.

People knew who Dorcas was too. Jamie heard them make comments when they were out. Paler than she looks on the telly. They must be rolling in it with those records, could she not get a better rig-out than that? Shabby, to be honest. But they're against fashion, those religious sort of people. Would you fancy your man, big Ronnie? Would you? Don't think she actually does too much anyway. Just sort of sings along now and again. Money for old rope. And then the delayed peal of laughter as she and Jamie exited a shop.

When the Christmas album came out, it even had a television advert involving a montage of burning candles, a manger and Pastor Devine singing in a forest. There had been a flurry of snow one morning and they had taken the opportunity to go to a forest park for some impromptu filming. The actual album cover had taken a while to shoot. The log fire had sparked and sputtered, at one time sending out a spark that singed the Pastor's trousers. Dorcas hadn't been well. She had been vomiting in the toilets and although she rarely wore any makeup, the photographer's assistant had to apply some because she was so pale. Smile Jamie, the photographer had said. Come on, smile. It's Christmas. Look up and smile.

Although everyone wore the same school uniform the differences were significant. Mods had tight trousers and thin ties, a flash of white sock between trouser and shoe. The few skinheads wore their ties the same way but shortened their trousers so that a few inches of boot could be seen. The crowd into heavy metal had tight trousers but their ties had fat knots. The form teacher brought in an old cassette player and allowed members of Jamie's class to bring in tapes to be played during lunch. Jamie sat eating his sandwiches with a couple of quiet boys who were Christians. Their ties were neither thin nor fat, but both wore a pin-badge to show they were members of the Scripture Union. The rule in the form room was that no one could play more than one side of a tape before it was someone else's turn, so the music ricocheted between mod and heavy metal.

There was a lot of concern about Satan at the time. It was said that many of the groups the young people were listening to were made up of devil-worshippers who took part in animal and even human sacrifice. On certain records, back tracking revealed subliminal satanic messages. A look at the hellish images on the album covers suggested that much of this music was of a depraved kind. In school the pupils had plenty to say about what was meant to be going on. On any elevated ground, black masses were taking place. If you went up the Cavehill, for example, and saw the remains of a fire, that could only have been the result of a dark activity. People were breaking in to the local churches in the dead of night and conducting satanic rituals on the altars. Cats were disappearing, dogs were disappearing. Had people not heard about the farmer out near Ballyclare? He had found three cows dead, bizarre symbols carved in to their sides. Stay up until midnight and stare into the mirror and say the Lord's Prayer backwards and you would see the devil.

The local papers ran stories on the spread of satanic practices and churches warned young people not to get involved. Satan, despite what some might say, was very real. One of the boys in Jamie's class said that at the church his auntie went to they hired a cement mixer and asked all of the young people who liked heavy metal music to bring all their records and badges to waste ground at the back of the church hall. The minister read some bible verses and they threw all of their stuff into a hole someone had dug and then the cement was tipped on top of it. But the cement didn't set for ages. It was really weird. It was as though the devil stuff wouldn't let the cement set. It was pure freaky.

Because of the relative infrequency of bands including the city on their tours, those who did come, such as AC/DC in 1979, or Siouxsie and the Banshees in 1980, were guaranteed a rapturous welcome. When tickets were released for the Bryght Gehenna concert, due to take place at the Ulster Hall on 15th April 1981, there was in some quarters delight. This group from Wolverhampton had been one of the star turns at Castle Donington Monsters of Rock festival the year before, and their bass player Gibby Crawford was from Belfast. Their album featured a hooded semi-naked woman in front of a scaffold. Their songs were both leaden and histrionic. The guitarist had inverted crosses tattooed on his arms and the singer, Denis Faccenda, had spent an indeterminate period on hallucinogens in Bolivia. The music at some of their concerts was so loud that people's ears seeped blood. Jamie listened to all this talk. The boys in his class were too young to get into the venue but everyone knew someone with tickets.

The posters around the town displayed Bryght Gehenna in Germanic script against a fluorescent yellow background.

There are still street preachers and singers in Belfast, as there were then. But it was better to appear before a congregation who gave undivided attention, not shoppers passing by, laden with poly bags. The Lord's word required concentration and it was sad to see the tracts handed out in the street trampled underfoot. It would have taken an exceptional circumstance for the pastor to take to the streets but the Bryght Gehenna concert proved to be exactly that. There were people who felt compelled to make a stand against everything that this group represented. Bryght Gehenna. The biblical reference to the destination of the wicked, Gehenna, the Lake of Fire, was not lost on the pastor. Jamie heard him ask Ernie McCormack if he had heard about Bryght Gehenna when they were driving along one evening to a performance at a faith mission. He had. Well, said the pastor, it's all very worrying. Don't think I've ever heard the like. And they're performing in the Ulster Hall. Ernie McCormack sighed. It's not satanic, Ronnie. It's just showbiz. That's just the way it is. Showbiz. The pastor said nothing.

On the evening of the protest, everyone was invited to gather outside the venue from 7:30pm onwards. Dorcas Devine wasn't well and couldn't go. The pastor stopped on the way to pick up some others and their placards bearing Bible verses. Two women bundled into the back and the one beside Jamie was his old Sunday School teacher. Even through her thick, decent coat he could feel her excitement. I'm quite fearful of what I might see, the other woman said.

On the way 'round to the Ulster Hall they encountered first a husband and wife from another church, who were there for the same purpose, and then, as they got nearer, some others from their own. It was a cold, bright night. The windows of a bar they passed glowed amber and when the door opened as a crowd left, there was a swipe of laughter, the smell of cigarette smoke.

The long queue snaked 'round the side of the hall. Other protestors became visible as they drew closer; they stood in a rough semi-circle at the side of the entrance. Some held Bibles, and there was a little, wan singing. Oh, Pastor Devine, a man said, rushing forward. Did you ever see such a crowd? Who would have thought there would have been so many of them! And indeed there were so many, the queue four or five people in denim and leather wide. One man at the front of the queue, his jeans didn't have a zip, but rather a criss-cross lacing arrangement, as though some mighty, mighty beast needed to be kept strapped down. One teenage guy kept coming up and doing strange signs with his hands. Jamie was standing next to the other woman who'd been in the back of the car; she stared ahead, mouthing the words of the hymn his father was singing as though she didn't see the sea of Bryght Gehenna fans in front of her.

Somebody started the chant. Terra! terra! terra! The stamping of feet and their arms in the air. Terra! terra! terra! descend. Terra! Terror! Tear her! Jamie had heard these words before, usually accompanied by people banging the desks with their fists. He knew most of the songs on the album, but the one he liked the best was Slave of Naamah: it began so quietly, just the guy singing, but then built up to pure noise. They would sing it tonight. What it would be to be in that crowd! It was the song that Bryght Gehenna often finished with, the final three minutes, a slab of sound. Suddenly a girl appeared from out of the queue, right in front of where they were standing. What's that say? she said, pointing at a placard held by one of the group. Can't read it. What's it say? Sub something? Sub what? Submarine?

The woman beside Jamie shouted out – Submit yourselves therefore to God! Resist the devil and he will flee from you!

Och aye, the girl said. Sure thing.

Hey big man! she shouted over at the pastor. Big man! Hey you!

And she pulled up her T-shirt to reveal large breasts which she jiggled, laughing. She turned 'round to face the cheers of the crowd. Cop a look at that then! she said. Hey big man!

The protestors gasped, appalled. Everyone stopped singing except for the pastor who continued without a beat. The sight had frightened some of them. When the doors opened into the foyer of the hall, the protestors stood until the last of the crowd had crossed the threshold. On the journey back home no one mentioned the incident with the girl. Jamie was asked about how he got to school in the mornings. He said that quite often he walked but he did get the bus if it was raining. There were two different buses he could get, the school bus or the service bus.

There was a lot of discussion about the concert the next day in school. It had been recorded as the loudest concert in Northern Ireland ever. There had been a fight and somebody had been stabbed. The bass player had had sex with a girl that somebody or other actually knew. The Ulster Hall had been wrecked, thousands of pounds worth of damage, and there was blood down the walls in the toilet. Bands weren't going to be allowed to play there ever again. Well, one of the mods said, why not ask wee Jamie Devine about what happened because he was the one who was actually there.

Serious, wee Jamie was there?

Yeah. Somebody in one of the other classes was saying.

Were they trying to like, you know, sacrifice him?

Sacrifice Jamie Devine? If only. Now that I would pay to see.

And so the story unspooled about how Jamie Devine and his full-on psycho da had been seen there by someone's brother and they were protesting against Bryght Gehenna. He was there with a bunch of old women all shaking signs and reading the Bible. The old women were screaming and shouting. Then a wee doll flashed her tits. The one time in my entire life, a boy said, that I've actually been jealous of Jamie Devine. Right in front of him, lucky bastard.

Don't know about that, somebody else piped up. I heard about that too and they said she was a boot. Was she a boot, Jamie, or was she not?

The Devine Family had a release pencilled in for the summer. They had some new songs that had been written by an acquaintance of Ernie McCormack, still gospel songs but lighter, more upbeat, more suited to the better weather. It had been decided that the album cover photo should be taken at White Rocks, a beach near Portrush. But on the day when the photos were meant to be taken, Ernie McCormack, arriving to drive the family up to the coast found them not ready to go. Dorcas Devine had locked herself in the bathroom. Make her a cup of tea, Ernie said. Jamie, can you make your mother a cup of tea? But Jamie, he said, you're not even changed yet! That's not what you're meant to wear. Where's the shorts and that wee casual jacket?

The pastor said, Get changed Jamie. Get changed now. Then the pastor went upstairs and banged on the door of the bathroom. Dorcas, he said. Ernie's here.

Well look, Ernie said, we can call it off. I can get a message to the photographer. It's dulling down away. Might be sensible to wait for a better day.

No, the pastor said. We'll be ready soon.

Jamie appeared in the outfit he had been given. He stood in the doorway.

Ernie saw the long, thin legs, the shins shaded with hair. He saw that the fly was only half up because the shorts were so tight. The jacket ended two inches from his wrists.

Not too sure about that actually Jamie, Ernie said.

His hair was combed severely to one side, too far over, a mockery of a parting.

This is what I was told to put on, Jamie said.

Ernie looked at Jamie's face, the gaunt cheeks, the rash of spots on his forehead. His hair seemed darker. Actually, Ernie said, I'm thinking maybe we should just leave it for today. Your mum's not well.

The pastor came downstairs. Dorcas is just getting her things on, he said. She'll be down in a minute. Jamie, you're ready to go. That's good.

But by the time they got up to the coast the wind was whipping the rain against the windscreen. Nobody, not even the pastor, wanted to get out of the car.

In school, Jamie sat by himself at the desk in front of the teacher staring at the board's half-rubbed out hieroglyphs. The two boys he used to eat his lunch with sat behind him but he didn't turn 'round. When they started going to a new youth fellowship they had invited Jamie along. He asked them what they did there, and when they told him scripture-based activities, he gave a laugh and said no thanks. One lunchtime the teacher noticed that her cassette player wasn't there.

Where'd you move it to, miss? one of the boys said.

I didn't touch it, she said.

Gonna be a rubbish lunch if we've nothing to listen to!

Somebody'll have borrowed it. Probably it's been one of the other teachers. They'll bring it back tomorrow I'm sure.

The talk in the classroom turned to the Twelfth in just a couple of weeks' time: some boys had been involved in getting the materials together, taking orders from the overlords about what needed to be placed where. They discussed the best construction of pallets and tyres for optimum fire. They talked about the flags to be burnt, the various effigies of people who were hated.

Jamie had started with dice. He got the bus into town and went to Woolworths where he walked up and down the aisles, feigning an interest in this and that, a couple of pounds from Dorcas's handbag in his pocket. He bought some sweets from the Pick 'n' Mix, smiling at the woman when she handed him back the change. She looked as if she half-recognised him. There was an aisle with notebooks and writing pads, pens, pencils, rubbers. Some rubbers were shaped like strawberries, others were in the shape of cartoon lions and elephants. There were rubbers that were also dice. He slipped one into his pocket, felt a thrill. Then he took another, and another. The cassette player was less enjoyable because it was bigger. He came in to school early when the classroom was still empty, put it in a plastic bag and transferred it in his locker. He waited after school until everybody had gone before he headed home with it.

He could have stolen the tape from someone's bag in school but he didn't want to do that. In the phonebook he looked up the addresses of record shops in the town, but the first one he went to didn't have what he was looking for. In fact it had hardly any tapes at all. He would have preferred a record – the cover! – but if he wanted to play it in his room he would have had to steal a record player. In the first shop the records were catalogued by genre. There were various different sections including a gospel one, and if he had looked there he would probably have seen himself. But Jamie found what he was looking for in another shop, where the man at the till was too deep in conversation with his two friends who leaned across the counter to notice Jamie reaching up for the cassette and slipping it in to his inside pocket. He could have slipped in half the shop without the man noticing.

It didn't work, staring in the mirror at midnight, reciting the Lord's Prayer backwards, even when it was written out on a sheet in front of him. He didn't see even the outline of the devil in the bathroom mirror, just his own face, disappointed and slightly relieved. Jamie turned round to see Dorcas at the bathroom door in her dressing gown.

I was just getting a drink of water, she said.

I'm just going to clean my teeth, he replied.

From the bedroom there was the noise of the pastor's faithful snores.

Jamie slept at the top of the house. His room had a desk, a bed and a wardrobe. Dorcas came in twice a week to collect his washing and hoover but other than that it was left undisturbed. A ritual began. When the pastor and Dorcas were asleep, Jamie got a bag of flour and marked out a small circle with it on his wooden floor. Then he put his things in the centre. The dice he would roll until they were sixes and he would place them so they made a triangle. He would have taken something from the church but always something plain: no ornaments, no crosses or goblets or things like that. The only thing he could get was an arrangement of dried flowers in an old jar. He broke off their heads and crushed them to dust. This was sprinkled at the edge of the circle. He had drawn a pentangle on a broken compact mirror of Dorcas's. That too was put in the circle. Jamie put on the tape of Bryght Gehenna. It demanded to be played loud, but he couldn't risk turning up the dial beyond three, four at the most. And then he took his place in the middle of the circle. He would wait until the second or third song before pulling down his pyjama bottoms. Sometimes the woman from the Pick 'n' Mix would present herself, or a pretty girl from the accordion band, but he would bat them away to think instead of the one from the concert who had bared her breasts. He could see them vividly, appalling and moon-like. He thought at other times of Denis Faccenda from Bryght Gehenna.

There were other Bryght Gehenna tapes Jamie wanted to listen to. He'd heard them talking about them in school. Live recordings. He went back into the town, to the same shop where before it had all been so easy. He scanned the cassette boxes, looking for the familiar jagged typeface, and there it was. He put it in the palm of his hand.

Hey! came a shout.

Jamie turned 'round.

Jamie!

It was Ernie McCormack, coming from the back of the shop. Next week, Jim, he shouted to the other man.

So, Jamie, what you up to? This where you're hanging around this weather?

Jamie shrugged. He felt the tape in his pocket.

You got a spare twenty minutes or so? Ernie asked. Because if you do, I got a load of stuff ready for posting I could do with a hand with.

Ernie's pokey second floor office was only a couple of minutes' walk away. There was an old typewriter at a table, but mostly it was just cardboard boxes, some empty, some full of records. There were posters on the walls for groups that Jamie had never heard of, a line of tickets dating back to the '70s.

Move those boxes off that chair, Jamie, Ernie said. Give yourself a bit of room.

The cardboard gave way when Jamie lifted it and he only managed to hold on to a few albums as they fell onto the floor.

Ernie sighed. Hard to shift, that stuff. Country singer-songwriter. But then everything seems hard to shift these days.

He gave Jamie a list of addresses that needed to be put on other boxes, once they'd been assembled from their flat state. There was a leaning pile of Devine Family albums under the table. Jamie could see the one with him sitting on the floor pretending to read a book.

How's your mum? Ernie asked.

Fine.

You rehearsing any new songs?

No, Jamie said. Weeks ago they had tried but the parts had to be switched because he couldn't reach the high notes anymore.

Ernie lifted a record with a cover of two women in white dresses sitting on a wagon. He looked at it and then put it down before reaching into his inside pocket for his cigarettes. A match rasped as it caught light. They'll hopefully do well, he said, taking a long, first draw. Although you never know.

He pointed to the boxes, the records piled up against the wall, the bulldog-clipped invoices and bills that sat beside the typewriter. Hard to know which way the wind is going to blow, he said.

Yeah, agreed Jamie.

So, Ernie said, the Devine Family. He paused. End of the road really for the Devine family. You know what I mean. You understand what I mean. Maybe your daddy can continue, maybe there's a market for it, small enough but a market. The three of you though ...

Jamie kept on folding a box.

End of the road, he said.

You got any sellotape? For these boxes?

Listen though. Listen to this. When you look back, you can be proud of what you've done. Even if people think it's shit. Even if a lot of people think it's shit. He reached for a Devine Family record. Because this stuff, this thing, exists longer than you. When you're gone it'll still be here. I'm under no illusions, we ain't producing the Sistine Chapel here. But something of some kind has been created. It's been created.

Sure, Jamie said. When he finished boxing up the records, Ernie gave him a five-pound note but he didn't say don't spend it all in one shop. He shook Jamie's hand. The windows in the town were full of white clothes and coconuts and fake cocktails. Summer was coming even if it was raining. In the arcade he went into the sweet shop to get a box of matches. Although Jamie was half expecting it, the old guy who served him didn't query what he wanted them for. The café in Woolworths was still open, so he would put in some time there until he got his bus. He could get an orange juice from that tank where the fake oranges bobbed, churned around by the paddles.

It was the end of the day and they had already started to put some of the chairs on top of the tables. Jamie took a seat in a booth at the back. The woman at the till had her back to him and the only other people at a table were two old women wearing hats. He took a sip of orange, and got the matches from his pocket. He lit one and held it against the plastic seat. Nothing happened initially, but then it started to bubble. Next the chemical smell and the plastic turning dirty brown. He shook out the match, then lit another one, did the whole thing again. He took a sip of orange. McCormack was wrong. To destroy was the real thrill. The seat was left scarred in six neat lines. He had tried to bring the flame as close as he could to the side of his hand before the pain became too much.

    Where have you been? Dorcas said when he got back. I was worried.

    Just went into town. Got the bus.

    Tea'll be ready in half an hour.

    Sure.

    Jamie?

    Yeah?

    Half an hour or so, she said, and her hand hovered at her temple.

    He waited that night until he knew they were asleep to go downstairs to where the candles were kept in case of a power cut. In his room he drew out his flour circle and arranged the candles in the shape of a pentangle. Their glow was beautiful when they were lit. Could you be thrilled and totally calm at the same time? Yeah, he thought so. He sprinkled the dead flowers, what remained of them. He sighed, thinking of Bryght Gehenna. McCormack was right really when he said they were showbiz. On that one point he was right. He wanted silence for what he was going to do, didn't need any distraction. To destroy was what was required. That seat, he had left it in some state. The matches in his hand demanded more than thin candles; he wanted to watch things distorting and buckling, that clean flames should consume and destroy. It was hard to know where to start.

THE CHILD OF PRAGUE IN THE PHONE BOX

Clooneyquinn, Co Roscommon, August 2018

Anna Leask

THE TURN

Aiden O'Reilly

I had an unexceptional Irish Catholic upbringing, at least as regards the waymarks now regarded as canonical. Getting the leather at the Christian Brothers all-boys school, visits from Father Fagan when the best china cups were laid out, being bundled off to mass each Sunday, the early summer thrill of the Corpus Christi procession, queuing to get my miraculous medal blessed. I was an altar boy, too, but at the convent chapel, not the parish church, so nobody knew. One week out of five I rose in the small psychotic hours before dawn, walked down the silent street and through the high iron gates. The sacristy door would be left unlocked. Once inside, I put on my surplice, lit the taper, and went out to the altar to light the candles.

The sisters were an enclosed contemplative order. I never saw their faces; I spoke through a mesh grille into darkness. The chalice, cruets, and altar linens would be waiting for me inside a wooden cylinder which rotated on a vertical axis. When it was open to the sacristy side it had the appearance of an architectural recess. When rotated to send items back to the nuns, it looked like a wooden column with no apparent purpose. This apparatus was called the Turn.

These nuns knew a lot about my family. They would inform me they were saying prayers for my sister's job interview, or for my mother's hospital appointment. Often I would have to pretend to know what they were talking about, and thank them for the prayers. My older brother was skilled at distinguishing the different voices. He knew which one was chatty, and which one would reliably neglect to turn on the sacristy heater. Whenever that particular nun was on duty, it was inconceivable to us to ask her to turn on the heater. The cold had to be cursed at and endured.

There would be about a dozen people at the mass. The nuns in their wine-red habits gathered on an upstairs gallery at the back of the church, partially hidden by a vertical array of organ pipes. At unpredictable moments in the liturgy they broke into song for the responsorial psalms. It was all quite pleasant. At communion time the priest went to a side hatch to dispense the host to the nuns, but again there was never a clear angle on their faces.

One particular morning the box of matches to light the taper (which was then used to light the candles) was not among the items in the Turn. I set out the altar vessels and linens, and then looked around the sacristy to see if perhaps the matches had been left out somewhere. I loitered around the Turn, waiting to see if they might appear. A mistake had never happened before in my two years serving mass. Time was passing, the priest would be here soon.

'Sister?' I said loudly into the dark grille.

There was silence, a rustling of cloth.

'Yes, Aiden, what is it?' a voice responded anxiously.

There was never another occasion when I had to unexpectedly address the nun. But I am certain she was there at all times waiting, sitting or perhaps standing, behind the grille.

One day at school a boy from a different class tapped me on the shoulder. 'Here, are you an altar boy at the convent chapel?' I was flustered for a moment.

I had never spoken to anyone about my early morning duty, had never even thought of myself as 'altar boy'. 'Yes,' I replied. 'Oh right,' he said, 'so am I.' I never spoke to him again. I've seen him present the weather forecast on RTÉ.

That Christmas I got a present from the nuns: a slab of chocolate, and a book with a wings-and-cumulus cover image and the title I Believe in Angels. It was so absurd a present that I read it from cover to cover. Strangely, I recall a section which explained that divine machinations were beyond human conception. We try to comprehend them with our limited earthbound minds, and one way of doing so is to think of angels. Bit of a Kantian influence there. Say what you will about Catholicism, it's nothing if not subtle.

But I didn't want my mother to find out I was reading such evident chicken soup. I stashed it at the back of the wardrobe alongside the other books I didn't want my parents to know about: Nietzsche's Zarathustra, Executive magazine, and a slim hardback entitled In a Dark Time, a strange anthology of writings and quotations on living under the imminent threat of nuclear annihilation.

I served mass for several more months, soldiering on in my solitary atheism. These Redemptoristine nuns had closed themselves off behind fourteen-foot stone walls to dedicate their lives to prayer. For most of each day and night they were busy directing intense beams of prayer at all the problems of the world. By what hideous arrogance did I presume to judge their lives and work to be pointless? It seemed a violent judgement to make. No matter how polite I was to the nuns, it couldn't salve my guilt.

Perhaps, I reasoned to myself, there was a scientific basis to telepathy, a subject I was reading about in the local library. Perhaps the nuns' kind thoughts and prayers exerted an influence via paranormal channels, and were not entirely wasted. Twenty-two of them in there, I had counted the hand movements as the priest dispensed the host, closed up until death. A teenager among them, so I had heard.

In Dostoyevsky's novel, The Brothers Karamazov, the middle brother Ivan relates the legend of the Grand Inquisitor. The legend speculates that in the Middle Ages a cabal of atheists held power in the top hierarchies of the church: they did not believe in God, but enforced a regime of thought that gave solace to the masses. Perhaps worse again than atheists, the legend continues, perhaps these inquisitors accepted God and Christ, but intentionally imposed their own system of superstitions and rituals because the common hordes of mankind are incapable of living up to the ideal of freedom Jesus represents, and the majority would be condemned to be forever miserable. The inquisitors repress all dissent for the higher purposes of peace and contentment.

What kind of chaos would be unleashed, I thought to myself, when the facts of science become more generally known and ordinary people stopped believing? (Somehow I was under the impression that the nuns, Christian brothers, teachers and priests were all in ignorance of the kind of books I was reading at the local library.)

At school, the religion class was regarded as a doss class because there was no exam and no homework. It was basically a talking session where we boys were treated by the Christian Brothers, occasionally at least, as adults. Lots of deliberations about what's acceptable and what's sinful:

> whether it's a sin to be drunk (no, but a sin to drink with the intention of getting drunk)
> is fighting sinful (only if cheered on)

should we take the Bible literally that a rich man can't get into heaven (no)

is it sinful to look at pictures of naked women (no, unless done with the ultimate intention of emitting).

Many earnest discussions, disarming honesties, and descents into farce as when, for example, in a discussion about contraceptives one boy said he knew his mother used them and threw the teacher into a tizzy. But the question of whether you believe in the premise that holds the whole thing together never arose. Except perhaps once, in the months before the final exams. The religion teacher was organising a special mass to offer up for good results. It was to be held in an oratory (a word I haven't heard since) built in to the newly-constructed PE complex.

The teacher wanted a few volunteers to compose a little poem/prayer and read it out during the mass. His eyes scanned the room. I was a well-behaved boy, not a rebellious bone in my body. I could never understand the perpetually vexed – those unhealthily pale, spotty boys who must always be bristling against authority.

'Aiden, will you do one of the prayers?'

'Ah, I'd rather not. I don't really believe in it.'

Another pupil offered modestly to take my place. And that was it, my rebellion against Catholic Ireland. It gained me no credit in the coolness economy of the schoolyard. It went entirely unremarked.

Retreat week was coming. We were informed that we would have a special visitor to the school. A person with intuition into the lives of young people these days. A thinker, a *writer*, a person of relevance in the wider world. A priest, but we shouldn't think of him as being just another priest. This man had had plays performed in the Abbey, articles in newspapers, and been interviewed on television. He would meet each of us individually. His name was Father Forristal.

Fifth and sixth years assembled in the new PE hall – a concrete plaque outside listed the American donors. We jostled and fidgeted, conscious of not being under supervision. Father Forristal was introduced and gave a brief talk, of which I recall nothing, apart from an aside that, if it wasn't for his health, in a week's time he could be giving a talk very much like this one to forty young lads very much like us out in Africa, except they would have fuzzy hair instead of greasy hair.

The months before this visit had been marked by an increasing thirst for the miraculous. Not just at school, but at home and in the country at large. There was schoolyard talk of UFOs and psychic powers, and kitchen talk of widows' curses and superstitions. In retrospect I can see that the moving statues of Ballinspittle were but a few months in the future. We were attuned to the magical in a way which seems remote now. It seems to me that this, more than moral attitudes, constitutes the greatest difference between that era and the present one.

So when one aging brother, who regularly entertained us with stories of his work among the lepers of Argentina, told us that the visiting priest had the gift of seeing inside teenagers' souls, we accepted this as fact. He would, we were assured, have an insight into what troubled us before we even spoke. In the one-to-one meetings he might ask us questions, or he might ask us to be silent, or he might spontaneously tell us our personal problems. Or he might joke and have a laugh.

In the schoolyard I kept my ears on alert as the first few pupils emerged with stories of their encounters.

It was my turn to meet Father Forristal. The principal's office had been temporarily rearranged for this purpose. The desk pushed to one side and a couch brought to the forefront. Just as we had been told, I entered a few seconds after the previous boy left. Forristal welcomed me and made some commiserations about the school heating system. He did not assume that I had had sexual intercourse and was feeling guilty about it, as the talk in the yard had led me to believe would occur. Nor did he begin a process of intuiting my habitual transgression by a tightening circle of insinuations that it did not involve violence, nor drugs, nor stealing. Instead he talked about electronics, satellites, and live television broadcasts. Maybe he had noted that my science results were good. The conversation meandered on without touching on anything that was close to the core of myself. So I began to answer reluctantly, with a minimum of words.

'Well, it's good to see you're doing well in the spring tests,' he said signalling the end of the conversation.

The whole meeting was a failure. He had not intuited anything, and I had treated him in the same way I treated any old priest or teacher. This was somebody out of the ordinary, I should show him respect.

'Father,' I said, 'I'm not a believer.'

He gave a nod, a touch inquisitor-like I thought, and still think, and said something about the upcoming exams, or the heating system.

Desmond Forristal's plays have not to my knowledge been staged in recent decades, but I have several times come across his book Maximilian of Auschwitz.

For a couple of years after the Leaving Cert I lived in London. Several of us Irish shared a house in Willesden. The phrase *Catlick Ireland* was nothing more than a cue for laughter, especially when uttered by English workmates. We played along with the clichés. Yes, the nuns tell girls they'll get pregnant if they sit on a boy's knee. Yes, you had to be careful buying condoms in case the chemist had punctured them with a pin.

It was all in the past – both my personal past and the country's. But the church wasn't finished with me yet. At that time I was working as a technician in a hospital. I'd made a big mistake in thinking that the real world had more to offer than university. And now I craved college as a kind of safe haven. There was only one place that offered what interested me most – a joint degree in philosophy and mathematics. And that was St. Patrick's College, Maynooth – the very heart and bastion of Catholicism in Ireland.

For two hundred years *going to Maynooth* meant undergoing the seven years' training for the priesthood. The university had admitted lay students since 1968, and to outward appearances, at least, was an entirely modern university. All clerical students were expected to study for a degree alongside their divinity studies. Most opted for science. And whether by chance or not, my best friends at Maynooth were clerical students. For four years we swapped lecture notes and had pints in the town pubs. I never felt I had to hide my true thoughts. They laughed with high amusement when I said theology was a training in mental slavery. They slowed and stumbled their words when I asked what urged them to become priests.

One friend questioned his vocation, and after a process lasting several months, left the seminary, moved into digs, and continued his degree as a lay student. At home in Sligo at weekends, whenever his girlfriend rang, his mother would cover the mouthpiece and shout up the stairs 'Satan's on the phone.' Another friend made his decision to leave when he came home one evening to find his fellow seminarians with their shoes off engaged in a sort of foot-tickling ring and laughing hysterically. In general there seemed nothing unusual about these students, and I always thought that if there were a Grand Inquisitor in the hierarchy, he couldn't have come up with a better plan for the self-extinction of the priesthood than to allow its recruits to mingle freely on a campus with a sixty per cent majority of females.

At the end of four years, I was handed my graduation scroll by the President of the University, one Monsignor Ledwith, member of an elite circle of theological advisors to the Holy See, who left Maynooth a few years later to become a speaker with a spiritual school led by a woman who channels a 35,000-year-old warrior called Ramtha who once led an army against the Atlanteans. In videos Ledwith talks in a disconcertingly familiar accent about his conversations with Ramtha and his years of research in theology. In another, more disturbing video, he staggers drunkenly onto the stage to rail against our capricious, psychotic God, and finishes the evening by dancing to Elvis Presley's It's Now or Never.

I had experienced Catholicism once as a system of solace, and a second time as farce. The church was staggering into oblivion. A wave of revelations of child abuse and cover-ups nudged the public perception of the church from farcical to sinister. The Redemptoristines where I once served mass now have a website which prominently displays their 'Review of Child Safeguarding Practice', even though, as the introduction to the document states, being an enclosed order they did not have any contact with children.

And yet all across the country, every day, priests are still called upon to stand at the altar and perform rituals. Holy communions, funerals, weddings. The congregation fumble through their forehead-lips-heart gestures, and emerge grinning to the sunlight: 'The man above gave us good weather, Father.' Those same friends who had mocked priests for the last twenty years were now queuing at the sacristy door to get their babies baptised.

An old college friend of mine and his fiancée were making arrangements to get married. They visited the priest at his home and explained that they 'weren't particularly religious'; that they wanted a church wedding mainly for their families. It transpired that the priest, not much older than themselves, had also studied science at Maynooth. He fetched some beers from the fridge, the chat rolled along familiar ruts. No problem, the priest explained, he could arrange a ceremony, a beautiful ceremony, where he would bless the marriage and invite the congregation of all shades of faith to join him in prayer. It would be in the church, and virtually indistinguishable from the holy sacrament of mass.

The couple left the house agreeing he was a sound person, very understanding and not the least cloying. A few days later they rang back to say they'd changed their minds; they wanted the full ceremony. The bride's mother had objected, said it wouldn't look proper, it would be over in ten minutes and there were guests driving a hundred miles to be there.

That's not what they told the priest, of course. They invoked 'family reasons' in a lowered tone. Some weeks later I watched that man make a puppet of himself on the altar and I blushed for him. Priests are people, too. Did he not perceive it was a mockery of his beliefs?

I got the email address of a priest who I had known as a clerical student three decades ago. I had once spent several hours in his room trying to explain the basics of Maxwell's equations to him. He didn't remember that detail, in fact he didn't give any indication that he remembered me at all. He said he never worried much about what people actually believe when they come to him for the sacraments. (I could sense a smile in the words he wrote.) There's a long history of belief and doubt being tangled up together. Those priests who leave the ministry, he maintained, generally do so for reasons of unsuitability. He said he didn't know any who left the priesthood and publicly ceased to be Catholics. He directed me to recent speculations on the future of the church made by Bishop Noel Treanor. Our email exchange petered out.

The old friend was reluctant to agree there was a crisis. Yet undeniably the church has imploded. In April The Examiner reported that many parishes across the country no longer have a resident priest. These churches can only hold mass every second or third Sunday.

For fifteen hundred years Christianity provided the answers to life's existential questions, rituals to orient life's stages, structures for social cohesion. In Ireland, it all seems to have disintegrated over the course of two decades with remarkably little turmoil. No chaos, no mass despair. No increase in violence or drug abuse. Suicide rates seem to track economic cycles more than anything else. And yet I find it hard to believe that a faith that animated society for fifteen centuries can dissolve so easily and so rapidly. I can't shake a sense of foreboding, a feeling that we are in a period of calm, and the consequences have yet to emerge. I think of apostate Ledwith raging against God.

WHY ARE WE IN THE ROOM?

A conversation with BEN KIDD and BUSH MOUKARZEL
By Mark O'Connell

Over the last few years, some of the most memorable nights out I've had have been in, of all places, a theatre, watching plays by Dead Centre. The Dublin/London-based company have an extraordinary knack for executing high-concept experimental premises in ways that are not just entertaining, but provocative and emotionally resonant. Co-founders Ben Kidd and Bush Moukarzel, who met as undergraduates at the University of Nottingham, have been collaborating since 2012, when their show Souvenir, a wildly enjoyable riff on Proust's In Search of Lost Time, played in the Dublin Theatre Festival. (Bush came to Dublin in the mid 2000s to do an MPhil in Psychoanalysis in Trinity – which is where I first got to know him – and never got around to leaving.)

Their work is thrilling and strange and deeply inventive. There is always some weird and clever gimmick that brings the audience into the show, but which the show then subverts and transcends. Lippy, their brilliant exploration of a real-life suicide pact involving three sisters and their aunt in Leixlip in 2000, begins with a post-show talk and gets steadily more disorienting as it proceeds. They've since been rifling the canon, staging shows that tackle, in one way or another, the presence (or the idea) of some or other great theatrical eminence. Chekhov's First Play is an anti-adaptation of Chekhov's famously unstageable Platonov, in which the audience, while ostensibly sitting through a more or less stodgy production of the play, is continually interrupted – via headphones worn throughout – by Bush's variously frivolous and profound 'director's commentary'. (Platonov himself, the play's silent central character, is played in each performance by a man pulled out of the audience and directed by Ben over headphones.) Hamnet, meanwhile, is a strange and affecting creation in which Shakespeare's recently deceased only son – played in the initial run by the incredible Olly West, an 11-year-old boy who had never acted before – kills time with the audience in a kind of meta-theatrical purgatory, eventually summoning the anti-ghost of his father.

This conversation took place in my office in Rathmines. Ben, having recently come down with actual tuberculosis during rehearsals for Dead Centre's Shakespeare's First Play at Berlin's Schaubühne theatre, joined Bush and I over Skype from London. My office is an unsuitable environment for humans at the best of times, but it is definitely not the kind of place you want to be if you have tuberculosis.

MARK O'CONNELL: Two of my most vivid memories of seeing your shows involve moments where everything threatened to come apart. In Chekhov's First Play, there's this moment where the wrecking ball comes out of nowhere and knocks over the set. I don't know if either of you remember, but the night that I saw the show, the wrecking ball never made contact with the set, and that spectacle of demolition was itself demolished. And then the night I saw Hamnet in the Peacock, during the moment where Olly is petitioning men in the audience to come up on stage with him to read a scene from Hamlet,

to play the ghost of the father, he kept having to ask and ask, and it seemed for a moment as though no one would come up, and that the whole thing would collapse. In both cases, it was only talking to you both after the show that I learned that these were, in their different ways, fuck-ups. But what this makes me think is that there's a certain volatility built into what you do. Using untrained child actors, relying on technical gimmickry, audience participation and so on. The possibility of things going disastrously wrong is quite significant in your work, and maybe even structural, is what I'm getting at.

Bush Moukarzel: Yesterday I had a conversation with Marina Carr, and we were talking about ideas of shows we might do in the future. I was talking through another show we might do in Vienna, based on Freud's The Interpretation of Dreams, and I was saying 30% of the show would be improvised, and we would join that up with the other 70% of the show that was scripted and rehearsed. The show would have an audience member speak about her dream, and then the show would somehow interpret her dream. Like a live analytic session. But Marina said, why would you have an improvised element? Why would you do that to yourself? And my answer was that it's like if you have a meal, and someone said, 'Why did you add chilli to that? I've had this before without chilli and it's really nice.' And I would say, 'Yes, but it's also nice with chilli. It's just another flavour you're bringing into the room.' So on a basic level, it's just another texture, or another tool that theatre has at its disposal, that something might go wrong. You might even argue, as in the case of Olly in Hamnet, an audience member not coming on stage to talk with him – although I'm backstage having a heart attack and thinking what the fuck have we done, putting this poor boy through this – that it added to the show, because people then tell you that it was a particularly lovely moment. And you then remember, ah, that's why we believed in these aspects of the work! So in one sense it's just a flavour. But there's a deeper answer that I would grapple for, which is maybe an attempt to answer what theatre is for.

MO'C: That was going to be my first question, but I decided it was unfair to shove you off the deep end right away. Now you've shoved yourself off.

BM: Well, I really think that's at the heart of it, because you might argue that the experience of seeing something palpably prepared, and which in that sense can't go wrong, is nowadays historically moribund, and doesn't bring the audience into any connection with the story you are trying to tell, and that these disruptive strategies of failure are access points to make the audience feel respected. Now this might be just a sort of historical fetishism of the moment, like with that David Shields book Reality Hunger. It might be that we're just part of this junket of people who are trying to get in on the Real. The idea that you need a little bit of the Real for it to be seen to be a contemporary work.

Ben Kidd: Historically that is probably a response on theatre's part to performance art. But at the same time that tension between the Real and the Not-Real – the potential for mistake, and the potential for brilliance if you spend a long time preparing for it – has always been part of theatre. It's a cliché, in a way. You've always had people saying, 'Well, it's live isn't it, there's a danger in the air, you just don't know what the actors are going to do!' Actors can be in plays they've been rehearsing for weeks, it can be all quite mechanical, but they have to tell themselves that they're making new decisions every night. I think theatre congratulates itself that the potential for mistake in the moment is what gives it its resonance and its possibility to speak to people. And as Bush was saying, that's something we really like exploring. And working with Olly in Hamnet was a case in point, because he is that lack of preparation personified. If you work with someone of that age, they can't not be. Then there's the element in the Chekhov show where the audience member puts the headphones on and comes onstage as Platonov and is following instructions. Maybe it's because I'm the person giving the instructions that I can sense the possibility of failure every step of the way. But some audience members just don't realise that the person they're looking at is one of them; they think it's rehearsed, they think it's someone *pretending* to be an audience member. But if they don't think that, and if they get it, it has a real potential to rupture. Theatre is always dealing with the tension between preparing something so that you do it really well, and at the same time taking advantage of the fact that you are in the same room as everyone else. Mistakes in that sense just couldn't exist in any other art form. You can't really read a novel and it goes wrong halfway through in the same sense as a play can go wrong.

MO'C: So the risk of failure then is not just an epiphenomenon of what you're doing, but is actually part of the thing itself.

BM: Completely. As Ben said, the whole of one type of theatre has been to rehearse something as thoroughly as you can so it looks unrehearsed. Then there was – as Ben mentioned, possibly from performance art – a sort of scepticism of that whole process, and the setting up of a real unpredictable event, whereby it's not rehearsed, it's just a scenario you go to and it happens there and then. In our instance we're just interested in all of it, in playing those elements against each other. All of that is a way of questioning the production's relationship to the audience. Is the production supposed to ignore the audience, act like it's not there, or is it supposed to cast the audience into the meaning of the evening?

MO'C: That clearly is one of the things that distinguishes theatre from other forms. You can't get around the audience. The audience is primary in a way that you surely have to be thinking about the eventual room full of people, all the time, at every level of creation, in a way that for instance I, as a prose writer, do not have to think about my readers all the time. You're explicitly grappling with that and trying to make it part of the work.

BK: Yeah. And whatever you make, there are ways you think about an audience that, hopefully as you get better, simply become techniques and crafts and rhythms. Have the audience been bored for a while, and is that okay? And that is, I'd imagine, an analogous process for a prose writer. Bush would often ask of a particular moment, Why are we here? Why are we in the room? That's got to be the primary question. The tradition of realist playwriting doesn't really wrestle with that. You start, the lights come up, a door opens, someone comes on stage with some shopping bags, and then they have a line to say.

BM: But that is literally the opening of Beckett's First Play! Obviously there's a couple of twists on that classic scenario, but don't knock coming in with the shopping.

[Beckett's First Play is the project Dead Centre are currently developing; it's about the life of Samuel Beckett during the time he was writing Eleutheria, the famously failed theatrical work that immediately preceded Waiting for Godot. Dead Centre's play takes Beckett's preoccupation with absence to its logical conclusion, and features only the voices of actors, with objects ghosting about on stage. The aforementioned bags of shopping, for instance, will be hoisted in on strings – and so on and so forth.]

BK: Well, my point is you can't just tell stories anymore. I think we have deliberately talked about why an audience is there. I remember going to see a play with a friend of mine, who isn't a regular theatre-goer. And he came out of the play and said, 'I just look at all these people on the stage, and they're all pretending to be someone else, and I just feel so awkward for them, so embarrassed!' He wasn't saying that, therefore, this is a moribund form; he was actually saying it as a reason why he doesn't like going. Because of the awkwardness and the embarrassment on their behalf.

MO'C: I think that's one of the really interesting things about theatre: the potential for it to be so alive is precisely what can make it feel so incredibly dead. A play can feel much deader than any other form of failed or bad art.

BM: Because they really should be alive. Because the people are right there. And because the tools of liveness – for instance, maybe just to turn your head in my direction and say hello, and bring everything into the present – are available for you at all times. So go for it! But then it doesn't happen and it can feel so alienating, and it's like, as you say, the living dead. But I feel that that's the kind of thing I would have told myself when we started making theatre, as a catalyst for energy around making a different style. Thinking 'How embarrassing to go to the theatre, and they not look at you and say hello! How embarrassing for everybody is this old style of 19th century naturalism!' But actually I don't feel that at all when I go to plays now. I think it's fine. It maybe doesn't set me alight, so then you try something else. Like, wouldn't it be funny if there was a horse in this? It's more just refining and looking for a different sensibility, rather than having a strong reaction against that traditional form.

MO'C: It's not like you're trying to do A Thing to the theatre, then. It's not like you have a manifesto.

BM: Sadly I don't feel like making an attack, no.

BK: The thing is you kind of know the sorts of shows the people who are coming to your shows are also seeing. There are millions of books that any given reader could be reading, so although you as a writer are probably in a conversation with certain other writers, you can't really be sure, in the way that a theatre maker can, of what your audience will be familiar with. All theatre makers who are good at paying attention are in some kind of conversation with theatre being made in their cultural environs. The whole Chekhov's First Play opening sequence revolves around something that not just regular theatre goers, but

hopefully anyone will appreciate, which is that this is a way you might do a Chekhov play. You might put them in old-fashioned costumes, and have them wander around and talk in a very proper way. That's deliberately in conversation with other people who are making plays as well, but also in conversation with other experiences your audience might be having.

MO'C: I'm intrigued by the dynamics of collaboration. Especially given that you're based in different cities, how does the working relationship happen? What are the mechanisms?

BM: In theatre there's this role called the dramaturg. And that role might involve anything from fact-checking the script, checking whether its propositions add up, testing the rhythms of a script or whatever it might be. One way we collaborate is that Ben might dramaturg things I've written. But that's purely because we started out in these roles. I'd written this long adaptation of Proust's book focusing on the Albertine story. And Ben questioned that script, and then we set to work on it, and it became Souvenir. That was the way we started working together. But now it's become much more complicated. Often now the role reverses, where Ben might write a scenario and I would scrutinise it. We get to the end point and we both sign off on it, and the author is always 'Dead Centre', and then we go into the rehearsal room. So the way we collaborate is a work-in-progress. But it does feel that if we want to carry on, I have to be careful not to be too rude. I can be rude to Ben quite a lot of the time, in the way you can be with a family member, but I wouldn't be with you because you're a friend of mine. So because we've become like family, I've ended up being complacent with Ben in a way I never would with a normal friend. So if we want to carry on, and so far we do, there's a sort of duty of care to sustain the relationship. But I speak to friends who make work on their own in what ultimately is a collaborative medium, and they sometimes say it's annoying that they can only bring someone on board late to read a draft after they've spent six months working on it, and the show is on in four months. The fact that from the get-go what we're writing and thinking about is already out there, between us. That's what's valuable about it.

MO'C: Do you have a conversation from time to time, about whether you're going to keep working together? Is it just a given?

BM: We don't have it pencilled in. You know, we're going into rehearsals next week for a new production of Hamnet, so we'll be talking about that. Then we might have more general meetings about Dead Centre, where we'll talk strategy for the next year, have we got the right applications into the Arts Council and so on. The one thing we don't do is really strategise long-term. We're not talking about what kind of company should Dead Centre be in five years, ten years. We don't have the duty of care meeting pencilled in after each project.

BK: We have each followed, moment by moment, the most interesting thing we could be doing with our lives for the next few months. And so far that has always been working on a theatre project and trying to get it made together. There is a strong sense of the accidental to how we work together.

BM: It is absolutely accidental. But on we go.

EIGHT NON-SEQUITURS

Images by Stephen Brandes

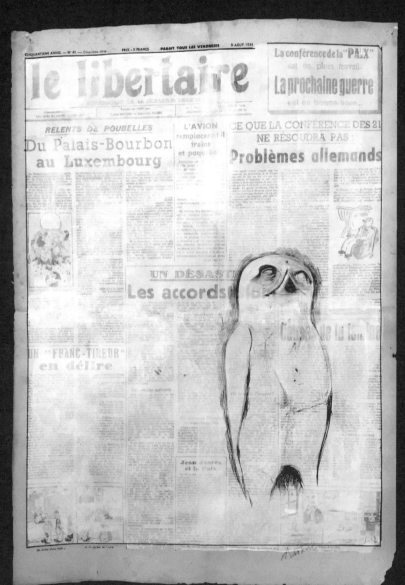

THREE SPINS, A WEDNESDAY

Danny Denton

Whirling forces that moved at speed. Shadows that multiplied and grew along the fringes of the hard shoulder, shadows probed by headlights. To fifth gear. The rattle of change in the tray eased. The phone rang again. She felt about her lap for the vibration, eyes steady on the road, and she found one earphone and got it in and answered.

'Are you nearly here, Mam?'

'I'm just coming off the dual carriageway, love. I'll be on the roundabout in a second.'

'Liar. I'll come outside if you're that close?'

'Don't come out, love, in case I get stopped at the lights. It's too cold to be waiting outside.'

'Just hurry, Mam. I'm already late.'

If the eyes could rest a moment ... She eased off, indicated, light failing on the wing. The sound of cars forged the evening, the darkness growing from the ditches, falling first on other fields and houses and roads.

To fourth on the exit, feeling the curve of the road within her, the hard shoulder tapering away to nothing. Whirling forces which moved at speed, slowing. The brief beat of cat's eyes beneath. She thought of Sadie then, clicking over the tiles at home, waiting for her dinner. She sighed and blinked and accepted the facts of road signage: SLOW DOWN. CHILDREN CROSSING. She fancied Dino's. Maybe between Lou and Daddy she would. Something light touched her belly and slipped down into her lap. A phantom trickle. No, the headphone. The streetlamps framed the night now, and the sign for the roundabout.

Don't say that word to me, Bee.

It was always gonna happen one of us, Jim. Anyway, it's not a death sentence, you know.

The words came round: whirling forces. And here was the sign for the roundabout, framed by streetlight. And the phone again.

'You haven't forgotten about me?'

'I haven't, Daddy. I'm just dropping Lou to work and I'm coming for you then. It'll be about half past.'

'I can't be holding the proceedings up.'

'I know, Daddy.'

Here's what she would do: she would drop her, then drop him, then pick the other up and drop her wherever she was going. She would get home and park and run up the steps to the house. That would get the blood flowing again. She wouldn't even turn on the hallway light; she'd just grab the lead and Sadie would come running and wagging her tail like a mad thing and hopefully not wet herself with the excitement. They'd walk to the bridge and back. The bridge.

Don't say that word to me, Bee.

Come on, Jim, we'll be fine.

I won't go to Comic Con.

For God's sake, Jim, I'm not going dying this weekend!

To the bridge and back. Twenty minutes. She'd remember the poo bags this time. Open the door; grab the lead; grab the poo bags; out and back in twenty; feed Sadie; fill the water bowl, and then onto the couch and get the soaps on. Lou was watching those same soaps; she wondered would yer wan tell yer man, and she wondered what Lou thought about it. Yes, a glass of wine and the soaps on. And maybe a fire going too. Not stopping for coal though. A fire or a blanket depending on how much coal was left. Sadie let onto the couch for a cuddle. No study tonight. No hoovering or washing up. Bed for ten, happy out.

Shit, but dinner too. Something quick. Dino's. Or if she didn't want to stop and go through the ordering and the waiting then maybe just toast. Peanut butter on toast and a cuppa.

She came to the roundabout – all her evenings on that roundabout. Whirling forces on repeat. The same old exits, always. The phone again. The fumble for the earphones.

'Love, I'm literally just coming around the corner now.'

'Come on!'

She turned into the complex and swung around the green, the windows of the block illuminated in the glare of the headlights. Through those windows, right now, lives played out in boxy apartments. She eveningdreamed of clotheshorses alongside sofas, towels slipped to bathroom floors, sticky toothpaste lids, mantelpieces and wood-framed photographs. *I won't go, Bee.* How many others – in there – were sick right now? There was a tremor in her belly, like worry. *I'm glad it's me anyhow.* Then Lou was yanking the door open, pulling the tote bag over her head as she fell into the seat and leaned across to kiss.

'Thanks so much, Mammy.'

Her heart beat. She started around the green again. The phone again.

'Answer that, will you, Lou?'

Lou took the phone out of her lap and pulled the earphone jack.

'Hey Grandaddy, you're talking to Lou.'

'…'

'She's driving.'

'…'

'We're on the way, yeah.'

'I already told him, five minutes ago.'

'He says he can't be late.'

'Tell him he won't be late. Tell him we're at the roundabout.'

'She'll be twenty minutes, Grandaddy.'

'…'

'You too, Grandaddy.'

Lou dropped the phone back into her lap. 'We're nowhere near the roundabout.'

'I spend my whole fucking life going around that roundabout.' To fourth. To fifth. 'Anyway, he'll keep ringing if I don't say something. He's obsessed with this shed thing. He has to be on time because he's *the timer*.'

Lou slurped from a pot of instant noodles. 'Don't begrudge him his happiness.'

'I don't! I'm the one bloody dropping him to it twice a week.'

'Okay, okay. Chill.'

'Don't spill that stuff in my car.'

She heard the sigh. Whirling force of exhalation. The lungs emptied in a moment of giving up. But it could only be a moment, because you had to inhale again. The body made you. You had to inhale and breathe again.

As they came back towards the dual carriageway a forest of pylons stood against the darkened sky.

'How is Dad getting on at Comic Con?'

'I haven't heard from him today, so good probably.'

The headlights of another probed the depths of her car, the backseat empty, her daughter's wild head of hair, the instant noodles tilted forward in one hand as she looked at her phone in the other.

'Are you supposed to be starting at seven?'

'Half six.'

'So you're *very* late?'

'Oh it doesn't matter, Mam. There's no one there at half six anyway.'

'...'

'Actually, Mam, do you have that forty?'

'Should be in my purse there.'

Lou flipped the glove box and took out the purse as they merged with the dual carriageway. To fourth, to fifth. Indicate. Over the right shoulder to darkness – safe to go.

'There's only twenty here, Mam? I'm not going through the change pocket.'

'Is there only twenty there? Oh. Sorry. Yeah, I gave Jo twenty.'

'What did you give her money for?'

'Grandaddy owes me fifty. I'll get it off him and drop it back in to you.'

'It's grand, don't mind it.'

'Sure take twenty now and I'll drop the rest in.'

'Hang on to it til you have it all.'

'It's no bother to drop it in, Lou.'

'No point coming back into town.'

If the eyes could rest a moment.

'Mam, we're in no rush.'

'I know.'

'Can you not drive at a hundred and twenty then?'

It wasn't easy to let the needle fall.

'How much longer will you be off work, Mam?'

'I'm not sure.'

'I love you, Mam.'

'I love you too, darling ... Did you remember to record the soaps? Will she tell him, do you think?'

As they came into town along the quays she noticed that there were great piles of suds – dirty suds – floating upstream like iceberg tips.

'Look at that, Lou.'

Lou shrugged. Her hair fell onto her shoulders in great piles. She held herself a particular way: bleak, uncertain, beautiful. She turned the blowers on and said 'Do you mind?' and hot air poured from the dash.

She heard her father before he was even sat into the front seat, seeming to fill the car then, saying 'Christ! You have the heat on full blast!'

'Get in, Daddy. Why'd you wait out in the freezing cold?'

'I prefer cold,' he said, 'than that heat. Heat is no good since the prostate.'

'I'll turn it off now,' she said.

He held out his arms in front of him and pulled up his coat and jumper sleeves so that they bunched at the elbow. 'Look! Heat rashes. Since the prostate.'

She glanced as she turned the dial; she'd seen the rashes already.

'I need to piss now.'

'Will I go back?'

'No, drive on. It's the cold. I need to piss constantly.'

'Will I turn on the heat a little then?'

'Do what you like. You're grand my side.'

She pulled out of the narrow lane and into second. To third. Away again along the road. It was not a flat landscape, but lumpy, stretched out like a ragged dust sheet over everything to be kept clean.

'We were fishing last weekend in Kerry,' he announced. 'Mikey Austin took us. He's got the prostate now too. He just needs to make a call on it, you know? We can't all be like the fish in Egypt, you know? The doc said that to me and I said same to Mikey. Make the decision and get on with it.'

'I read somewhere yesterday that once you make a positive decision, positive things start to happen.'

'I owe you forty,' he remembered. 'I'll give it to you Thursday.'

'No rush.'

'You're still off work.'

'Not back yet.'

'Take your time my princess Bee. Life is good and long to be working.'

They came up towards the dual carriageway again, and to the roundabout again – night after night, the cycle a kind of joke – and the signs commenced the ritual of appearing from darkness onto the headlights, like miracles.

'I can't get warm,' he said, looking at his forearms like he was looking deep into his soul. 'We're coming back from Kerry anyway and we see this crash. A whole family in one car. Into a white lorry. A child came out the back window. I didn't even see where it landed.'

'Jesus, Daddy.'

'The roads in this country have a lot to answer for.'

'Jesus.'

'Impossible to tell who was to blame.'

'Did ye stop?'

'I called 999. It was a shock of a thing. Here, will you take my dishwasher?'

'Your dishwasher?'

'I'm the only one in the house. I won't use it.'

She glanced. He was looking through the windscreen with some kind of intent, head tilted to the left. As if something was in his way and he needed to see past it. Or as if he had to line his view up with the hard shoulder. She felt the cat's eyes rumble and corrected herself.

'Sure isn't it handy to have?'

'I wouldn't put it on. I *like* doing the washing up.'

'Sure what would Jim and me want a dishwasher for? We're only two.'

'Your mother liked it. I never asked for it.'

'...'

'It would make it easier for ye to keep on top of things.'

'What?'

'Your house. I'm worried is all.'

'My house is fine, Daddy!'

She began to cough and couldn't stop for a minute. Coughing, she could only think about stopping coughing. The needle fell to eighty. Something silver passed like a train on the right. The night was full dark now, the tarmac jaundiced in headlights.

'You've always three in that house anyway,' he said. 'There's always some crisis with one of them. Three's a dishwasher.'

'Daddy, I'm not taking your fucking dishwasher.'

'Now,' he said, pointing to a looming block off the road, his sleeves still bunched up over the elbows. 'Who owns that hotel?'

'Is it not Declan Driscoll?'

'He's got the prostate too.'

The cough jacked again and her father pulled a plastic bottle of water from his large coat pocket and put it in the holder between them. 'Here,' he said. '*Always* dehydrate.'

Coughing thanks, she tried to hook the wetness of the lung.

'How's Jim?' he asked.

'He's grand. He's off at Comic Con.'

Don't say that word to me.

'What's that?'

'A kind of conference I suppose.'

'A conference? Since when does Jim go to conferences? Here, look, there's a space, look. You'd want to get that cough looked at. It's the last thing you need. There, yeah, leave me there. I'll walk in from here. Thanks, love. Give yer auld dad a kiss. Drink some water there. You're grand, you're grand. Bye now, love.'

'Josie? I'm outside. Are you nearly ready?'

'…'

'No rush.'

While she waited in the car she looked through the messages from Jim, her phone a beacon within the gloombosom of the car, itself within the gloombosom of the road. The selfies of him in full costume, a hotel lobby at a strange angle in the background, as if it were a dream. There was the passing hush of cars – all these cars moving through the night like dust that swarmed through light. Sadie would pull and drag at the lead, mad for road. She'd walk her, feed her, then they'd settle on the couch for the soaps. No hoovering or washing up tonight. Would yer wan tell yer man? Would she?

It was always gonna happen one of us.

As if the body held self-destruction within it, like a pearl.

Josie climbed in, stuffing her hands back into her coat pockets, pressing her chin down into her collar, and said, 'Heya. Thanks.'

'No bother, love. How are you?'

'Grand. You?'

She indicated. She moved into the clear space – streetlight, pavement, windows and darkened brick – and shifted to second. To third, feeling in her shoulder the curve in that road, feeling it in her gut as though it were part of her, as though she were the car.

'Where are we off to, love?'

'Oh.' Josie lifted her head as if awakening. 'Do you mind if I stay with you tonight?'

Gone, the soaps. Gone, the toast, the couch snuggle, the glass of wine. She'd hoover. She'd do the dishes, try to think about dates, and test results, and treatment. She'd find clean sheets, make the bed for Josie.

'Of course not, love. Of course not.'

The black, winding road all hedges and trees now, reaching up into the nothing. Lights to full beam for a moment, and off.

'I was thinking of take-away for dinner. Dino's.'

'You can't afford take-away, Mam.' Each word not a sigh, but a sigh. 'Neither can I.'

The curve of the road. The trees reaching overhead, forming a tunnel, holding the road in that bosom of dark. It would be wrong to put on the radio now. The silence and the night would have to be filled with her own words. To full beam again for a moment. Whirling forces that moved at speed. On into the darkness; on the other side of the darkness, the soaps. Would she? The curve of the road. To fourth again. The phone again.

THE GERMAN PRINCESS

John Gallagher

Her name was Mary Carleton. Or else it was Maria de Wolway. Sometimes she went by Mary Steadman, though people said she'd been born Mary Moders. She was the daughter of a grand family in the city of Cologne – well, either that or she was the daughter of a Canterbury fiddler. She was rich, except she wasn't. She was a model of wifely virtue to several husbands, provided they didn't mind the overlap. She forged the most beautiful letters.

People loved her. She was charming and witty and fashionable, and anyway it wasn't their valuables she'd made off with. When she won her first great court case, they cheered and clapped; while she sat in prison, they queued to visit her. Her jailers made good money from her: when people came to get a look at her, they charged a fee. Once, she was recognised in the street, and the star-struck crowd nearly pulled her out of her coach. They'd sing songs about her long after she was dead. Some of them had watched her die. Whatever her real name, they called her the German Princess, and she was the most famous con woman in Restoration England.

Mary Carleton – I'll call her that, because it's the name under which she became a sensation, and the one she used most reliably to tell her story – burst onto the public stage in 1663. Just three years before, King Charles II had returned from exile to take the throne, putting an end to two decades of turmoil: his father had lost his head; the three kingdoms of England, Scotland, and Ireland had exploded into violence; the people became participants (whether they liked it or not) in a new, radical political experiment. Their world, they said, felt turned upside down. In a decade when the scars of civil war had barely healed, and when London suffered fire, plague, and war, Mary Carleton showed what could be done by manipulating the bonds of trust that made the city run smoothly. She showed how a woman could become someone else.

Here's the story, or at least one of its many variations:

A German ingénue arrives in London from Cologne. Tired from her journey and in need of refreshment and accommodation, she heads for the Exchange Tavern. To the tavern-keeper, the woman who's just walked in the door seems well-dressed, rich, a long way from home. Later, he'll intercept her letters and confirm these impressions. By the time he realises that she forged them herself, it'll be too late. For now, it's an opportunity too good to resist.

The tavern-keeper starts to plot. He dresses up a young man named John Carleton – his friend's son – as a fine gentleman. Carleton, accompanied by a pair of footmen, is introduced to the German Princess. He pays her compliments; they dine. Everyone else in the room knows their roles: they call him 'my lord' and treat him with respect. In short order, he proclaims his love for her. His father and the tavern-keeper prevail upon their guest to assent to marry him. They've been eyeballing her clothes and her jewels, and now they won't let her leave the house. The net is tightening around the German Princess.

But one grifter recognises another. When she wrote her own account of these events, Mary Carleton (as she continued to call herself) claimed to have spotted the ruse a mile off. She would take them for all they were worth. 'Let the World now judge,' she wrote later 'whither being prompted by such plain and publique signes of a design upon me, to counterplot them, I have done any more then what ... a received principle of Justice directs: *to deceive the deceiver, is no deceit.*' After persuasion and coercion, she assented to a hasty secret marriage. The scammers were overjoyed. They put the couple up in plush accommodation, her father-in-law paid for some beautiful new clothes for the newly-wed bride, and they settled down to wait for the money to roll in from her estates in Germany.

At this point, things start to go wrong. The money doesn't arrive. Matters aren't helped when her husband's family receive a letter accusing the German Princess of imposture and bigamy. The author claims to be a figure from her Kentish past, writing – 'If it be the same woman I mean, she speaks several languages fluently, and hath very high Breasts, &c.' Her father-in-law, furious at the idea that he's been duped, takes his revenge. He and his men assault her, calling her a 'Cheating Whore' while her new husband stands by. She wrote that 'devested and stript of all my cloaths, and plundred of all my jewels, and my money, my very bodyes, and a payr of silk Stockings, being also pulled from me, and in a strange array carried before a Justice.' She is thrown into prison, to await her trial.

So it is that, in 1663, Mary Carleton goes on trial for bigamy. The catalogue of her supposed husbands is difficult to keep track of, and it depends a bit on who you ask. There was William Ford, a shoemaker of Dover; a surgeon, Mr. Day; and a man named Steadman from Canterbury. Later, there would be more. But her husband's prosecution got nowhere. He produced only one serious witness, a fellow called Knot, who claimed to have given Mary away at her first marriage to Mr Steadman. Steadman himself didn't show. Apparently he couldn't afford the coach.

In contrast to the prosecution, Mary Carleton's performance in court was a masterclass: one account reported that she held herself with 'such a grace and gallant deportment' that those on the bench couldn't believe she could be 'of any low birth or parentage.' The account continued: 'She stood at the bar ... playing with her Fan before her Face, beholding the bench with a magnanimous and undaunted spirit.' She stood there, with her cheeks 'a perfect vermilion'; she cracked a joke when an elderly witness failed to recognise her; she dropped in a reference to St Paul to show off her more than ordinary education. She suggested, very gently, that the prosecution's witnesses were in her husband's family's pocket. When she was acquitted, there began 'a great noise throughout the whole Court, and most of it was to her great applause and brave acute wit'. She had choreographed a perfect piece of Restoration theatre.

Mary Carleton became a media sensation. And she fed the beast herself: during the trial, she paid a scrivener to come to court and take notes on all the proceedings. When it was done, and she had triumphed, she had the transcript printed. A pamphlet war was now brewing: one little book, hot off the press, described her on the title page as 'the crafty whore of Canterbury.' It boasted stories of her multiple husbands and her many crimes: how she had been imprisoned in Newgate for cheating a vintner of sixty pounds, and had robbed money and valuables from a French merchant and a Kentish gentleman; how she had almost been transported to Barbados, and how all her jewels had been found to be counterfeit. An outraged counter-attack was swiftly fired off, calling itself A Vindication of a Distressed Lady, and lamenting how 'the World is so deceived ... by the Reports that are disperst abroad every where concerning the

Behold my innocence after such disgrace
my ??? show an honest and a noble Face
Henceforth there needs no mark of ???
the right Counterfeit is herein sh???
1662
??? tatis meæ proximo 22° Ianuar stilo novo vicesimo primo

JOHN GALLAGHER

Person intended in this Discourse.' Tales and counter-tales were published; she and her husband wrote dueling pamphlets of their own.

A woman who had made her name by toying with anonymity was thrust into the public spotlight. Her biographer wrote that 'so great Novelty had not been known or seen in our age, nor in any other age as I can read of, I never heard of her Parallel in everything … [she] was the only talk for all the Coffee-houses in and near London.' In 1664, she agreed to act as herself in a play based on her life – a performance within a performance. But Samuel Pepys, who watched her in April of that year, was disappointed, writing that 'never was anything so well done in earnest, worse performed in jest upon the stage.' In the bright lights of the theatre, her performance suddenly seemed less convincing.

What happened next is hard to pin down. Later accounts of her life brim with stories of new 'pranks' she pulled off during this time: she duped the king's watchmaker and stole a chunk of his stock; she won the heart of an elderly man who thought he could reform her, and made away with his cash and goods, lying low at the other end of town until the hue and cry died down. 'She had a running Brain,' wrote one observer, 'and the whole City of London was too little for her to act in.' She was said to have gone to Holland and defrauded people there, and in 1671, after being caught for another petty theft, she wound up being transported to the Caribbean. She managed – exactly how is unclear – to make it back to England, but when she beached up it wasn't long before she was caught again. This time, she was the victim of a fatal coincidence. The man who picked her up was the warden of the Marshalsea prison 'and surveying her face more seriously he remembered her Physiognomy.' The city's anonymity had failed her: the German Princess was unmasked by her own notoriety.

Writing today, when I try to tell the story – as if there's only one story – of the German Princess, I run up against the same problem as one of her early biographers. He wrote exasperatedly that 'If I should promise to give you a true account of her whole life I should deceive you, for how can Truth be discovered of her who was wholly composed of Falsehood?' It's not that everything that was said about her was a lie: it's that there's always another compelling competing account, each one undercut by the next. She had so many names, was accused of so many crimes, wrote so spiritedly and convincingly in her own defence, that it feels impossible to pin down anything approaching a historical truth about this extraordinary woman. She had a sense of herself as a fictional character: she compared herself to the heroine of a picaresque novel or an explorer of *terra incognita* – 'What harme have I done in pretending to great Titles?' She wrote and rewrote her own story in ways that mean that she can still con us three centuries later. But sometimes I think it's healthy to be reminded of the aching presence of everything we can't know about the past, and of how easy it is to be seduced by the only side of the story that survives. Reading her today, I think of her presence in the courtroom as she smilingly upended the case of those who tried to pin a story on her.

Mary Carleton lived in an age of impostors, and in a city that seemed to breed them. One chronicler of her life called London 'that little World of People': as the city burst its boundaries, becoming broader and denser than ever before, it was getting harder to know exactly who your neighbours were, or to learn a stranger's identity with any certainty.

When I first came across Mary Carleton, I was in New York. It was the summer of 2017 and, though I didn't know it, just around the corner from where I was pounding iced coffees and reading faded 17th-century pamphlets, the story of a modern-day German Princess was entering its final spiral. A woman calling herself Anna Delvey had taken banks, hotels, restaurants, and lawyers for a brilliant ride: posing as a New York socialite, she had spent tens of thousands of dollars she didn't have, courted celebrities and almost conned her way into a multi-million dollar real estate deal. They're putting her life story on Netflix: a few weeks ago, she managed to post an Instagram photo from inside Rikers Island, where she's in prison. Reading about her, I couldn't stop thinking about how much her story and Mary Carleton's had in common, even at three centuries' remove. They both understood that in a big city, you can become anonymous. That if you know how to talk and what to wear, you can short-circuit networks of trust and recommendation. That greedy people are the easiest to trick. Mary Carleton's biographer had written that 'she may very well serve as a Looking-glass, wherein we may see the Vices of this Age Epitomized' – but those vices weren't just her own. She gloried in tricks that played on the avarice of others, and humiliated those who thought they were smarter than she was – *'To deceive the deceiver, is no deceit.'*

In the end, they got her for a robbery in Chancery Lane. She was quickly found guilty and, this time, sentenced to death. She tried, at the last, to 'plead her belly' – to argue that she was pregnant, and so couldn't be executed. For some condemned prisoners, this worked; it didn't work for her. In January 1673, on a Wednesday that she said was the anniversary of her baptism, she was brought to Tyburn to be hanged. One account of her death reported her final speech: 'I confess I have been a vain Woman; I have had in the World Glory and Misery in abundance; and let all People beware of ill Company. The World hath condemn'd me, and I have much to answer; pray God forgive me, and my Husband likewise.' To John Carleton, the man she still called her husband, she left 'Only my Recommendations; that he would serve God and repent. … I forgive him.' She had asked that those who attended 'would be so much friends to Justice, as not to give credit to all vain Rumors that were reported of her', but around the execution ground, they were selling ballads – cheap sheets of paper packed with scurrilous tales of her misadventures, all set to a most hummable tune called The German Princess's Adieu.

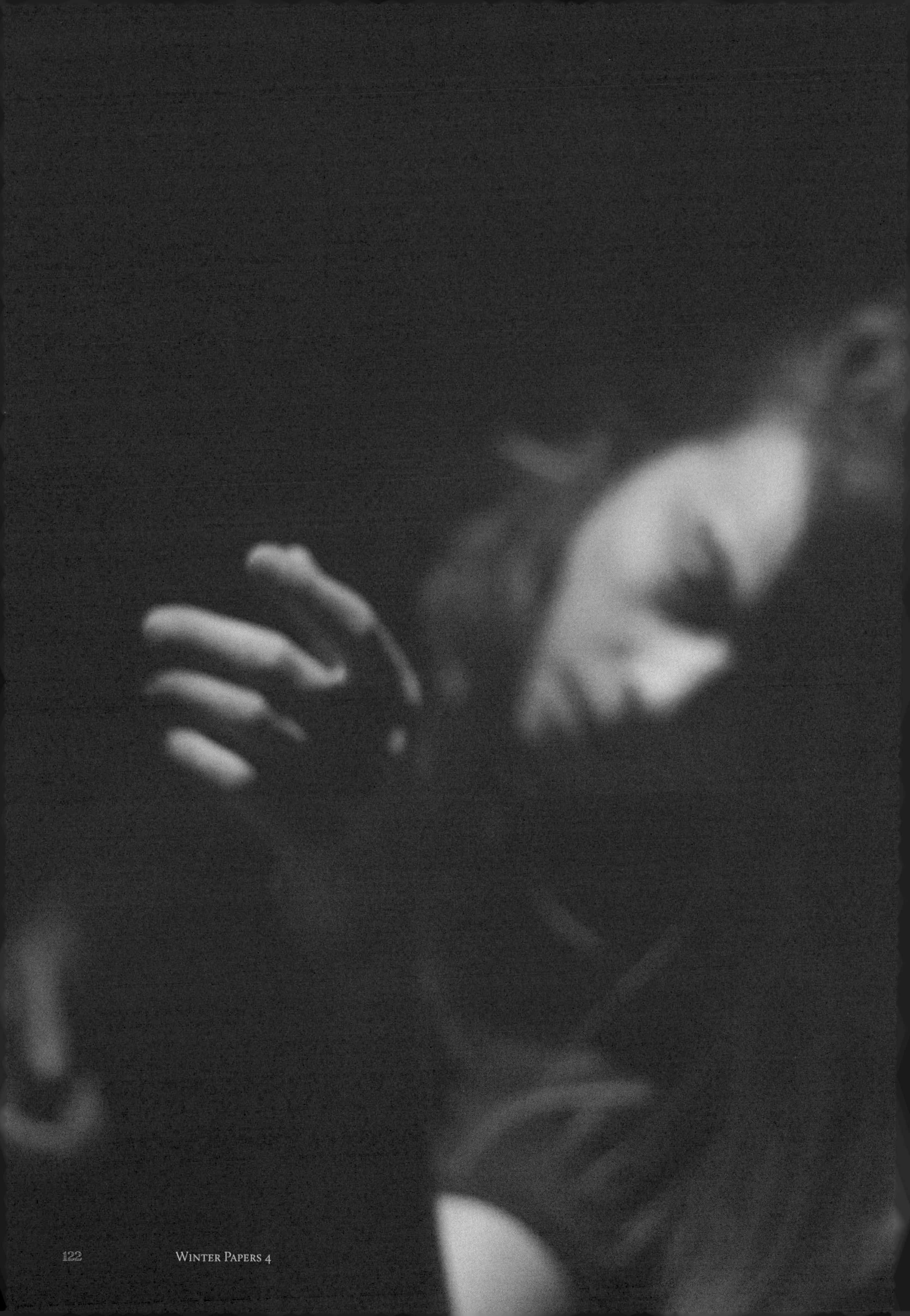

A DANCE TO MAKE A DREAM

An interview with MARIA NILSSON WALLER by Róise Goan

Maria Nilsson Waller is a dancer and choreographer from north west Sweden who has been living between Ireland and her native country since 2009. Her practice encompasses works for theatres, found sites and occasionally film, and she regularly collaborates with artists from other disciplines. She is currently preparing a new work, Flora and Fauna, which will premiere in 2019. In her work, she explores landscapes both physical and emotional, and the wisdom of the natural world as it manifests in the body. We met at my house in the centre of Dublin, on the hottest day of the summer so far, at the end of June.

RÓISE GOAN: *Maria, I wanted to ask you about something I think about a lot and I think you do, too – what has where you come from got to do with your work?*
MARIA NILSSON WALLER: I think it has a lot to do with it and I think it's kind of coming up again and again for me as an artist. Where I'm from in the north west of Sweden is quite remote, and dance-wise, it's been a bit of a black hole til now. There's a lot of traditional music and a bit of theatre ... but really, it's like a hunting, fishing, skiing kind of region. Mountains, lakes, forest-ranger Sammi people. Nature is everywhere – you walk through the one city there on your way to school and you see the seasons changing, you see the skies, the trees. I think that land or that region is really immersed in my bones, in my cells. I don't know if it's the light.

From the beginning I wanted to be a dancer. I had this, like, inexplicable passion for dance, so I left at 15 and I got into the Swedish Ballet school, and since then I've been mostly living out of a suitcase, but I've always had this connection to that place, and the memories of it. It's kind of how I see the world. I think in a lot of my pieces, whether more or less consciously, from the beginning, it's about recreating nature on stage or bringing landscape in. Also, I think about how, as a society, we relate to nature. There is a shifting understanding, especially in Sweden, where there's such a strong tradition of walking in the forest as a recreational thing, but there's a shift from where people used to feel like nature is this beautiful, positive thing to it becoming a scary thing that people are afraid of and now they feel unsafe in nature.

I've perceived in your work that sense of extremity. Nature in that environment seems quite extreme, where you have total darkness in the winter and white nights in the summer. I've maybe had the idea that you experience nature in a kind of heightened polarity? Does that make sense?
Maybe. My piece Last Land was really looking at Antarctica and the desert and those extreme polarities. But then the second part of that triptych, Founder, was about me arriving in Ireland and trying to make sense of this place and this life on an island surrounded by water. Where I'm from it's the mountains and forests – I wouldn't really be a sea-person. Ireland is also extreme. It's about sponging up the space around you, the space that you live in. You can't have a body or be a dancer without space. For me, it's also about looking at the unknown or the unexplored, so with Antarctica, I'd never actually been there. It was an excuse to absorb some of these places, trying to perceive them or put

myself there from an imaginary perspective, and having a sense that nature might be animated. Looking at mythology and where science kind of ends and faith and mythology begins. Pushing at that border at the end of the known. The bottom of the sea is still so mysterious. Antarctica is still very extreme. Man is small, nature is big, that kind of thing. Those are the frontiers where life is still an adventure.

Why is it important for an artist like you to communicate that to an audience? Does the urgency come from your lived experience? Is it about trying to articulate yourself and where you come from, or is it about the conversation with an audience or both?
I do think it's urgent and I think it's become very obviously urgent with climate change and the feeling that we are actually destroying, we're actually provoking the earth into a state of imbalance. I think it's urgent because we really need as a race to learn to listen to nature again. Maybe this happened in the past because you were somehow in a better relationship with nature, perhaps you were dependent on fishing in the river. You knew the rhythms of the tide and what you needed. We were co-existing and we have lost that. So it is urgent. With my next show, Flora and Fauna, it's not so much about the unclaimed territories – it's more about nature and your own body, actually. It's about human nature and the need to listen not only to the surrounding environment but also to start to tap into your own nature where you'll find that your body has all this intelligence that is part of the natural world and its evolution. It's also about learning not how to become animals, but to access your own animal instinct and your bodily intelligence. In dance and in the physical training that goes with it, you do kind of get to that stage when listening to your body becomes like learning to listen to nature again. I think I'm kind of educating myself through my work. While it started off with a fascination for the mysterious, it actually brings me closer to my body and to a much bigger quest.

You have made a lot of work for and with children. Sometimes in the arts there's an unhelpful binary created between artists who make work for an adult audience and those who make work for children and young people, and it can be difficult to navigate between those spaces. I always think that children are the scariest kind of truth tellers – you always know where you stand with an audience of children. Can you tell me what has motivated your work for them?
I don't really see a big difference between working for children and working for adults. If the work has quality, if it's something authentic, you'll receive it whether you are an adult or a child. I'm trying to tap into the adult sense of imagination as well as that of the child. With children as well as with adults, we know that we are performing, and they know that they have come to the theatre to see a 'performance'. We all know that it's a game, but it only works if you engage, if you can draw the audience in. Then you can start to make people see the thing as if it really was. In reality, we are using newspapers as props, but we all see Antarctica.

When you start to enter that imaginative space, it's an incredible feeling. The way you can collectively create worlds and engage and play. I feel like there's not enough scientific research here because what is imagination, actually? It's an incredible thing, this creative ability that we have. When we are children we interact like this naturally, so we can learn and explore together but somehow we become adults and we stop doing it. I'm trying to keep the child in me alive or trying to bring out the children in the audience. I think it's so important to give kids and everyone, really, access to creativity as a language, as a tool to express and to explore. I think you really learn something about what's going on inside yourself and if you know yourself well, you can connect with other people around you.

Dance being a physical practice is so important because our society is becoming more and more virtual and digital, we are more and more removed from our bodies. Dance has such an important role to play because it brings us back to the body and gives us access to nature, to our own instinct.

With kids, it's such a joy to come into a classroom and to give them tools to express themselves and be creative. They are allowed to run and slide all over the place. When you're dancing you work with your brain and your concentration and with order and chaos. You see these messy kids who are used to being told to sit down and try to do better at school and for once they get to shine, they get to use all their energy in a way that's not competitive but creative. And you see shy girls, the ones who wouldn't be great at sports, who wouldn't want to be physically active in competition – they get a space to use their bodies and to be big and brave through a creative process. I learnt a lot about the values of dance as an art form and as a practice by teaching kids.

It has actually been really important financially for me as well, it's helped to sustain myself as a practising artist. There's a Swedish programme for creativity in schools where basically any school can apply for special arts funding that they can only use to invite local artists in to work with children. So it's a way of paying artists to do something within education. By having the artist in residence you get to share and explore and experience rather than just buying a show for example. We have probably had two thousand kids in our workshops over the last few years and in a place where dance has been sort of non-existent that feels like real groundwork in terms of educating and giving people access to dance. When they grow up, they actually know what contemporary dance is. They will have created choreography, they have a sense of what that is not only because they have seen it but because they have tasted it.

I read about a project you made called See The Man with members of a football team. What led you towards that collaboration and what was the experience like?
They started this project where they engaged with artists to try and make the players braver and better human beings. Basically the philosophy was if we become better human beings, we will become better players on the football pitch. So they started having this art project every year.

Wow – are they a professional team?
They are a professional football team. That region had never had a professional football team so when they started off, they were back in the 4th division. So not a great team, to be honest. Then this guy came in – the captain of the team – with this idea where he was, like, 'I'm going to make a team here and we're going to become the best team in the world, basically, and we're going to do art and that's what's going to help us.' It was all the vision of this one incredible man. After three other projects they really wanted to push themselves so they asked me to do a dance project with them. They really wanted me to push them outside their comfort zone, because that's where you become brave. So the premise was do whatever you want, but it is going to have to be challenging for the players.

To be honest, in the beginning, I wasn't sure if I was going to take the gig but

I'm really glad that I did because it was an incredible experience to work with a group of 40 men, the whole team, professional football players but also the coaches, the chefs, the administration, physiotherapists, everyone who worked for the team took part. I worked with them in the same way as I work with children or professional dancers, really – no difference.

I was trying to use the project as a way to introduce the world of dance to them, so they could access that language, have a sense of it, taste it. There was a whole process of not seeing them as players who are bought and sold but trying to bring up their human qualities and their human values as well as their athleticism. I also worked with José Miguel Jiménez on a video aspect of it, with interviews that would portray their humanity, their feelings, their faces, as well as their physical skill.

We created this 45-minute version of Swan Lake with them and it was incredible. And they were so respectful, you know? I was in a room with 40 men and there was no disrespect. We had a lot of fun and there was a lot of laughter, but they were really an incredible group. The captain would talk about how football careers were short, but that their time with the team was not just about becoming good players, but becoming good men. And through this process, they have climbed every year from the 4th division right up into the Swedish Premier League. And that was all happening while we were working with them and then the year after, it was surreal, seeing them entering the Europa League. They played Arsenal! Arsenal came to my hometown! It was incredible to see how a football team can really create a sense of community, a sense of assembly in the town where people in the area have an excuse to join together, to love something together.

To join those two worlds a little bit – the art world and the sports world – to me that's what should happen. I think that arts and sports are replacing the space that church would have had in a community. The traditional weekly get-together where you sit next to a stranger or your neighbour that you don't necessarily know well and you get fed with some kind of message that you can ponder, you know? And it's about life and its meaning and not about working and earning money. It's about the bigger questions. And I think that space is still needed because we need to figure out how to be here, how to make this society work, how to tackle our challenges in a global sense but also in a very local sense. We need those spaces to gather and to think and to hear different voices.

That's also something that I'm taking with me to the art world from that project – it's about bringing people together, building a good community. You create whatever reality you want to try to make a good working space. It's super important, I think. The show is just a show but the process and the people that you work with, and how you work with them, and how you lead and how you look at money, how you treat people, what kind of values you bring with you, how you respect people's time – that's the art I want to master. Now, more and more, it's about making a better dream, in the way that we work as well as in the work that we make. And because it's only art, because it's only a game, we can follow whatever rules we want and create bigger dreams, better dreams, different dreams.

THE ATTENTION OF OTHERS

Jill Crawford

The production company had rented a maid's room for Suze near the Jardin du Luxembourg in the 6th arrondissement. Yesterday she'd had to simulate the delivery of identical twins and she'd pushed so hard that the muscles in her stomach and abdomen still throbbed and twanged. Tomorrow she had a sex scene with a slave. It was a soft-core medieval soap opera, but the costumes and settings were so ornate and sumptuous that they'd smuggled it onto the BBC. It was set in courtly France. The script was terrible, and she'd tried to refuse it, but her agent had said it was essential to dabble in the mainstream and she didn't have to go full-nude, as in her first series – Suze had been distressed when someone had uploaded that footage to YouPorn.

There were perks to a higher profile. Since the previous series aired, she'd been invited to sit beside a dead rock star's daughter on the Chanel front row at Paris Fashion Week and an elegant rapper had chaperoned her to a film premiere. People inundated her with clothes, for which she'd never much cared, but she liked the parties: so many beautiful people who could help, so many famous and half-famous people.

She stripped and stepped under the shower. Fine javelins of water scorched her skin. Hopping out of range, she banged her funny bone against the smoking glass door. It shuddered in response. She adjusted the temperature to tepid and washed her flesh and hair before stepping out and into flip-flops.

Techno, playing queerly softly, wafted into the studio from outside as she passed through the room. Listening, she wrung her long black hair into a hand towel and wrapped it up. She nudged the apartment door closed with the back of her heel. The building felt empty. Ivan with whom she shared the corridor went out to work all day. She broke off a banana and perched, naked and damp, with the cold fruit in her lap, on the edge of the futon, scrolling through music on her phone. She and the man she had been seeing had split a slat of the base of the futon while fucking. The frame now wheezed when you sat on it and there was a slack hollow in one part of the seat. Alex was also somewhat famous, which made things more balanced, but that wasn't why she was seeing him. He was an intriguing person, regardless of who his mother was.

Benjamin Clementine – just right. She hiked up the sound and placed the phone next to her on the cushion. The song gushed out of her small cubed speaker and lapped against the walls. Her fingernails were bare – polish wasn't allowed for a period film – but she'd paint them for tonight, not just for him, but for her, because it always undid him, and she enjoyed that. A bright tomato shade called Fired Up. In bed, Alex liked to elevate her at the end of his hands and feet as if he were her pedestal. Then, she was suspended above him in the air, nude, wavering. Her limbs would tense, and he would feel to her like a foreign element within which she moved, some viscous realm, distorting gravity and pulling her askew. He worked with blockchains. He travelled all around the world because of blockchains. And he had helped occupy Wall Street. It was gripping, he assured her. She consumed the banana and tossed the skin. Wait, what on earth? A cat slunk out of the shower compartment and minced toward her, tail erect; a ginger cat with a broad, pleased face. It looked exaggerated, cartoonish – as if it were a fabrication.

'Hey,' she said. It blinked. 'Who are you?' Actually, this was a French cat. 'Que veux-tu?' It sealed its eyes. Slender elastic lashes pinged from the pale rims of the closed slits. From within its depths the cat's body trilled. 'Salut,' Suze murmured, raising her hand slowly, fingers spread. She barely touched, more lingered above, the slanting amber fur on the spine. The tips of the shafts prickled against her palm. When she set her hand flat upon the cat's back it sprang off the futon and vaulted onto the kitchen table. 'Hey! Get down from there.' But the cat remained still, apart from the ringed and flicking end of its flamey tail.

Feeling suddenly vulnerable, she dragged the hair towel off her head and pulled it across her breasts, clamping it under her armpits. Where had it come from? She wanted it out. She reopened the door of her chambre de bonne and approached the cat from the far side, from the direction of the shower room. Its nose twitched. It sissed: malice. She clapped, loud. 'Yip! Skite!' She clapped louder. 'Vas-y!' She grunted, barked. The cat did not flinch. She stamped a foot on the ground, making a shallow whack. The cat sat firm on the table. She removed her flip-flop and batted the table's edge – a fine bloom of dust. The cat let out a narrow strangulated screak, and the ears flattened. 'Sors. Get out, beast!' The cat stayed put. 'Fuck you, cat,' she murmured. Suze lifted her fist to thump it, but her arm caught, suspended. It would not. She daren't. She stood, hand in the air, at a loss, surprised at herself, as Benjamin Clementine moaned. His voice raved and cooed and seesawed, melodious and wild and bizarre – was he laughing at everyone or merely himself?

The music staggered and bluntly stopped, the cat evaporated out along the corridor, and Suze shut her door. Muted techno could be heard again. Absurd thing – how had she missed it? It must have entered through the window. It hadn't morphed through the wall or swum up the throat of the toilet.

She put on underwear and a bubble-gum pink and apricot bralette with two minute inscrutable holes over one breast, like punctures left by a snake bite – moths? She split her legs across the floor on a towel to stretch her hamstrings. The script lay between them: lines. She was playing a powerful and cryptic monarch with elaborate hair and a small girth, a woman of considerable beauty and very few words, sprinkled between the voluminous chat of others. Tricky to learn. To anticipate each cue, she had to memorise her own lines, plus those of all the others in the scene. She had to know the scene so thoroughly that she could intuit the thoughts that gave rise to the words that sprang from her tongue without pause in scant gaps between the speech of men. Rhythm was key. Her character was exhausting: the bandying back and forth; the strobing internal heat she had to evoke; her stark need that had to roll out from within; the constant angling of a woman who understood her precarity; the preservation of a face that was beautiful, still, unintelligible, 'like Sophie Marceau in Braveheart', the director had said: exhausting.

On top of that, there were all the interviews in which she must play herself: endless performances in which she must be delightful, and plausible, and muse-like. She wanted to go home. She wanted to curl up in a cave. She wanted to hole up in her family's lost house in Saint Malo, to watch the bloat and frilling of the ocean. Makeup. Dresses. Dresses on the brain. She was sick of dresses. She wanted to wear nothing but denim cut-offs for the rest of her life. She wanted to move unweighted and bare and oblivious like a young child, happy in mere skin.

There was a rap on the door. What the fuck? 'Oui? J'arrive.' She pulled a T-shirt over her head. No one had ever knocked on the door of this room. She hardly knew anybody in the building and Alex only ever accompanied her home after whatever they'd been doing, then left early in the morning, claiming he found it claustrophobic. She opened the door to a young woman with bulging cheekbones edging a frenzied, glassy, reckless expression.

'Ça va?' Suze asked.

'You see the cat?' The young woman spoke in poor English with a strong accent, flat and curt.

'Your cat?'

'Not my cat,' the young woman said. Her eyes, a leaden-blue, were dilated, panicked.

'Was it orange?'

'Yes, yes!' the young woman gasped. Her jaw looked too big for the rest of her. She was wiry, underfed.

'I think it came in through my window,' Suze replied.

The young woman's face eased. 'Hah, tank you, tank you.' Feathering lines fanned from the corners of her eyes. A deep vertical crevasse stretched between her brows. Her lips were bracketed by two intense lines.

'But it's gone now,' Suze said. 'I let it out.'

'What? No! Why you do that?'

'I didn't know. Is it your cat?'

'Non, non, non.' She tugged at her brittle-looking hair.

'Ivan's cat?'

'Yes. Ivan. It went through the window.'

'I didn't know. I didn't know he had a cat.'

'What am I tell him? What I do?' A clump of the young woman's fawn-coloured hair came away from her scalp. She clasped it in her hand, staring.

'Uh, you say it got out,' Suze said. 'That's not your fault. Cats always try to escape. It'll come back, I'm sure.'

Then there was a flicker of recognition. Perhaps the girl had seen Suze in something, maybe the Gap ad campaign. Had Suze seen the girl before?

'He'll understand. It'll come back,' Suze said. 'Did he tell you to keep the window closed?'

The snag in the bony face suggested she had indeed been instructed to keep the window shut and had failed to do so. 'No, you lost it. It was *you*,' she choked. 'You let it go.' The words spluttered out.

'Now wait. I had no idea. It wasn't my ... I know you're upset, but.'

Her lips curled back: '*You* are the blame. I tell, I tell him.' She suddenly poked a finger into the soft part under Suze's sternum.

Suze batted her hand away, and it smacked against the door.

'Aie!' the girl wailed.

'Stop, just stop it,' Suze panted. 'This. This is too ... You've. Go away. It's too much, OK. I don't even know. Who are you?'

Suze narrowed the parting of the door to push the girl into the corridor. The girl pushed back. As they bent toward each other, pressing in opposite directions, the girl spat. The spit shot into Suze's face, scalding her upper lip where it landed. This girl could do anything. Suze bit down and shoved until the door clicked shut. With the back of her hand, she rubbed the hot saliva from her mouth then wiped the hand on her T-shirt and washed her hands at the sink with neon lemon gloop. She sensed the girl still standing at the other side of the door. She waited.

At last, the two needles of light beneath the door merged and broadened into one. The young woman had withdrawn. Suze's scalp had seemed to lift slightly away from her skull as if it were being prised up to create a small gap which let in a cold draught before being replaced. She dressed hurriedly, quite shaken. She thought she might varnish her toenails at least, but her hand was unsteady, and she'd muck it up. The paint would pool around the cuticles and speck the skin around her toes and splatter the script, upon which she'd place her feet to spare the floor tiles. Fuck it. She tugged on socks and baseball shoes. When she cracked open the door, the corridor was empty. Her heart throbbed beneath her breast.

She left, heading first to the Musée de Cluny which was dim and absorbing and otherworldly, and afterwards loitering in the medieval garden until the air prickled with rain, before, at last, studying her script in a brasserie on the Île St-Louis. She couldn't settle, and the lines spiralled without soaking in. A waiter whirled to answer a customer's call and Suze spilt her glass of apple juice. It doused the lap of her jeans.

After her four o'clock appointment in Saint Paul with Cecile, the costume designer, who leant her a denim skirt, she met Alex for an early dinner near his place in Belleville. She ate enormous amounts of bread; he looked disapproving but watched her do it. She did not mention the cat or the strange girl. As she'd hoped, they slept at his apartment. In the fume, lift and dip of him, she almost forgot, but when she rose to the brink and flopped over, crashing, she broke into sobs, sparking and trembling.

'Eh, eh,' he said, clasping her cheek, touching each rib as though to set it back in place, rocking her, rocking her, rocking her. He held her tightly without asking the cause of the eruption. He wasn't keen to get involved. His divorce had spent him, and there was still his son Rudy to fight over.

Early next morning, her driver Tarik picked her up and took her to the studio. The new makeup artist, an Israeli with dreads, made her hold frozen spoons against her eyes to reduce the puffiness.

After filming, late the following evening, she returned to her chambre de bonne. Several fierce handwritten notes, presumably from the girl, had been fed under the door:

'SALOPE', 'TUEUSE', 'JE TE VOIS, CHIENNE.'

The room felt unbearably cold. In her panic, Suze had forgotten to shut her window. A wedge of light spilt across the cavernous shadow that filled the central courtyard. Someone was watching a movie in the blue-dark of the opposite apartment. She did not deserve this. She had nothing to do with what had happened to the cat. How was she supposed to know? She'd have to move. Yes, she'd go. The production company would have to find her somewhere else. She couldn't call Alex because they only saw each other twice a week and never on adjacent days. Maybe Cecile would let her spend the night. On reflection, she almost doubted herself. The cat seemed unreal, made-up, almost like a cartoon animal. So too the hostile girl with premature cracks in her face. Where had she seen her? She reminded Suze of the homeless one who begged by the bakery on the Rue Vavin, near where her friend, Aurelie, lived. Aurelie was in L.A.

Seated in the rattan chair in the corner by the window, she watched another note slip through, face down, secretive. She listened for breathing on the other side of the door. When she closed her eyelids, a fuzz and a burr rose between her ears. Some insect zipped about, smouldering. Outside, a larger thing flapped past and, below, the hose was trickling. The superintendent hadn't closed the tap after watering his vines in the courtyard. In their cages, his little flamboyant birds chittered and piped. She thought she could hear the short breaths of the girl. But after a while, she bent to the floor, stretched, and drew the note to her.

A drawing of a stick body whose circular face contained two arced lines for eyes, each a skinny crescent. On the head were six strands of long, straight, black hair. There were two little balls for breasts with dots for nipples. The legs of the stick figure flared wide, horizontal, as if she were doing the splits. The end of a tail peeked out from behind the stick back, and a pair of triangular ears sprouted up from the head. The eyes knifed her: two slashes; slitty. It was intended to remind her. Sickening. She thought of what her mother had told her, the little she'd said about coming first to Germany from Guiyang, and then to France, and then to England; how those curving eyes had visited her again and again wherever she played. Children had recited rhymes and jokes, stretching down the edges of their own eyes, stretching them across their temples towards their hairlines, and it hurt, it hurt. Though her mother didn't say so, Suze understood. She had it once too from a flat mate at university. They'd argued about him using the washing machine after midnight. He'd done it and laughed, said he was kidding. Her dignity, then. She couldn't. She'd slapped his face. 'Calm down,' he'd said. 'You're so touchy. It's what you look like. Get over it!' And now this note to single her out, to tell her how she seemed to others.

She'd appeared on the cover of the Sunday Times magazine. She'd posed on the carpet beside bona fide stars. They'd described her as a 'starlet' – a small female star. They said she was 'modern'. She'd thought she moved apart from those who'd spit into her mouth. But, the lost cat was Suze's fault. Now, she was to blame for all that was wrong in that girl's life. I know what this is, Suze thought. From the courtyard, someone roared up the dark corridor that rose from the ground between the apartments to the sky. Suze pounced on the window and sealed it. The girl could have climbed right in, as the cat must have done. The shutter slurred on its descent. She was left quiet in the cubed room in lamplight. A moth flapped about the shade. A big moth, the biggest she had seen, with a body that was long and thick, with scintillating, scaled wings. She switched off the lamp. Its wings whirred in the gloom. She should let it out. She ought not to trap it in here all night. It might need to drink or eat. It might run out of air and die before morning. If she swatted it with her hand, it would drop to the ground like a slipper, soft and heavy and muffled. She sensed its wings flicker across the inner part of her upper arm.

When she first went to bed with Alex and before he'd touched her there, he'd whispered – 'Is it true?' He had wanted to know if what he'd heard of that part, of that part of someone like her, if that part was so narrow and good. She had giggled and said – 'Are you crazy? Don't be stupid.' And then she'd placed him inside her, and he'd said she felt only as different as any woman did. He had forgotten about that. And she had continued as if he hadn't wondered, hadn't asked right out.

The moth was beautiful, its outline furred. It beat frantically in the black with her; her body lifted and dove. Another note hissed under the door.

All night the notes came. She sat at the base of the shower with her eiderdown about her, waiting for the creak and the hiss of the next note slipping through. It wouldn't have mattered if they were blanks delivered across the threshold, in. The vigilance it took. The readiness she needed to receive each one. She had to steel herself in case one might blow her open, blow through her. You know this, she whispered. The monstrous bloom in the gut, the twist of apprehension, shame. She had wanted to be picked out. She chose to be known. She had surrendered to the art, to the craft, and, at last, to the business of trading body and emotion, giving herself to an audience, owned by them.

With the shutter down, the light didn't enter when morning came. She sat in the dark in the shower, waiting for the cat, knowing the cat would appear again. She must keep her senses peeled. The cat will visit when she least expects, the moment she forgets. The cat may be conjured out of walls, out of toilets, out of beds, out of nothing to do with the cat. She called Alex; he didn't answer. She called Alex; he didn't answer. She called Alex; he didn't answer. She called Alex; he texted 'What's up?'

fin

OCTOPOLIS

Photographs: Yvette Monahan
Text: Rosie O'Reilly

Octopolis[1] was born from conversations between the artists Rosie O'Reilly and Yvette Monahan on octopuses and consciousness.

We are mesh-mates with the sea. Life was born in the chemistry of the ocean and we still carry it inside us. When we ground ourselves in this connection – swim in the woven fabric of our evolution – the separation slips away and we become fully aware of the ancestry we share with the ocean and its inhabitants. The boundary between sea and land slowly disappears and we find ourselves in a mesh of kinship and species. We find ourselves in the gaze of the octopus.

The first octopus I ever knew by name was the infamous Inky; he escaped from his enclosure in a national aquarium in New Zealand by breaking out of his tank, slithering down a 50-metre drainpipe and disappearing into the sea. The aquarium staff were not surprised by his escape and are still hopeful he will come home. He is, they say, 'that type of octopus … all personality.' This story and many more have of late prompted a focus on octopuses in science, philosophy, literature and beyond. In his 2016 book, Other Minds: The Octopus, the Sea, and the Deep Origins of Consciousness, Peter Godfrey-Smith journeys through the evolutionary pathway of cephalopods in search of what these animals can teach us about other minds and the origin of consciousness. To examine this evolutionary story is to ask big and timely questions of our place in the world. Consciousness – the possession of an 'inner' model of the 'outer' world, or the sense of having subjective perspective on the world – is, in his view, just a highly evolved form of what he calls 'subjective experience' and is possible outside of the human perspective.

That octopuses have an experience of what it means to be an octopus has become the focus of much attention in lab studies over the last decade but for Godfrey-Smith his observations uniquely began in the wild – in Octopolis. This is an underwater site on the east coast of Australia, so named because of its likeness to an octopus city, a place where the usually solitary creatures gather in great numbers to feed. Octopolis gives an unusual insight into the social interaction of these animals. Struck first by their interest in us (in one tale, he recalls an octopus leading a fellow diver around by his arm to show him its den), Godfrey-Smith begins both a scientific and philosophical journey into the intimate sensory life of the creatures. Cephlapods, he tells us, represent a different evolution in the nervous system, their nervous systems are 'more distributed, less centralized, than ours … much of a cephlapod's nervous system is not found within the brain at all, but spread all over the body.'[2] What does that mean for an eight-armed animal? In conversation with Louise Allcock of NUI Galway she explains that 'its central brain only contains one-third of

1   Octopolis is the name given by philosopher Peter Godfrey-Smith to a research site he discovered off the east coast of Australia and is detailed in his great book Other Minds: The Octopus, the Sea, and the Deep Origins of Consciousness, 2016. William Collins. London
2   Godfrey-Smith, Peter. Other Minds: The Octopus, the Sea, and the Deep Origins of Consciousness, 2016. William Collins. London. *P67*

the octopus's total nerves. The other two-thirds are in its arms and each arm has a 'mini brain' at its base. Hence an octopus arm can feel and react independently.'[3] The octopus, it seems, has a sensory experience of the world that sits outside the usual brain/body divide, its thinking limbs experiencing the world as they move through it.

The fact that they live outside the usual body/brain divide, have a phenomenological experience of the world that is radically different to human experience yet express intelligence associated with a three-year-old child is surely why these creatures occupy such a place in our mythologies and imagination and are the stuff of legend in lab studies. Renowned for their curiosity and craft, Godfrey-Smith's work documents octopuses refusing food they dislike and pushing it out through water valves in their tanks to get rid of it, as well as turning lights out with squirts of water.

So why is it that the story of this curious being is so misunderstood? The philosopher Timothy Morton gives us clues in his book Dark Ecology, where he begins to dismantle the very idea of 'nature' so that we can understand the social constructs that have put 'nature' as something over there, estranged from us. The idea of 'nature', he tells us, is a legacy of Romanticism, which appeared during the Industrial Revolution. This was a period when unintended consequences played out and externalised costs such as pollution and radiation took shape in the human psyche. At this point Romantic Irony appears and 'the narrator becomes the protagonist, unnervingly aware that the world they have constructed is fiction.' This period signals for him the beginning of a separation between the world and us. He references Tolkien's Lord of the Rings as an example of the persistence of the Romantic narrative and points to the fictional world of the Hobbits – organic and wholesome in their form – as designed to sit outside the 'otherworld' and never to interact with it. The narrative reverberates with the divided worlds of 'nature/the octopus' and 'us'. The romantic 'world outside' places nature as an entity to be guarded or an entity to be fought for, but never an entity that is similar to 'us'.[4]

So much of the framing of nature falls into this trap. We are confronted with images of 'nature' in wooden boxes, glass jars and tanks, and on online databases, preserved post-mortem or framed outside our world and even their own. This sort of aesthetic framing is Tolkienesque, where nature is to be observed from afar. For Morton the realisation of this framing is a sensing of a Dark Ecology and there is no return. It takes the form of a film noir with the

---

[3] Extract from conversation with Dr Louise Allcock, Lecturer in Zoology, Ryan Institute & School of Natural Sciences, NUI Galway.

Do octopods have subjective experience?

Neuroscientists have recognised that octopuses have neural circuits that deal with important components of consciousness such as decision-making. They display behavioural traits associated with consciousness including sleep and exploration of novel items. Some researchers even think octopuses have individual personalities, but not all agree. It is not proven, but it is certainly possible that octopuses do have subjective experience.

Do they taste with their skin?

Yes, they do. Octopuses have chemoreceptors in the skin and these are particularly concentrated around the sucker rims, so that when an octopus touches, it is also tasting. Early experiments using sweet, sour, and bitter tastes showed that octopuses have a sense of taste that is 100 times more sensitive than ours.

[4] Morton, Timothy. Dark Ecology, 2016. Columbia University Press

detective investigating an external situation only to realise they are implicated in the plot. It is here in this darkness that the narrator realises there is no 'other'. This for Morton is the important message for our time; *nature never existed*. It was never the other; it was always us. Morton tells us, 'Don't fight it. Find a way to tunnel down. Find a way to see how things sparkle all by themselves.'

Tunneling into the world of the octopus it is impossible not to feel things sparkle. Staring through the glass at a captive octopus (Leonard [5]) in Bray aquarium I get lost in a web of flesh, arms and suckers. It is impossible to know where things begin and where they end. They coil and recoil, evoking the great spiral motif so iconic because of its repetition across all life from star constellations to our DNA, and echoed again in the first expressive stone markings recorded by our kind. The non-human and human bound together, entwined as companions, twisted in an ever-moving spiral.

Tunneling down further I feel I am in his gaze and I wonder:
What does he make of the times we are now living in together?
What would it be like to see with your skin?

Asking these questions sends me into a speculative spin where this boneless, shape-shifting being teaches us to understand the world through many different lenses, axes and planes. Perhaps the Bronze Age Greeks knew this when they adorned their pots with the octopus's figure, its eight arms stretching around the earthen vessels as if to protect the valuable contents. The octopus seems to have boundless possibilities as a symbol of the thinking we need in these times. All-sensory, with a tentacular understanding of space and time, this is a creature whose boneless body seems to challenge borders with every movement, shape-shifting to escape entrapment, curious and inquisitive. This is a being with a sense of taste a hundred times greater than ours, when its arms and suckers reach for our skin it can taste our ancient chemical history. It is very possible they can taste the sea in us and they know we are kin.

As I leave the tank a visitor snaps with an iPhone …
   I point to the sign: 'No flash …
   (long pause) his eyes are sensitive.'

[5] While photographing the octopus Yvette named him Leonard Cohen, thinking about the lyrics to his song Anthem: 'There is a crack, a crack in everything, that's how the light gets in'.

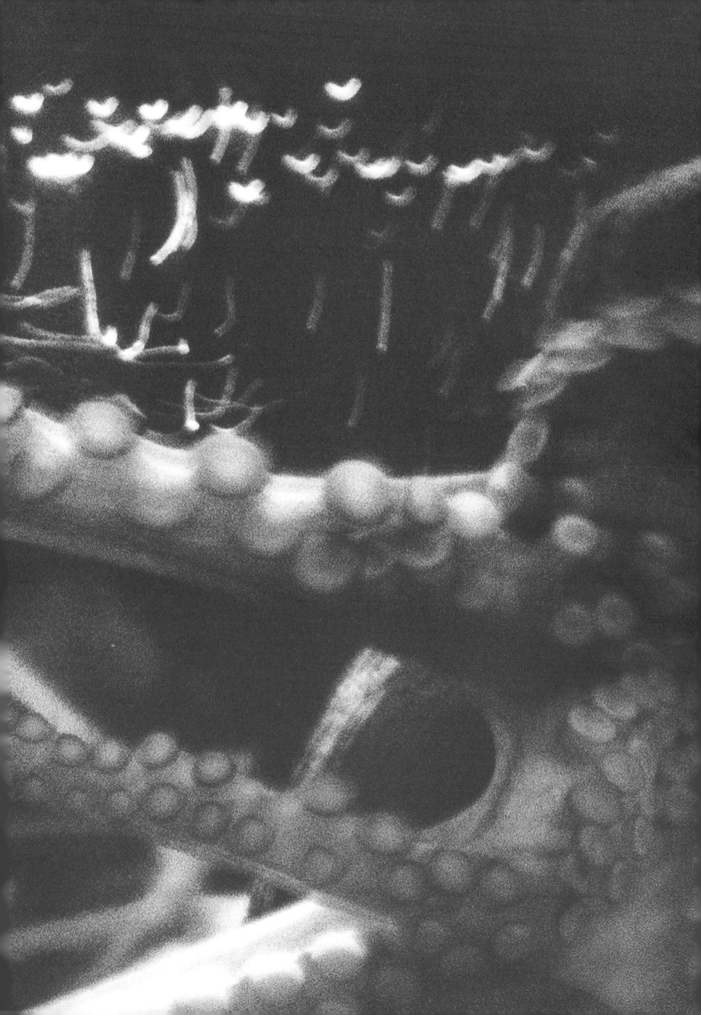

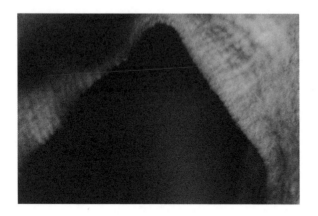 

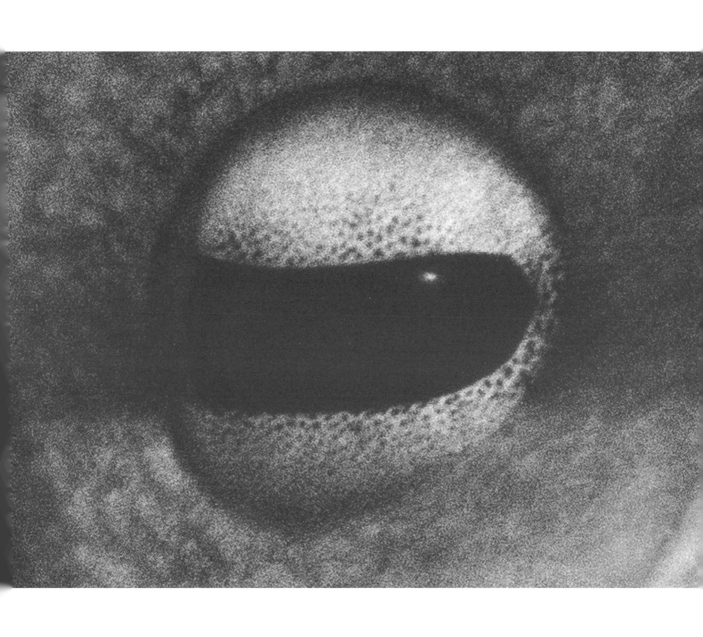

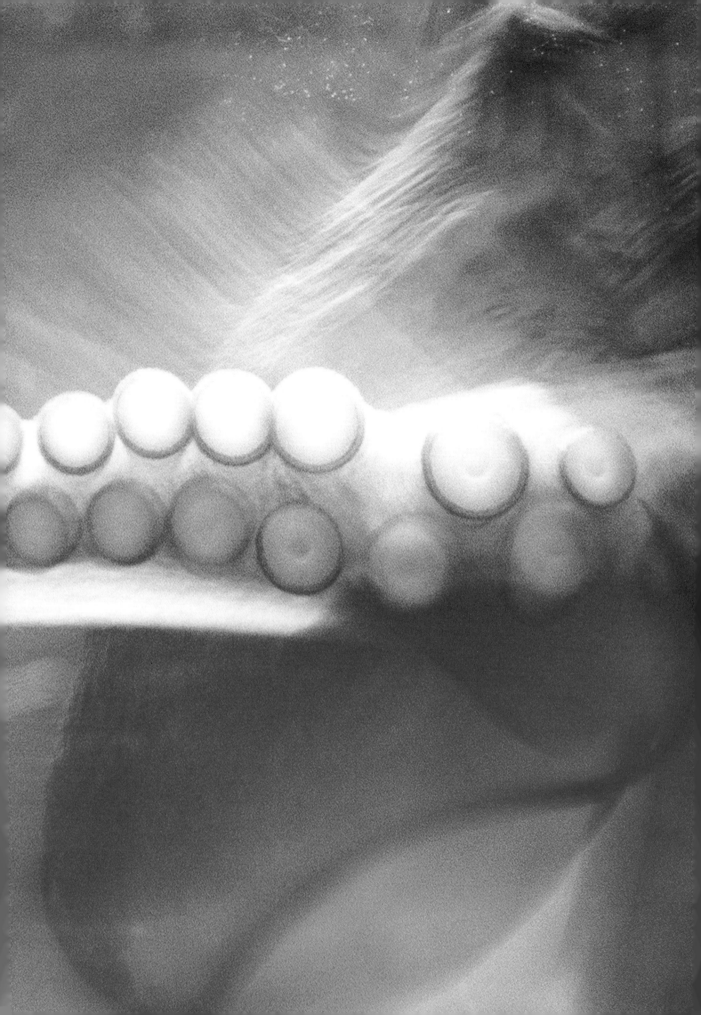

COMMON GROUND

An interview with DÓNAL LUNNY by Siobhán Kane

Dónal Lunny has been at the forefront of traditional music for 50 years, from his early work in Rakes of Kildare, to the legendary Planxty, the Bothy Band, Moving Hearts, Mozaik, Coolfin and, more recently, LAPD and Ushers Island. Renowned as one of the most pioneering musicians to emerge from Ireland, he is also a gifted composer, arranger, and producer, working in many different mediums, and with artists such as Kate Bush and Elvis Costello. He helped to popularise the bouzouki in Irish traditional music, and the instrument has now became a staple of the form, and his ability to fold in a modern sensibility to an older tradition has created some of the most innovative compositions and performances over the last decades. We talked over a couple of unusually balmy July days, in The Library Bar in Dublin, about his way of working, creating, and seeing the world.

SIOBHÁN KANE: *This year has been a special one for you, getting the BBC Folk Awards Lifetime Achievement Award.*
DÓNAL LUNNY: I was thrilled about it, but as well as that, I was contacted by Folk Alliance International, an American organisation, they decided that they hadn't given a lifetime achievement to anyone outside of the States, and I'm the first! So I am up there with Dylan, and Pete Seeger and all of these great people. They performed the presentation in Clonakilty, in De Barras, which was magical, and Lankum were singing that night – they were absolutely stunning.

It's interesting that in the same year the BBC gave you the lifetime achievement award, they also inducted Nick Drake into the Hall of Fame – there's a kind of fault line there.
There's a real link. And then seeing Lankum in De Barras as well – there are lots of connections that come through. I sometimes think I don't connect enough with younger people, although I've been enough lucky at the same time. I'll put it another way – I would like to connect more. And I do get opportunities.

You have been connecting, in less obvious ways, for some time. For example, your series last year, Tracing the Celtic Songlines, for RTÉ, kind of dovetailed into the 1992 BBC series you were part of, Bringing it all Back Home.
That's true. For that last series, the Isle of Man was a complete eye-opener. It's fascinating to visit these places and see what their take was on their Celtic identities. On the Isle of Man, there were people speaking real Irish, proper Irish ... it's actually understandable, but it died out, technically, when the last native speaker died. He was recorded by English-speaking scribes, they wrote it down phonetically, this was in the last 30, 40 years. So something like 'tá mé' would be written down 'taw may'. It looks indecipherable, until you speak it, and then you realise you're speaking proper Irish. And there were people playing tunes there which are identifiable jigs and reels. Historically, there wasn't much traffic between the Isle of Man and Ireland, but they also have great dancing there, they know how to live!

Photograph by Hugh O'Conor

In terms of your own background informing your music, how far did your parents' northern roots and identities, Enniskillen and Donegal, influence you?
I think it welled up as time went on. There was a subliminal presence of tradition in the house. My mother didn't learn English until she was 13 or 14, she came straight out of a Donegal Gaeltacht, and then my dad was learning Irish, and when he met my mother he *really* started to learn Irish *(laughs)*. His Irish was very serious, and it was part of their thing, their romance. My mother had a collection of old songs from around the region, Donegal and the Rosses, and my father loved the songs. We all heard them when we were small. Irish was our first language and we went to Donegal for two months of the year, from mid-June to mid-August. It was our other home.

And then I encountered traditional music properly in Prosperous, Kildare when I was in my late teens. We had the Clancy Brothers and so on, and you could sense there was a movement. Then an illustrious group of the time emerged, who were in fact one of Ireland's first boy bands *(laughs)* namely The Emmet Spiceland, who made singles of lots of traditional songs.

The Emmet Spiceland was an amalgamation of two groups, wasn't it?
We were Emmet Folk first, consisting of Brian Bolger, Mick Moloney and myself. Mick is a proper ethnomusicologist who now teaches at NYU, and we meet very occasionally, he's brilliant. Around the same time as Emmet Folk, there was a duo called Spiceland, with two brothers, Brian and Mick Byrne, so a merger took place *(laughs)*. Emmet Folk disintegrated, and Brian and myself joined up with the brothers and we became The Emmet Spiceland, then Brian dropped out, so we made a trio.

We won a national folk ballad competition – one of the deciding factors was that we were very smartly dressed *(laughs)*. We were fops! Dandies!

You have always been so open to playing with other musicians but it seems as if meeting Andy Irvine was an explosive, seminal experience?
The connection with Andy was quite profound musically. He had done a lot of travelling in eastern Europe and brought cassettes back from there, and the music absolutely transfixed me. I was so taken with these weird tunes, where you were on the wrong foot all the time. They were very challenging to play, but I learned them and then Andy himself started writing these songs that very often had beats missing, or bars added. They were quirky, idiosyncratic constructions which didn't always fit into a regular 4/4 or 6/8 thing, but had corners that you had to know and traverse. It was a challenge to learn these songs, in a great way, to see where Andy was going to go. There was an unspoken magic. The friendship with Andy has always been a touchstone. There was a long period of time when I hadn't seen him, for five or seven years, he was constantly travelling, it was around the time of Moving Hearts and our paths just didn't cross, and I missed him.

We had first played as a duo, and we ran a club in Slattery's on Capel Street called 'the Mugs Gig' – 'mug' being an idiot. That was a brilliant year *(laughs)*.

Soon after that, Christy Moore came back from the UK where he had been for five years. In the year before he'd left, we had shared a grotty bedsit on Pearse Street, when I was still at the art college. It was a terrible place, with a wash basin full of dirty cups, and Christy high-tailed it to England! When he came back, Andy and I got recruited for his record Prosperous. And all of us knew Liam O'Flynn from the actual Prosperous, where Liam grew up and lived, and in the aftermath of that album, four or six months later, Christy came to us and said 'hey guys' and we got together to create Planxty.

It must be deeply strange to think of Liam now gone [Liam O'Flynn passed away earlier this year]. How brilliant it was that you got to reform Planxty in 2004.
It's very sad, but it was wonderful that we managed to get back together, and I loved the fact that we had time to make it good, to bring it back fairly close to where it was the previous time.

Christy really recognised the potential of Planxty. I don't think any of us realised where it would go. We were taking our own tradition, and doing something else with it.

Was that a very conscious thing, to not essentially modernise a traditional form, but to bring in a modern sensibility?
That's right. I always felt that I've been influenced by having been in the art college for five years, doing design, and being in the presence of artists – the emphasis, or the aspiration, was always to be original.

That was the thing, you don't grab someone else's idea, you find your own. I believed that and it filtered into the music. It's hard to describe, but there are parallels in everyday life, for example, with fashion, you might use the same cloth to make clothes, but it's the way you design it, and you might use the same words to write poetry, but you make it your own.

With the music, outside of the fact that there was a deep instinct, I wasn't aware that we were doing anything hugely pioneering. We were doing our own thing and loving it, and I loved where we were at, and having the opportunity to do this with a traditional background. But 90 per cent of what I was listening to was contemporary music, jazz, and rock music.

Which kind of feeds into the modern sensibility – what kind of things were you listening to?
My all-time favourite band is Steely Dan, and then it was people like Van Morrison, particularly his early stuff, and artists like Elton John, The Band, Bob Dylan, Joni Mitchell ... I shared the same soundtrack with a lot of people. I adored it, and I lived it. I also loved jazz for its sophistication. I didn't understand it, I loved its mystery – it's instinctual music. To my mind, it's of a different order, and the best people were so far ahead from where I was at, people like Miles Davis and Thelonious Monk. But there were great musicians here in Ireland who I think were, and are, giants by anybody's standards. I remember Louis Stewart playing the Mugs Gig and he was monumental, and at the time was listed among the world's top jazz guitarists.

I played some trad jazz in the art college – Daragh Ó'Lochlainn's jazzy jam band was brilliant fun altogether, I can't remember where the gigs were *(laughs)*. Maybe the Pembroke, places like that? It was fantastic. Daragh was so bubbly and enthusiastic, he is sadly long dead. He taught me typography in the art college, and I was learning rhythm guitar for jazz, and I just loved it all. Daragh was the son of Colm Ó'Lochlainn, who had compiled Irish Street Ballads, that was the bible for Christy Moore and myself and thousands of people around the country. Colm also owned the Three Candles Press, and designed the letterhead, and Daragh taught typography, so it was all in the family.

It's evident that there was a real counter-culture in Ireland in this period, very

different to the main narrative put forward at the time, which would have been a legacy of what Seán Ó'Faoláin called 'a dreary Eden'.
This is true. I have to confess that I saw that 'main narrative' as the norm, that was the plateau of the country, but then there were pockets, usually where there were students, that were independent, not necessarily anarchist, but bohemian. In the art college there were so many free spirits. The student strike for us in Dublin coincided with what happened at Kent State University. There was this eruption that was taking place in France and in the States.

It was at art college we realised we could actually stand up and resist, or object, to the status quo.

Would you say that what was happening in America, in particular, really influenced you at the time?
I think so, but there was also something bigger happening. In a funny way, it's a climate thing, in the way that tides of different politics sweep across the world.

We are experiencing one right now, where you have the Far Right rising, and it's really, really dangerous. It is hugely ironic that at the same time the Far Right is rising, as it did before the last two World Wars, you have a Department of Education in Ireland that is in the process of abolishing the teaching of history in schools. It's total folly – we need to remember what happened, to remind people what happened.

Do you think we are regressing?
We are going backwards. We are in times where 'greed is good' is what many people believe in. Absolutely. I have heard the mantra 'the market will fix it' so many times, and applied to so many situations, but it doesn't, it fixes it for those that already have, not those that haven't. Those people are left out, and when you hear it from the top of the country, it's scary.

Now the market has shifted to tech giants, who are diverting retail onto the internet and skimming money off the top. It's happening in the music industry – Spotify and YouTube are not paying artists, and billions are being diverted away. Protests are being made about these things, but there isn't even a ghost of a sign that the Irish government is looking at this seriously or doing anything about it.

Iceland is a utopia compared to Ireland. We have a real connection with Iceland. I went there for the first time 15 years ago. I love the mood and the climate in Iceland, it's just a wonderful place, and has so much going for it.

Do you think we have the potential to harness elements of that kind of utopia?
Of course we do. I think young people and kids need to be let know that they have the power to change things, and to get out and say it. A catalyst is needed to trigger people, to let people know they have the power to change politics.

And yet there are musicians out there, mining the Irish musical tradition and trying to shape it to reflect our times, like Lankum, and The Spook of the Thirteenth Lock. They are politically engaged, and I suppose themes of exile, heartbreak, and economic hardship sadly continue to be topical.
You can only hope that people will come along and express their beliefs and want to make change. I am only half-joking when I say that if Mary Lou McDonald promises to build houses I will vote for her.

We are in a very scary time. There are people who have no safety net, nowhere to go, and no immediate opportunity – the opportunities have to be made.

You've been instrumental in making the bouzouki a staple of Irish traditional music, part of the chain with Johnny Moynihan and Andy Irvine – you've really helped to popularize it.
It's been one of my proudest achievements. I designed a Greek bouzouki with a round back – it wasn't redesigning the wheel, but I recontextualised a flat-backed instrument for Irish music and people really leapt at it.

I think that's progress, but there are real purists in Irish music who don't want change, they feel it's all carved in stone already, it's always about looking back. I realised early on it's possible to go forward and to change, but also take the best of what was there before and add your bit to it.

Andy's work is a great example of that.
Absolutely. Some of his compositions seem like they are the old standards but clearly they share in the conversation that's going on. A lot of new stuff was coming out informed by older stuff, but with Andy, it was coming from his head, streaming out of his head *(laughs)*.

You've been prolific as a producer and arranger as well, and synonymous with the Mulligan label. How did that come about?
Mulligan started because of The Bothy Band. One of the employees of Gael Linn spotted the opportunity of starting a record label with the purpose of releasing a Bothy Band album. We thought it was a good idea, as no one then could tell us what to do, or take control. About 30 albums came out altogether, and I was across around the first 17 of them, producing for Mulligan. It was a great era for productivity and lots of lovely things went on, and then The Bothy Band ran into the sand, through lack of focus and management. People didn't know what we were – we were high-energy trad, they didn't know how to market us! We were doing something different without realising, but we ran out of energy after five years.

And then Moving Hearts started.
Yes, Christy had a large well of material, but a lot of it wouldn't transfer to the Planxty mould, it just wouldn't fit. So after we had made an album or two in that incarnation, I started going on about us getting a rhythm section, percussion and bass, something acoustic and ethnic but without bringing in the usual shite of a drum kit, which would confuse the issue, and blur it all back into some kind of hokey rock music. Anyway, I couldn't find the people or the way to do this. I tried recording it and failed really, and Andy, Liam and Christy, as Planxty, were saying well, we really don't know what you're talking about. They didn't connect with that aspect at all, and I don't blame them. But Christy came back after a while, and wanted to get these other songs in, like No Time for Love, Russian Roulette. He couldn't get them into Planxty, and Liam was profoundly apolitical, and fair enough, he felt there was no place for politics in his music, a lot of people are like that. I do think it should be interconnected – politics and music – but it all depends on how you do it.

When Moving Hearts kicked off, it instantly became a rock band, we had drums and bass, but those musicians had never played trad, it was kind of ironic. But then Declan Sinnott, a man I love, who played with Horslips for a while, a lot of his peers were on the west coast of America, like Robbie Robertson, playing that kind of cool rock. Well, Declan has all of that down, and brought it back to Ireland, so there was a kind of coming together of all of these things in Moving Hearts.

I wasn't on the outside, but I was running to keep up, even modifying some notion I had of how trad music could be transformed into a contemporary form. I think that's really important, otherwise the kids won't go there, it will be in a museum, and will have nothing to do with romance and sex, and it has to! Kids have to somehow connect with it – it has to be cool in some way.

You are always pushing limitations and expectations in music, whether through bringing in a less obvious instrument, or sensibility, or technology. Did being a producer fuel this?
I think so. I have seen where sounds go through fads and become the fabrics of a certain time. One thing I used to tune into and still do, really, is the quality of the snare in rock music, which has changed with the times. When it got to the '80s, there was a big metallic explosion that went on and on, and synth sounds were huge in the '80s, too but once fashion moves on, it becomes passé, and people move on.

I think that producing went out of fashion in the last few years, as people can make records in their bedrooms. Record labels stopped giving budgets for studio time, except for frontline artists. So producing took a back seat, but it's coming back again. I'm working with Daoirí Farrell at the moment, who is a phenomenal singer, and he plays the bouzouki, and as we worked through the material, I started waking up to some ideas to embellish the songs, and that's been coming along well. Daoirí really links back to the singing of Frank Harte.

Frank Harte was a seminal figure in Irish music, leaving such a legacy as a song collector and singer.
Frank and I had a great relationship that went way back. We did six albums together and he was avowedly non-professional – he didn't make money from what he did, it was non-commercial. So we were cutting one's cloth to fit the very modest budget, which was a very healthy discipline to learn. I would confine myself to one or two things that I would do with him. I've taken that experience into other work.

What other pivotal moments as a producer and musician have you experienced?
I have met loads of great people but Kate Bush pops into my head straight away. Adorable is the word I'd use, she is a really lovely person. She was just very alive and attuned to what was happening when we were working together.

I think it was Bill Whelan who made it happen. I remember she was on a certain track for a while, and I just loved the fact that she had a Fairlight synthesizer, which was absolutely Elon Musk level at the time (*laughs*), it was a thing that no one had, they cost a fortune, and you had to programme them very carefully. It wasn't an intuitive thing, you had to type things into the keyboard, spell them right, it was very exacting, but she got on top of it, and could use it. She could sample sounds into the keyboard, and this was absolutely unprecedented.

I had a Minimoog which was nicked on me! I got it from Eamonn Andrews' studio and it was the first Minimoog that ever came into Ireland – I played it with Shaun Davey, and a little in Moving Hearts.

Her Irishness was explored in your project Common Ground, in 1996, which was put forward as 'voices of modern Irish music', with people like Bono and Adam Clayton, Kate Bush, Elvis Costello, Tim and Neil Finn, among others.
Do you know, I don't even have it on tape now. And I don't have Coolfin either. The masters are in EMI – they could give me copies, I suppose. Gerald Seligman there had the vision for the project. He was the person who approached me about it in the first place. He commissioned me to do it, and encouraged it. He was ambitious enough about it that he suggested Bono and Kate Bush, and you know, it didn't take much to persuade them. It was simply calling them up, talking about it, getting through the nuts and bolts of the situation.

In recent years you had another configuration, with LAPD, and found yourself playing festivals – has that been an energising experience?
Without a doubt. It's been massive. We did an unforgettable gig in the Body and Soul crucible at the Electric Picnic a while back. It was fantastic, but it was like being thrown to the lions! In that kind of situation, it's like surfing, you have to keep your balance. Maybe it's not ideal, and if you listen back there'd be a lot wrong with it, but it's more about the moment, and being in the moment, which is what you often look for.

What do you think you are most proud of over the last number of decades?
I have to say that I felt that Coolfin was unfinished business. I had embarked on another batch of writing that had fed into that situation, I loved the band, it was so great, and it was different to any of the other bands around. We tried to get back together a few years back, but people like Ray Fean are in huge demand, it's practically impossible to get us all together. But I would maybe try again, although I would be very reluctant to do so without the original cast.

I also think Ushers Island has massive potential but again, it's one of the most difficult bands to assemble – the component individuals are so busy, like Mike McGoldrick, and John Doyle is even busier, because he can be, because he has an eidetic memory, so he's very much in demand, he's carrying around 15 repertoires inside his brain. What a player! If we could get back together, it would be lovely.

I also think the Atlantic Arc Orchestra has something, as it is such a unique collection of people. Pauline Scanlon singing, Jarlath Henderson … it is a vision of people from Celtic countries, a huge amount of people, like Ewen Vernal from Scotland, who is phenomenal, and plays with Capercaillie, I just love his stuff. John Blease as well, who is playing with Robert Plant at the moment. Great people, massive potential.

I am a bit of a nostalgist and I can't help but feel when I hear songs like O'Donoghue's, which immortalised Dublin in 1962, that things seemed much better then, in a way.
(*Laughs*) I was better then! There is a slight degree of sentimentality to what you're saying, but so much truth in it. I think it *was* better then, but I am reluctant to admit that to myself, as I know that one must make the most of now.

I remember Andy, 30 years ago, constantly saying 'ah, the good old days', and he was saying it back then! But Andy's sense of travelling kind of bends your sense of time. If you stand still for too long, it gets you down. I think one must keep moving, and keep being open to new things. Have you heard Kamasi Washington? I have only just discovered him, and he's just something else (*laughs*).

STARVING

Lisa Harding

'When you're starving for love the world is a dangerous place,' Maya said, eating a rice cake smothered in fish paté and smoked salmon, drizzle of lemon on top, cracked pepper. Susan nodded – she had heard it all before. The phone rang.

'Hmmm? Oh, I'd love that. You are a darling. Who? Kaufmann? How delicious. Eight o'clock at the Royal Albert? Yes. Fabulous. Yes. Bisoux,' Maya said, making kissing noises, clapping her hands with the insistence of a deranged woodpecker.

Susan watched the theatrical display with a mixture of indifference and indulgence. Maya continued, her mouth stuffed with popped rice: 'Opera – one of the delights of my life. I always wanted to be an opera singer. I had the talent and I wasted it. My dysfunction meant I spent a decade in the wilderness. We don't want that to happen to you.'

'I have no intention of being an opera singer, ever.'

'That's right, and right now you have no intention of being anything, ever.'

Susan stared out the floor-to-ceiling window at the Chelsea rooftops and saw only a grey mulch. Daylight in London was dreary in March. She shrugged at Maya and went back to staring out at the monochrome sky.

'What do you see out there?' Maya asked.

'Rain and rooftops.'

'Change your perspective on life and your perceptions change also. I see a magical fairy tale scene every time I look out the window,' Maya said, her Polish accent betraying her. Maya had held herself up to Susan often as a shining example of assimilation, and reinvention. Reinvention was a buzzword in here. 'Look at how the raindrops shimmy and dance. Look at that majestic gothic skyline. Have you any idea how privileged we are to live here?'

Susan thought about that: Chelsea, with its pavements blasted clean every morning, its designer boutiques, manes of glossy hair bouncing up and down its leafy boulevards, its frustrated pooches straining at their leashes. She was an outsider, just like her father with his upwardly mobile pretensions and loudly booming voice, trying to cover over the cracks of his past. Her mother – despite the Chelsea mansion and the maids and the cellar full of the best vintages – withered here. She was forever lamenting the loss of the sea and became a brittle blonde with over-dyed hair, a closet full of Louboutin shoes and bags, a habit of sipping delicately and sighing loudly, and bowel cancer. She was dead within five years of moving to manicured Chelsea from the wild open spaces of the west of Ireland.

Susan couldn't remember making the decision to come here – that was probably because Marcus, her father, had decided for her – just as she couldn't remember making the decision to sit in this black leatherette swivel chair, with tissues carefully arranged on the glass-topped coffee table beside it. Maya was always trying to make her cry; she couldn't remember the last time she cried.

'I liken the level of trauma you have experienced to a concentration camp survivor,' Maya said.

Susan thought how ridiculous, how could she possibly know how a concentration camp survivor feels. She wondered for a moment if perhaps Maya's family were survivors, maybe that's why Maya had decided to become a psychotherapist. She also wondered how on earth the insight was supposed to make her feel better.

'I had a dream I gave birth last night to a female baby Jesus, with your face,' Maya said. 'I interpret it to mean I am giving birth to a new way of being for you. A spiritual rebirth.'

Susan laughed so hard she felt her eyes watering. An excuse to reach for the tissues.

'Are you laughing or crying my dear, or both?'

'I don't know. This is ridiculous. Do you know what I dreamt last night? I dreamt I was standing on Chelsea bridge about to jump when I decided against it. Something about the way the light from the moon lit the river and made it kind of silky and beautiful. I stopped and I stared, and I felt fine, until you came behind me and started to push ... Now what could that mean, I wonder?'

'That you are on the brink of jumping into a new way of being, and you need a little nudge?'

'Brilliant,' Susan said as she got out of the spinning chair and stood tall and stretched. 'I think I'll say goodbye for now.'

'I don't recommend it. That dream was a premonition.'

'My thoughts exactly,' said Susan as she handed ninety pounds cash to Maya for the third time that week.

'Thank you, my dear. I only want what's best for you. I am here for you any time you need help. And remember – you are starving. Make sure you feed only from the finest source. Don't go to the hardware store for bread.'

'I'll bear that in mind,' Susan said, as she went to the door and pulled it politely behind her. At least her temper was under control. At least the crazy Pole had helped with that. Not with the other though. Not with that. Maya was right – she was hungry, and it was an appetite that could not be sated. At times she felt like she might be consumed by her own monstrous greed. She could feel the stirrings of the gnawing in her stomach and knew what had to be done. The rain was hard and driving, and she didn't have an umbrella. As she walked, the grey light was fading to black, and the streetlamps flickered a wan amber, warming up for the night ahead. There was something about night-time in London, it shimmied and sparkled under false spotlights, like an actress about to step on stage after a long day's sleep. Susan would have liked to block out all daylight hours.

She walked, dripping wet, into a shop so exclusive that price tags and security tags were deemed vulgar and where the shop assistants knew her by name. They offered her a warm fluffy towel and a hairdryer, fawning over her, smelling her father's money. She wouldn't be returning here after today. The rule was to never target the same place twice. Susan tried on five dresses, bought one, and stuffed the other in her Louis Vuitton shoulder bag. This gave her a momentary buzz, though nothing like it used to. An assistant thrust an umbrella at her as she was leaving: 'You look like you could do with one of these.'

She entered a plush brasserie, underground and ornately gilded, and saw her father scanning the room.

'How's my beautiful girl?' Marcus said.

Susan sat on the opposite side of a dark red velvet booth. She looked at her father who was looking for someone else. A tiny Asian woman with pert features appeared and smiled at Marcus. It was a simpering, supplicant smile and one that Susan knew well.

'Mandy, this is my beautiful daughter, Susan.'

The women nodded, and Mandy slid in beside Susan's father, rubbing against him like a cat.

'How's the shrink? Any good?' Marcus asked.

Typical, thought Susan, that he should expose her this way, and how typical that his latest woman was called Mandy. The last one was Shirley. He liked them small and submissive and preferably Asian.

'Great, Dad. You've hit the bullseye with this one. Really sorting me out.'

'She'd want to, the money I'm spending on her.'

'As you say, Dad, she's the best.'

'Only the best will do, darling,' he said as he clicked his fingers at a young waitress wearing a tiny skirt. 'A bottle of your best cuvée,' he said drawing his fat tongue over his thinning top lip. Susan noted that Mandy tensed. Poor cow.

'That's a lovely dress, baby,' Marcus said.

'I just bought it,' Susan said.

'Retail therapy,' he said, and he laughed hollowly. 'Mandy likes a spot of that too, don't you, Pussycat?'

Mandy curled herself into him and rested her tiny head on his wide chest with its greying tufty hair. Susan thought how ridiculous that he would dye the hair on top of his head and leave the rest. She looked at Mandy and wondered how old she was, and what exactly her father offered her – the same as herself probably: an apartment, and clothes, and jewellery – but only as long as she lasted. How ironic it was that she was the one in therapy and that he was paying. Paying was power, and Marcus wielded it well.

The three ate in silence mostly, punctuated by a practised giggle from Mandy. She was small enough to look up at him from under her heavily-mascaraed eyelashes, even sitting down. Marcus ordered three bottles, and Mandy had less than a glass.

'I don't think you should be drinking,' Marcus said to Susan, pouring her a fourth glass as he said it, winking at her.

'That's right, Daddy, I shouldn't.'

'What the hell,' he said as he cheered her, downing his glass in one gulp. 'Any men?' he asked.

'I shouldn't be doing that either.'

'Call that a life! A shag and a bottle of wine – the answer to all humanity's ills.'

As the drinking progressed, her father became louder and more demonstrative, cuddling her close to him, professing his daughter was his one and only true love. She had heard it all before and savoured the dominion she held over these other women. Theirs was a special bond and no new plaything was getting in the way. Susan looked over at Mandy's tight, upturned face and wondered what she hadn't done for the attentions of men like this – men like her father. She was pretty sure Mandy, and all the other women like her, couldn't enjoy it. Theirs was not an equal transaction, although her father liked to tell himself it was. How lucky she was that she didn't have to do anything for money. Anything she did was from choice, not necessity.

As they were leaving, a colleague of her father's approached. Marcus slapped him on the back and introduced her as his 'most prized possession.' He didn't introduce Mandy, and she hung back, knowing her place. The man asked if they'd like to join him for a drink, but Marcus said he had business to attend to – nudge, wink – but he was sure Susan would like to stay.

'Bye, Princess. Don't do anything I wouldn't do.'

'Bye, Daddy. I won't,' she said, and blew him a kiss. That didn't leave much out of bounds then. She rolled her shoulders back and smiled widely. Her teeth were recently whitened, on the insistence of Marcus, who couldn't stand stained teeth. And hers had been. Too much everything; blasted clean now.

The man was tall, and wore a beautiful slate-grey suit, and shiny cufflinks, and a wedding ring. She thought momentarily of Maya and the black swivel chair, and the incident that made her father finally take notice. She couldn't remember a thing about the night, but she could remember the look on her father's face the morning after, when the latest housekeeper had called him to the scene. He kicked the two men out – *the filthy cunting bastards* – and sent her away to clean up her act. Therapy was an extension of this cleaning up, alongside the visit to the dental hygienist, the well woman for the morning-after pill, and a once-over in the STD clinic. She wondered briefly how Marcus had made contact with Maya, apparently an 'expert' in her field – although what field, exactly? Phantasmagoria?

She woke the next morning in a plush suite somewhere in Knightsbridge. It was still dark outside and the man's heavy arm was cradling her to him, crushing her ribs. She managed to wriggle her body free without waking him and dressed in the dark. She couldn't find her panties; she'd leave him a memento.

At home, she showered, surveyed her bruises and cuts. She had asked for it like that, and although the man was reticent at first, he quickly warmed to her theme – they all did.

Her housekeeper was hoovering the bedroom when she emerged from the shower, and insisted she eat something. Susan agreed, just to shut her up, and when she wasn't looking she stuffed the omelette into a napkin, and later flushed it down the toilet. Marcus had hired this latest, Maria, a Phillipino with a big heart and a big arse, her father's words, not hers, to make sure she ate and didn't live like a pig. She could never see the point of cleaning: you did it, and then you have to do it again. It offered no thrill, although she did quite like to slip into cool clean cotton sheets. She dreamt that morning that there were fish swimming out of her vagina. One of the fish had a face like the man of the night before. She put him in an aquarium by the side of her bed and fed him bits of the omelette. He didn't know when to stop. He floated to the top, burst.

Susan lay in the dark, running her hands over her sore body. She watched the shaft of light that slipped through the rim at the bottom of the black-out blinds; it was like a laser beam, seeking out its target. She moved her body so no part of that interrogative daylight landed on her. Her mobile rang, and she looked at the number. Marcus; Daddy. She pressed the silent button, and let the phone vibrate on the bed sheets. She had no idea of the time. Life happened according to a series of whims, an internalised tick-tock of desire, and right now she felt nothing at all – no want, no need to do or be anything, other than lie here. A night like last night left her sated – for a while – and then the ravening appetite would build again. She thought of Maya and realised she would miss her if she didn't go back for their sessions. Maya would revel in the drama of her previous night's escapades, elevating the sordid to operatic. More than anything she would miss her histrionic empathy. Yes, she would call her later so they could discuss their dreams. She drifted back into a fitful and fish-laden sleep.

When she woke again, her throat was dry and she stirred herself enough to reach for the stale glass of water on her bedside table. She turned on the lamp and checked her phone. Three missed calls from Marcus, and two from an unknown caller. She listened to her messages and heard a contrite and sober voice playing the concerned-father role. How could he have left her alone with that sleaze, and was she okay, and if she didn't call he would be around any moment to check up on her. The other two were from the sleaze, asking was she okay, and how he hoped she wouldn't say anything to her father, and would she perhaps like to do it again sometime. The doorbell rang, and she shouted down to Maria to please answer it, and to tell whoever it was that she was out. Marcus's voice boomed from the doorway as she heard him greet Maria warmly, and asked her to fetch him a scotch-on-ice. He shouted up the stairs to her:

'Maya phoned me. Where the hell were you today? She's worried about you. As am I. Get your ass down here now.'

'Yes, Daddy.'

Susan made sure not to wear a scrap of makeup, and not to dry her hair. She came down with her bathrobe carefully arranged to show her father a bruise or two.

'Scotch?' he asked her. 'Jesus, what the hell happened to you? You look like shit.'

'Don't start, Dad. Not a great night.'

'That bastard …'

'You pretty much dangled me in front of him like bait. What did you expect him to do?'

'I thought you looked like you could do with a bit of company. That's all.'

'With a renowned sleaze.'

'Can't you just say no?'

'You know my history, Dad.'

'Did you learn nothing at all in that place?'

'I am my father's daughter,' she said, and perched herself on the arm of the sofa beside him. 'I am also a woman, Dad, and sometimes a man doesn't take no for an answer.'

'Christ, when are you going to learn to protect yourself?'

She shrugged and looked away, and circled a bruise just above her knee, with her right forefinger. Marcus finished his scotch in one gulp, and gestured to Maria to get him another. He stared at her, in a way that meant she knew she had his full attention.

'How's Shirley?' she asked

'Her name's Mandy,' he said.

'And how is she? Is she good?' She shifted her weight on the armrest so that her robe fell open.

Marcus stood abruptly and went to the bay window. He opened the curtains a crack and Susan saw that it was dark outside, and the street lamps were cranking into action.

'I have to go to a meeting. Promise me you'll see Maya later. I have paid in advance for three months intensive, five days a week,' Marcus said, turning to face her.

'You didn't answer me, Daddy. Is she good?' She stood, her robe flapping loosely at her sides, leg bent at the knee, leaning into her hip.

At that moment Maria walked in with a tray of sandwiches and tea.

'Put some clothes on. You look cold,' Marcus said, clearing his throat.

'Yes, you look cold,' chimed Maria.

'I am not cold in the least, Daddy,' Susan said, trying to draw his eyes back to hers.

'Make sure my daughter eats something, Maria. She looks hungry,' Marcus said, and he turned to go.

TARAHUMARA

Text: Dylan Brennan
Photographs: Liliana P. Brennan

Arriving dusty in a cold sweat, swirls of dry earth inhaled. The winter sun beginning its descent. The valley of mushrooms, the valley of frogs: the boulders of Tarahumara country, capriciously sculpted by unending winds, look like things, look like faces.

We made it to San Ignacio de Arareko having walked out from Creel after breakfast. Grey bricks and a stone cross, the squat geometry of the church. Children playing asked to be photographed. The authorities had provided informational wooden boards for walkers and cyclists. Images, maps and useful phrases in the Rarámuri tongue. Photographs of locals outside the church. Their faces, and some of the phrases, had been scratched out.

*

The first time I saw Creel was on a computer screen. A single lens camera documented the arrival of armed men just after dawn. They moved in formation, as if they were police. One of them seemed to be in charge and the others lined up at his truck window to receive clumped portions of cocaine. They needed to be wakeful. They were looking for something, looking for someone. Each armed with an AK47, they stopped cars, searched citizens. The camera followed them, zooming in to areas of interest. The camera was controlled by someone, someone who watched the whole scene. They made their way down to a large white rectangular building with many windows and split up, attempting to enter from various angles. The camera captured the steam of their breath, moved to the right for a moment to the digital gold of the sunrise flooding a dry field. Then back to that building. Eight people killed, including a fourteen-year-old girl. Bullets from a distance usually sound harmless. Dry bangs like firecrackers. Flashes from their weapons. They lit the place up.

I remember the evening Angelus on the television in the 80s. An icon of Mary with child, unmoving and a minute of bells. Followed by the news. At some point this was changed to short films of everyday people going about their daily routines. A woman washing dishes, a farmer in a field, children in a sand pit. The bells of Mary accompanying them in their activities. Supposedly provoking a quiet moment of reflection, a time out from the material world. This is what I thought of months later as I sat on the floor of a Mexico City museum watching To Have Done with the Judgment of God, a film by Venezuelan artist Javier Téllez. The artist arranged for a Rarámuri translation of the eponymously-named Antonin Artaud radio play to be transmitted on a station in Tarahumara country. He filmed contemplative scenes of locals cooking, walking by a creek, killing an animal, dancing, strolling, chatting. All the time interspersed with the wild declarations of the Frenchman's final work –

> *I prefer the people who eat off the bare earth the delirium from which they were born.*
> *There where it smells of shit it smells of being.*
> *And where does this foul debasement come from?*

Chú ani? ¿Qué haces?
Ketási namuti. Nada.

Pili mu rimúli? ¿Qué soñaste?
Wiká nmuti. Muchas cosas.

Ácha ukumea ve? ¿Lloverá?
Ketási ne machi. Isabaga ra 'ichaa. No sé. Siéntate y hablemos.

Népi rataame rawe. ¡Hace mucho calor hoy!
Ábela wabe ola a'acháa kabaga. En verdad hace mucho calor. Vente a la sombra.

We kusuchani chuluki! ¡Cómo cantan las aves!
Pe 'bela uki ba'yea ale ko. Estarán llamando la lluvia.

Népi wakichali pachi! ¡Cómo se ha secado la milpa!
Ábela wa'ione ba wi kiti. En verdad se ha secado por falta de agua.

Pili olá isaligame? ¿Qué estarán pensando acerca de la lluvia?
Ketási ne machi. No sé

Áchá nata ale uki kiti? ¿Estarán pensando acerca de la lluvia?
Ketási ne machi. No sé

Pili olá ketási omawálua? ¿Por qué no ha llovido?
Wiká temali ma ketási natéame ne____ jóvenes a no valoran eso.

Natéame: valioso
Lokáma: tomar pinole
Kulipi: en seguida
Ralámuli: tarahumara
Chú ani: ¿qué dices?
Piri: qué
Rimuma: soñar
Ácha: ¿acaso?
Machí: sé, sabes, saben.
Népi: muy, mucho
Rawé: día
Wabé: muchísimo
Kábé: donde
Kusumea: trinar
Pe: pues
Ukí: lluvia
Alé: tal vez
Wakichéame: secarse
Ba'wi: agua
Olá: hago, haces, hacen
Natá: pensar
Temali: jóvenes
Echíl: ese
Kobisi: pinole
Uche: de nuevo

The film is beautifully shot and the juxtapositions jarring. One thing remains unclear, what the local population feel about all of this. Antonin Artaud was an interloper convinced of the supernatural qualities of the Rarámuri people. After reading an Alfonso Reyes poem titled 'Tarahumara' he got in contact with the renowned writer to inquire as to whether a trip to Mexico would be feasible. He would give a few lectures in the capital before taking the train north. He wanted to experience at first hand the 'magical force' of a 'pure race'. He arrived in 1936 sweating in the throes of heroin and opium withdrawal symptoms. The Rarámuri language is notoriously difficult to learn or translate but Artaud claims to have found a 'mestizo' that helped him. Artaud's stories of his Voyage au Pays des Tarahumaras are almost certainly a mixture of fact and fiction, if not completely imagined. Apocryphal or not, his disjointed chronicle of his time in the Chihuahuan highlands is worth reading for the outlandish delirium of his prose. He may have been losing his mind. Just a year later, skeletal, penniless and bewildered, he would be expelled from Ireland as an undesirable alien after his attempt to return the staff of St. Patrick to the Irish people.

*

Píli olá ketási omawálua? ¿Por qué no h——————?
Wiká temali ma ketási natéame pe—————jóvenes a no valoran eso.

Nearly all of the phrases had been vigorously scratched at but these two, in particular, seemed to have provoked the most violent reaction, the plastic surface having been dug into and partially removed. I may not have transcribed them correctly. They are difficult to make out. The first phrase in English would be something like: 'Why have/has ... not ... ?' The second phrase: '...the young people to not appreciate that.' Maybe the phrases enable a visitor to ask why the Tarahumara have not fostered traditional values in their young people. But that wouldn't make much sense. I asked an old man to explain and he said he didn't want to. Maybe they just don't want outsiders talking to them.

Earlier in the day we visited a cave in which two families live. Clay trinkets for sale and the morning smoke of something recently cooked. I spoke to one of the residents. She was young and told me that it had snowed already twice that season and that the wintertime is tough. Her name was Esther. She told me that an older woman who wouldn't speak to us was named María. Esther was patient and answered my questions. She told me that twenty six people lived in the cave and they received regular visitors. We bought a tiny clay cup and spoon. Esther was selling some cloth tortilla warmers with a word written on them: 'Kuira.' I asked her what it meant and she said, in English, 'hello.' Maybe the younger generation have realised there is now no way around it, they have to put up with the interlopers and our stupid questions. We left and I shook her hand and said 'kuira.' She laughed and spoke to some of the other ladies and then they laughed too. What I should have said was 'ariosibá,' which I think means goodbye.

ORANGES

Cathy Sweeney

One
The orange was at the bottom of the fruit bowl. It was lying underneath two bananas and three apples. That is probably why it began to rot. The darkness at the bottom of the bowl. And the heat.

Two
It was my wife who ate oranges. For breakfast every morning she had an orange, then a bowl of cereal, then a mug of coffee. She cut the orange in four, then sucked each segment before removing it from the skin with her teeth.

Three
My wife had gone to stay with her parents in the countryside for two weeks, taking the baby with her but leaving the orange behind in the fruit bowl. And me. Alone in the apartment in the heat.

Four
My wife and I had argued about me staying in the apartment while she went to the countryside with the baby. She said there was no way she was spending two weeks on her own with her parents and the baby. Then I said okay we'll all go to the countryside to get out of the heat. Then she said we need a better apartment, one that is not so hot, maybe with a garden, so the baby wouldn't be cooped up. Then I said it was hard to work with the baby in the cooped-up apartment and it was work that brought in money. And that is how I got to stay alone in the apartment for two weeks.

Five
For three days I watched TV in my underwear, ate pizza, drank cold beers, watched porn on my laptop, masturbated, and took the dog out for a walk so late that there was no one to see me not picking up after him. I left the blinds down on the windows and spoke only when my wife phoned to ask how the work was going. I said it was going fine.

Six
It was on day four that I noticed the orange was rotting. Underneath the smell of pizza and beer and semen there was some other smell, a sweet rusty odour, like death, if death was a confectionery. I lifted the two bananas and three apples out of the fruit bowl and saw the orange, sagging and fuzzed over in grey.

Seven
I left the orange where it was and ate the two bananas and three apples. I was tired of pizza. I tried to watch TV but there was nothing on and I had sworn off porn due to my rapid descent into extremes.

Eight
On the morning of day five, I woke early. The sheet had mangled itself around my torso and my mouth felt like it was full of flies. I got up and showered and drove out the motorway to the supermarket. Inside the supermarket everything was cool and quiet, and the trolley glided through the aisles while I stared at products like they were objects from a dream I could no longer remember. Nappies and detergent and bumper bags of dog food.

Nine
In the fruit and vegetable department an entire bay was full of oranges. Tangerines from Peru. Mandarins from South Africa. Satsumas. Breakfast oranges from Valencia. Common oranges from Spain. Blood oranges. Seedless oranges. Oranges with their leaves still attached. Bargain oranges, their skin a bit mottled looking. So many oranges. I was amazed.

Ten
I bought about forty oranges. It was a lot. My thinking went something like this: I don't eat oranges. My wife eats oranges. This is my chance to eat oranges. To see if I like them. Maybe I like them. I bought about forty oranges because I wanted to taste each variety, and some oranges were only sold grouped in nets or cellophane bags.

Eleven
I cannot explain why, but when I got back to the apartment, instead of putting the oranges in a bowl or in the fridge, I filled the kitchen sink with them and let the rest spill out over the draining board and worktop. They looked nice. My wife phoned. I said the work was going well. Much better. That I'd had a breakthrough. My wife said she missed me and put the baby on the phone. I could hear it gurgle.

Twelve
The next day I went back to the supermarket and filled the trolley with oranges, loaded up the boot of the car with bags of them, went back inside the supermarket, filled the trolley with oranges again, loaded up the back seat of the car with more bags of them, and put the last bag of oranges on the passenger seat. The woman on the till in the supermarket remarked that I was buying a lot of oranges. I said I ran a small business making orange juice and that my supplier had let me down.

Thirteen
When I got back to the apartment I put oranges in the bath, in the sink in the bathroom, on the kitchen table, on the chairs, on the book shelves, on the TV stand, on the coffee table, on the dressing table in the bedroom, and in the baby's cot. Then I went back to the supermarket and bought one more half trolley of oranges. There were two reasons for only buying one more half trolley. One: the supermarket had a greatly reduced stock of oranges. Two: my wife analyses the statements for our joint Visa card in the same way that scientists analyse microbes in a lab, so I was using my own card to pay for the oranges, and it was almost maxed.

FOURTEEN
I arranged the last of the oranges in various spots around the apartment. In the washing machine, under the bed, along the wainscoting in the hallway. Wherever oranges fell, I just left them there. The only place I purposefully did not put an orange was in the fruit bowl. I wanted to leave the single rotting orange to die in peace.

FIFTEEN
After all this activity with the oranges I slept for two days, only waking to talk to my wife on the phone or to walk the dog. My wife said the baby missed me. She said that the baby was unsettled when she was put down to sleep at night, as though she was waiting for me to say the Dr Seuss poem. I always said the Dr Seuss poem to the baby at night. I was lying in bed when my wife said this, and I could see the baby's cot in the far corner of the room. It was full of oranges. It was day eight.

SIXTEEN
I dreamed that all the oranges in the apartment turned into lotus flowers but when I bent to smell them there was dog mess in the petals.

SEVENTEEN
The dog is acting strange. When my wife phones I tell her that the dog is acting strange and she says to put the dog on the phone. I put the receiver to the dog's ear and I can hear my wife saying things like good boy and mummy will be home soon. The dog starts to bark. I feel guilty about the dog and that evening I take it for a long walk. I bring baggies with me to clean up the mess.

EIGHTEEN
The apartment has started to smell. At first the oranges had no scent at all. Except for the one in the fruit bowl which now looks like a small misshapen rat. The smell is bitter and clean, and the air felt like when I was a child and went back to school after summer and opened the first page of a new copybook.

NINETEEN
I read somewhere that there are five things people cannot smell if they are dying: peppermint, leather, rose petals, fish and oranges. I am not dying. It is day eleven and my wife will be home soon. On the phone in the evening with the blinds pulled up to let in the last of the sun, I tell my wife I miss her and to give the baby a kiss for me. Neither of us mention work, or money or moving to a bigger apartment.

TWENTY
The oranges have started to rot. Their decay is taking place at a much faster rate than I expected, much faster than that of the orange in the fruit bowl which now looks like the tongue of an old person. It must be because they are all touching against each other, each orange affected by the orange beside it, either all fresh or all rotting. The smell is sour but not unpleasant, like soil from a grave, but not the grave of a child or of a person killed in a terrible accident, but of a person who lived a long time and was ready to die.

Twenty One
It is nearly time to clear away all the oranges. Some of the surfaces in the kitchen and the bathroom will have to be scrubbed with sugar soap and a few items, like the mattress in the baby's cot, will have to be replaced. I am making a list so that when I drive to the retail park I'll get everything I need. Gloves. And large black plastic sacks. Maybe a small shovel.

Twenty Two
It is day thirteen. My wife phones to tell me what train she is coming home on. She will be home the day after tomorrow with the baby. They have stayed one extra night in the countryside because train tickets are cheaper to buy on week days. I write the time of the train's arrival on the margin of the calendar in the kitchen. We both go quiet on the phone, but we don't hang up. I can hear the baby making noises in the background.

Twenty Three

That night I sit on the couch, but I don't turn the TV on. I just listen to the darkness. The smell of fermenting oranges in the apartment is powerful but I have gotten used to it. Everything is ready to clear them all out in the morning. Even the one in the fruit bowl. It strikes me that I never tasted any of them. I don't think I like oranges. The phone rings but I let it ring. My wife leaves a message reminding me about the arrival time of the train.

Twenty Four
I stay sitting in the darkness for hours. The dog shuffles in from the hallway and slumps at my feet. He is tired from a long walk earlier in the day. The air seems cooler. I sit there doing nothing, but I feel different. Like I am alive. Now. In this moment. Like if I peeled my skin off and left it beside me on the couch watching TV, I would still be real.

A FAREWELL TO MEATSPACE

Ian Maleney

> The world has arrived at an age of cheap complex devices of great reliability; and something is bound to come of it.
> — Vannevar Bush, 'As We May Think'

Because I had been tired too long and quarrelsome too much and too often frightened of migraine and failure[1] ... I found myself, twenty-seven-years old and breaking, sitting on the freezing ochre tiles of our kitchen floor, hoping that I could pull myself together before Niamh came home from work. It was close to six on a dark February evening. I was wearing pyjama bottoms with a heavy jumper to keep out the cold. I'd spent roughly eighteen of the previous twenty four hours watching the final two series of Halt and Catch Fire, a television show about some people involved in the computer industry in Texas in the mid 1980s. I had been awake for all but two of those twenty four hours, sleeping fitfully on the couch at dawn. I'd spent the last three hours crying, first in bed, where I'd been for most of the day, and then here, in the kitchen, while I attempted to wash dishes and return some semblance of order to my life again. I began to cry when a character in the show had died and soon realised I couldn't stop. I don't cry often, and when I do, the jag is typically brief. This was different: the tears kept coming. For hours I felt only moments away from collapsing, blind, into further floods. I couldn't explain it to myself, and I couldn't explain it to Niamh either, when she found me there at the sink. I can only imagine what she thought when she walked in; I must have looked like the victim of a major tragedy – as if a family member had died suddenly, or our cat had been hit by a car. When she asked what was wrong, I could reply only with a summary of the plot of Halt and Catch Fire. I was so confused. I was weak, and making no sense.

We ordered Chinese and I tried to explain. I said the show was very sad, which it was, and very beautiful. But that couldn't account for the state I was in. I said I wasn't really upset about anything in particular. Nothing had happened exactly, but I was nonetheless overwhelmed. I knew I was frustrated; I felt stuck, as if the orbit of my life had reduced and slowed until I stopped moving altogether. It had been the darkest winter on record, and I had fewer reasons than ever to leave the house. I had no money. My best friend had left the city. I was avoiding people I knew and liked. I had too much to do but felt paralytic with boredom. Work was a joke. I was going nowhere and I felt like I'd wasted years of my life in a manner both stupid and juvenile. Niamh asked if I was depressed. I said I wasn't sure what that meant.

*

A few years earlier, in the cold, quiet days of December, I had picked up HTML5 & CSS3 For Dummies. Niamh had taken it out of the library in the hope that it would help her finish a college project. I was procrastinating and the book,

[1] Joan Didion, 'Letter From Paradise, 21° 19' N., 157° 52' W.', Slouching Towards Bethlehem, 1968.

all eight hundred pages of it, suddenly looked interesting. I said I'd waste a few minutes reading it, maybe I'd even learn something. I knew almost nothing about web design, or programming of any sort. I used the internet every day, and I spent almost all my time on my computer – wouldn't it be good to know a little more about how it worked? I have always liked to know how things work. When Niamh got home, several hours later, she found me still sitting at the table, two hundred pages into the book, working my way through a tutorial. I hadn't moved in hours; the house was dark.

Maybe all obsessions start this way: small, unnoticed, lukewarm. My intentions were strictly diversionary. And yet, within a month or two, I was hooked. The first steps in web design are handy like that – the challenges are straightforward, and feedback is immediate. It doesn't take long to get something nice up on your screen, and there is satisfaction in achieving even that. Though I'd been using the internet since I was a child, I still felt something akin to what the internet pioneers must have felt when they made and shared their own web pages twenty years before. The basic act of creating a document which you can share with others, a document over which you have near-total control – that is exciting, liberating. After a decade of using forums and social networks, the blank simplicity of a handwritten HTML page seemed like an open field to me, full of potential. Words, music, images – everything could live inside this document.

By spring, I was spending many of my spare hours learning how websites are put together. I began to see just how difficult it really was to create things which would live on the internet – code doesn't work the same in every browser; screens come in all different sizes; people have slow connections and old computers. There were more stumbling blocks than I could have imagined, but the rush of overcoming those hurdles and solving a problem was incredible. It was addictive in a way I'd never experienced before. It drives you on, totally ignorant of time or hunger, until you eventually look up at some ungodly hour to find you're starving and your legs are dead. I could see why people once talked about leaving meatspace behind and becoming one with the code and the network it runs on; I've never felt so disembodied as when I've been staring at a text editor for ten hours without a break. When it's going well, the thought and its representation on the screen are indistinguishable: idea becomes code becomes whatever you want it to be. You need only your eyes and your hands – the rest of the body falls away, useless, until the mind burns itself out. Pure focus. It's the most cerebral and least erotic activity; by the end, you feel numb, chloroformed, static. I find it can take days for the body to wake up.

*

Halt and Catch Fire is not a show about computers; it's a show about ambition. This is what makes it sad. It's a show about failure, and this is what makes it beautiful. It begins in 1984 with a hardware engineer named Gordon Clark, and a salesman named Joe MacMillan. Both work for a computer company called Cardiff Electric in Dallas, Texas. Their boss, John Bosworth, is a wisecracking Southern good ol' boy. Gordon's wife, Donna, is an engineer across town at Texas Instruments. Joe becomes romantically and professionally involved with a prodigiously talented young programmer named Cameron Howe. These five characters are the show. There is a plot, but the details aren't relevant here. What matters is how these five people interact with each other and the world, and the ways they think of themselves.

The show ends in 1994, the world transformed. It takes just thirty hours of television to cover ten years of these lives. In that time, I became worryingly attached to these people. In the weeks after I finished watching it, I would constantly think about something Cameron had done, or something Gordon had said. I thought a lot about their personalities, and how they navigated their lives. I thought of them almost like friends.

All of them are builders. They build computers and companies; they build the world as they want to see it. They recognise the new when they find it. Each of them has an ability to look a short way into the future, and the means to follow that vision. They do okay for themselves.

As I fell deeper into these people's lives, I envied them. Not for any particular talent or success, but for living and working in a context that allowed their ideas to become real, and to impact the world. That's the great promise of technology – it will change people's lives in a way that is vivid and immediate and communal. Living a marginal and circumscribed existence at the edge of a couple of failing industries, in a city I was growing to despise, I wanted badly to feel like there was a way forward. The show could be a map. I watched these five people change and I thought about how I had changed, how I wanted still to change more, to change everything. I thought of Gordon, in the very first episode, and his desperate, wounded assessment of his life:

It's not enough.

*

Ray Dalio is the founder of Bridgewater Capital, one of the world's largest and most successful hedge funds. He is one of the richest men on the planet. This is Ray Dalio's five-step process for getting what you want out of life:

1. Have clear goals.
2. Identify and don't tolerate the problems that stand in the way of your achieving those goals.
3. Accurately diagnose the problems to get at their root causes.
4. Design plans that will get you around them.
5. Do what's necessary to push these designs through to results.
   — Ray Dalio, Principles: Life and Work, 2017.

This is designed as a loop – when you get to the end, you start again. Constant self-improvement. Constant realisation of more and more ambitious goals. It's admirable, and practical, but I can't seem to get past the first step.

*

When you study literature, you're expected to read your way through a thousand years' worth of writing. Not all of it, obviously, but enough to get a sense of what happened, when it happened, and why. You're given a précis that grants you the ability to make comparisons, and the freedom to pursue a particular area of interest. In this sense, the study of literature is focused on the past. There is an archive, or a canon, and you work in and with that most of the time. You might choose to work with contemporary literature, but you would do so only with extensive knowledge of the historical background. New forms and new ideas are rare. You learn to quote and to reference, to support whatever you have to say with what others have said before you. This can be stultifying or overwhelming. It can lead to a fetishism of minutiae. Most importantly, the study of literature is not an education in how to write. It is not, strictly speaking, a practical qualification in the production of novels or poems; it is a largely impractical qualification in the art of reading. I received this kind of qualification myself.

By contrast, Alan Kay, one of the primary inventors of personal computing, calls today's tech scene a 'pop culture': 'Pop culture is all about identity and feeling like you're participating. It has nothing to do with cooperation, the past or the future – it's living in the present. I think the same is true of most people who write code for money.'

Among the people who create websites and iPhone apps, there is almost no interest in history. There is little value placed on knowing where things have come from, how they were developed, or even who made them. The people who do seem to care about this stuff are often old, or fugitives from other disciplines – people who started out in the arts, or physics, or maths, and only later found themselves involved with computers. In those areas, knowing your history is important. It's taken for granted. For most people, however, the goal of computer programming is a steady, well-paid job; a bump up the ladder, or a way out of whatever they're doing now. Traditional computer science qualifications are too theoretical, and they take too long – they're not practical. Better to do an online course, or an intensive bootcamp. Education is delivered on a need-to-know basis. Research is minimal; better to learn while building. It's an iterative process: get something out into the world, however janky, and improve it as you go. Monetise it if you can. What happened five years ago is ancient history, it's irrelevant. What happened fifty years ago might as well never have happened.

*

5:55pm. I spent most of this time in bed thinking and putting my effort into aligning my goals.
I have so many burdens right now and so many regrets.
— Marko Grdinić, from the commit logs of The Spiral Language

*

'Computers aren't the thing,' Joe says, in Halt and Catch Fire. 'They're the thing that gets us to the thing.' In the last, lingering days of winter, I realised I had no idea what *the thing* was any more. I wasn't sure I ever did. I was certain only that what I was doing, what I had been doing, was going nowhere. I'd spent the better part of a decade scraping by as a journalist, accumulating bylines, padding a CV, stacking up extracurricular activities in the weirder end of music and books. And suddenly I thought – there is no point to this. I can keep doing this forever and it will not change, it will not improve, it will not get me what I want. And, the coldest truth of all, I didn't know what I wanted. I didn't have a goal; I had no ladder to climb; I had no real ambitions. And that, I thought, was really upsetting. That, I suppose, is what floored me.

*

The modern world has a solution for the un- and the under-employed: learn to code. Feeling frustrated in your service industry job? Learn to code! Let go from your manufacturing job? Learn to code! Considering a postgraduate education in the arts? Forget about it – learn to code! 'All the prejudices and stupidities that churn beneath our vague, signifying human language will be wiped away by the world that's coming, expressed in the blank mathematical intricacies of code,' writes the English journalist Sam Kriss. 'Your age or race or gender don't matter; they belong to the age of objects. Just learn how to code, and you'll be fine.'

People who can code are valuable. They work for companies that make a lot of money. They, in turn, make a lot of money. This is the gleaming lure in the murk of modern existence: learn to code and you will be valued. Your existential dread will vanish. You'll never want for gainful employment. If you're really good, people will be begging you to come work for them. They'll come with money. You'll have leverage. You could even be one of the lucky few who builds an idea into a business and joins the ranks of the self-made billionaires. Learn to code. You can do it.

*

I am watching the final episode of Halt and Catch Fire. Donna is sitting on her daughter's bed, talking to Cameron:
– If it's what you want to do, it's what you want to do.
– Yeah, man. You do what you always did, you're going to get what you always got.
– If the elevator is broken, take the stairs.
– It works if you work it.
– Unless it's more and more of what doesn't work.

*

Big ideas don't come out of thin air – you build up to them. The imagination needs a foundation. A history of falling short, a bedrock of mediocre ideas – the internet now has no use for that past. The economy which sustains our technology today – a venture capital economy, an advertising economy – is a bet on the future; a bet that things will stay largely the same. A bet on greater efficiency, bigger markets, better margins. The products might change, but the ideas do not. There is so much money invested in these ideas, there's more than enough to go around.

This is what makes that world so attractive and, at the same time, so repulsive. Now, when I am close to that world, when I spend my days reading blog posts about database optimisation and code-splitting strategies, I can almost touch the security it promises. I think of programming as if it were some kind of life insurance. I don't want to get rich; I just want to have a future I can rely on. I want to solve problems. I want to feel useful, valued. I want to be part of something bigger than myself. I don't want to live out my life in opposition, because it's exhausting and it's badly paid. It curdles into resentment, and that's no way to spend your time.

But I can't shake the disgust either; disgust at how shallow the world of technology can be, how bland the profiteering, how dangerous the implications of its so-called innovations. I can see, too, how often it is boring, insignificant and artless. I scan the pages of Hacker News or ProductHunt, and I think, *Christ, who are these people? I'm not like them*. I want what that world can offer, just a piece of it, but I don't want to be complicit. 'You become what you do and say; you don't become what your reservations are,' wrote Dwight McDonald. That's the gamble I'm weighing up. I lie awake at night and I wonder, how could all this be different? How could I be different? I ask myself, where will I place my bet?

*

Ray Dalio says that you should 'convert your principles into algorithms and have the computer make decisions alongside you.' Collect all the relevant data in your field, tell the computer to look for certain patterns, and let this complex system guide you in your decision-making. The result would be an optimal blend of technological objectivity with human wisdom and intuition. You could use this when choosing which investments to make, or how to improve productivity at work. You could even 'ask what lifestyle or career you should choose given what you're like.'

*

It's been six months and I still don't know how to write about what I felt while watching Halt and Catch Fire. I spent this morning rewatching its final episodes for the third or fourth time. Dropping in on the last few hours of that world, I remember just how quiet it becomes. The show is stripped of all extraneous characters – the offices are empty, the lights are dimmed, and the drama is reduced to little more than hushed conversations between two or three people. The music fades out, leaving only what these people are trying to say to one another. What I find so moving, and so unusual, is the way every word is tempered by the words which have come before. People speak to each other with the weight of ten or twenty years behind each sentence. Their choices have had, continue to have, consequences. None of this is explained – it's just felt in every pause. You can see it on their faces, when they look away. You can hear it in the hum of fluorescent lights and refrigerators; the crunch of a car door; the cold snap of heels on tiles. When someone breaks this kind of quiet to speak, you listen.

You listen because people don't say exactly what they mean. The words they say rely on words spoken before, perhaps years in the past. They reference people or ideas outside the scope of the conversation. They say the wrong thing because they're stressed out, or distracted, or just unable to articulate what they really think. They hold things back because they want to spare another's feelings, or to keep a secret. The words themselves are just part of a bigger picture; hand gestures, facial expressions, body position – they all modulate what the words might mean. Most of us understand this intuitively, most of the time at least. This fallible, partial connection is just how we communicate with each other.

This is not how we communicate with computers. Whether you're writing a complex program or a simple web page, you have to tell the computer what to do. You have to be explicit about every step. The computer will not infer anything from your intent. It will not take into account your mood, or the time of day, or that your father just died. It is utterly inflexible, and resistant to coercion or duplicity. This is what makes it reliable, and inhumane.

*

Cameron is tightening the straps on a trailer; she's packing her bags. She is telling Boz about recursion – the idea that a function calls upon itself repeatedly in a programme. 'In order to solve the big problem,' she says, 'it uses the same small problem over and over as a solution to increasingly complex issues.' Programmers write recursive algorithms to help computers find and organise information efficiently. Recursion can be used to animate objects across a plane, or to parse complex streams of abstract data. This is what computers do best, because computers are good with loops. Computers can keep doing the same thing, over and over again, until they turn up a solution. All you have to do is tell them what to look for.

The birdie in the phone box with the Child of Prague